ANYTHING GOES

𝕿𝖎𝖒𝖊𝖘BOOKS

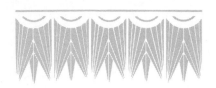

ANYTHING GOES

The Jazz Age Adventures of
Neysa McMein
and Her Extravagant
Circle of Friends

BRIAN
GALLAGHER

Library of Congress Cataloging-in-Publication Data
Gallagher, Brian.
Anything goes.
Bibliography: p.
1. McMein, Neysa.
2. Illustrators—United States—Biography.
3. Magazine covers—United States.
4. New York (N.Y.)—Intellectual life.
I. Title.
NC975.5.M36G35   1987   741.6′092′4[B]   87-9954
ISBN 0-8129-1215-2

Manufactured in the United States of America
9 8 7 6 5 4 3 2
First Edition

Book Design: Jessica Shatan

For Marian

Acknowledgments

Particular thanks are due to Neysa McMein's daughter, Joan Barag-wanath Leech, and her stepson, Albert Kingsmill ("Barry") Baragwanath, both of whom spoke to me with complete candor, and who provided valuable materials for this study; to Elise Goodman, my agent, who first interested me in the project and supplied information to get me started; to Hilary Cummings, Manuscript Curator of Special Collections at the University of Oregon, who tracked down material relating to Neysa McMein in the Jane Grant Papers; and to Jeannie Kay, who did extraordinarily helpful research in the public records of Quincy and Adams County, Illinois.

Contents

OVERTURE: 1923
1 "A New Groom Sleeps Clean" 3

MARJORIE AND NEYSA
2 Marjorie Moran McMein of Quincy, Illinois 23
3 The Creation of Neysa 34
4 War and Its Afterwit 45
5 A Very Modern Salon 69
6 Neysa and the Pretty Girl 88

NEYSA AND JACK
7 Living a Life with Handsome Jack 105
8 When Jack Was Away 127
9 Sands Point and the House That Jack Built 148
10 Games and More Games 168
11 Neshobe, India, Egypt, and Other Expeditions 186
12 Neysa and the Withering of the Wits 205
13 Passings 216

Epilogue 229

Sources 233

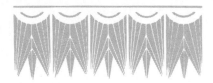

OVERTURE
1923

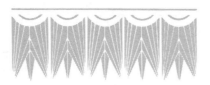

=1=

"A New Groom Sleeps Clean"

It is not true, as some reports had it, that Neysa McMein went on her honeymoon with ten, or even seven, men. Discounting occasional hangers-on, the number never rose above five. It is true, though, that her husband was not one of the men with her. She might have married in haste, but she was going to honeymoon in leisure—surrounded, as usual, by a group of men friends. A new husband would only have spoiled the party.

There she is in the grainy honeymoon photographs, looking very pleased, supremely content, hardly the newlywed pining for her absent spouse. She is sitting in a Parisian café with a nattily dressed Jascha Heifetz looking older than his twenty-two years, and a bearish, owl-eyed Alec Woollcott, all three of them bundled up against a chilly late spring day. She is standing, half-turned, with the light catching her tawny, large-featured beauty, on a road in the French countryside, flanked by Heifetz and Woollcott and a bereted Marc Connelly. It was May 1923, and Neysa McMein was thoroughly enjoying herself, an art that she had been perfecting ever since that day a decade earlier when she had chucked over prospects of a comfortable, dull life as a commercial artist in Chicago and joined a vaudeville troupe headed for New York.

Neysa's earlier life, like that of a number of Americans born toward the end of the nineteenth century, seems very much a rehearsal for the 1920s. Of the period between the Armistice and the Great Depression, F. Scott Fitzgerald wrote in "Echoes of the Jazz Age": "It was an age of miracles, it was an age of art, it was an age of excess, and it was an age of satire." He might have added, had he wanted to be absolutely complete, that it was also an age of commercialism, publicity, and political quiescence.

Neysa McMein, as much as any American of the time, typified this contradictory decade. She was charming and eager and sophisticated, but she could also be disarmingly provincial. She was liberated and self-supporting and casual—a few would say notoriously casual—in sexual matters, but she was generally apolitical and still clung, at least nominally, to the rather conservative political tenets of her Republican upbringing in western Illinois. She led something of the bohemian life of the artist, but she knew that the magazine covers she drew were slick, commercial products, and so she made sure to be paid well for them. She took an unpretentious delight in having famous friends and in being famous herself, as an auxiliary member of the New York literati, but she could not always see how her fame and that of her friends was a compound of genuine achievement and the insistent, pervasive kind of publicity that first began to be practiced on a large scale in the 1920s, not least by her set at the Algonquin Round Table. Most of all, she was, in the fashion of the 1920s, "young," even though a strict accounting of her years would have disqualified her as a representative of "Youth."

By 1923, Neysa had been a famous and popular bachelor girl for six or seven years. George Abbott, who was not to meet her until the end of the 1920s, recalls how in her heyday, "every taxi-cab driver, every salesgirl, every reader of columns, knew about the fabulous Neysa." Harpo Marx thought her "the sexiest gal in town," and joined the long queue of her admirers: "The biggest love affair in New York City was between me—along with two dozen other guys—and Neysa McMein." Another who was smitten, novelist and screenwriter Charles Brackett, puzzled at the perplexing simplicity of Neysa's charm: "Why the bare word 'hello' from her lips, and the way she brushed back her tawny hair with her wrist, should be so luminous with charm was incomprehensible."

A number of women, on the contrary, found Neysa decidedly less compelling. The more gracious of her rivals described her as a femme fatale, if one of the indigenous variety. The less gracious typed her, in the words of one distinctly unsuccessful rival, "little better than a tart, that one. . . . a professional beau-snatcher." But to a young, shy, socially self-conscious Helen Hayes, Neysa in the 1920s was a marvel, a beauty who could have had any man she chose, a woman who would inevitably put any other in the shade. In her moment, Neysa McMein was a woman who could not be ignored.

Neysa's opinions were sought and circulated, her intentions chronicled. In her twenties she announced her plan to marry at thirty and rear five children. At thirty she proclaimed a change of mind: she would remain a "bachelor maid." *McCall's* asked her to name the twelve most beautiful women in America and then commissioned her to do their portraits for its covers. It is perhaps an indication of her influence, and its limits, that nine of the twelve sat for her. Neysa, in her turn, sat for a number of fictional portraits. Edna Ferber made her into the free-spirited artist, Dallas O'Mara, in *So Big*, the bestseller of 1924. Her great friend Janet Flanner, the *New Yorker* correspondent, combined some of her own history with a good deal of Neysa's to create the heroine's story in *The Cubical City* (1927). In Charles Brackett's *Entirely Surrounded* (1934), perhaps the most perfunctorily fictionalized roman à clef in American literature, only Neysa, as the beguiling Leith O'Fallon, survives the author's thoroughgoing satire of the celebrated satirists of the Algonquin set. The lesser portraits, fictionalized or not, are too numerous to chronicle.

Besides doing covers for *McCall's*, Neysa spent a year (1932–33) as that magazine's film reviewer, and with her finely developed visual sense did a quite credible job. In announcing the appointment, *McCall's* simply informed its readers that Neysa would "tell you how a famous person reacts to current cinema offerings." For close on two decades, fame for Neysa McMein was often something more tangible than its own reward.

It did sometimes appear that Neysa knew everyone who was anyone in New York, particularly in the 1920s, which is to say she knew a fair portion of the important people in the country—and not a few of those in from Britain. Of course, many were just passing acquaintances who took Neysa up on her offhand and freely dispensed invitations to drop in at her studio and join the crowd that gathered there, full of wit and hijinks, late every afternoon. Of that celebrated locale Alec Woollcott wrote whimsically, in a 1934 appreciation, "In the years just after the war, when the pattern of the life I know in New York was beginning to take its present form, the Bureau of Missing Persons at police head-quarters first adopted the custom of starting each quest for a mislaid citizen in Neysa McMein's studio." Had the police been looking for many a prominent visitor to the city—H. G. Wells, Charlie Chaplin, Bea Lillie, Noel Coward—they might have had to look no further.

The woman who was able to draw that glittering crowd to her large, haphazardly furnished studio on West 57th Street—over the Swiss Alps Restaurant and opposite Carnegie Hall—was as striking as any of the models they were likely to find there posing for one of her "pretty-girl" covers. Neysa was, very much in the fashion of the period, beautiful in a wide-mouthed, tall, athletic way. Three decades after her death, Marc Connelly, himself nearly ninety, still vividly recalled her in an interview: "Neysa couldn't have been more popular. She couldn't have been love-lier. Everybody loved her. She was perfectly beautiful, [a] tall Amazonian sort of person, handsome as could be." Perpetually untidy in her smock, and usually eccentrically dressed out of it, Neysa triumphed over her disarray. Her golden hair seemed incapable of staying neatly pinned in place, and her face, hands, and smock were covered with a fine, multicolored drizzle of pastel dust. Yet, even in this deshabille and surrounded by the usual chaos of her studio, Neysa's clear green eyes seemed to indicate a sense of serenity and sureness that struck many as uncanny, almost primitive. Most visitors soon noted the strong likeness between Neysa and the large Persian cat that was always about her in the studio.

For a fast friend of the literati, Neysa was rather unliterary herself. While she could turn the occasional phrase and coin the occasional witticism, one of her major roles in the Algonquin set was to serve as an appreciative audience for the prodigious wit of others. In that combative assemblage, it was probably only Neysa and Harpo Marx—who was not only unliterary but virtually illiterate—who could laugh wholeheartedly at the wit of others without feeling a pang of envy at a verbal cleverness that was not their own. Another of Neysa's roles—she had a baker's dozen—was to provide regular doses of unfeigned enthusiasm for wits who could at times be rather bloodless and cerebral. She rode elephants in circus parades, she judged beauty contests, she dashed from her studio in pursuit of fire engines, she opened movie theaters, and she gave nearly daily, and often public, verification to Woollcott's fond estimation that she was lacking in "the apocryphal virtue called dignity."

A few who met Neysa, but who did not get to know her well, thought there was something a bit contrived and affected about her carefree behavior. Anita Loos, who was a provincial of a different sort than Neysa (being a Californian by birth and a skeptic by inclination), represents as well as anyone this minority opinion. As she wrote from the vantage point of the 1960s:

> [Neysa] was a magnificent young creature, a Brünnhilde with a classic face, tawny hair that scorned a brush or comb, and a style of dress for which her inspiration could only have been a grabbag. But all New York knew she was the heroine of a succession of romances with extremely prominent men. When Neysa invited me to her studio I accepted, but I confess to being critical of

her; to me Neysa's unkempt appearance seemed phony
and even a little conceited; it was as if Cinderella had
purposely gone to the ball in rags, knowing they'd make
her all the more a sensation.

Loos, as the unsympathetic often do, exaggerated. Neysa did indeed
know, even cultivate, "prominent men," but with just which of them
she carried on love affairs was hardly something the whole town, or even
some of her closest friends, knew. Neysa might have been sexually
liberated, but she was also discreet. Had she gotten to know Neysa
better, Loos would have learned how Neysa had come to New York with
romantic notions and a rather unglamorous background, determined to
create herself anew and live her life at a higher pitch. That Neysa by
and large succeeded in this endeavor is not quite the same thing as her
being "phony," despite the degree of artifice involved.

One of the things Neysa came to New York to be was a fully eman-
cipated woman: socially, sexually, and economically. With her, the
matter was more personal than ideological. If she was a feminist, and
there were a fair number of women who identified themselves as such
in the 1920s, Neysa was one only by example. It was not that she did
not participate in some aspects of the women's movement—Neysa was
an ardent suffragist and a willing, if less than ardent, member of the
strongly feminist Lucy Stone League—but that she seemed to participate
in such things instinctively rather than intellectually. The "woman's
question" as such did not preoccupy her. It may even be true, as her
close friend Jane Grant suggested, that Neysa postponed marriage chiefly
because she desired no curtailment of the parties, long weekends, and
foreign excursions where she was often a center, if not *the* center, of
male attention. Neysa may have wanted her own rights and may have
wished those same rights for her sex, but she held no strong brief against
the opposite sex for withholding them.

Despite the feminist ferment, the 1920s were still a difficult time for
women seeking their freedom. The very day that the news of Neysa's
odd and offhand marriage broke in the New York newspapers, the *World*
carried a story headlined: "College Seniors Define Dream Woman That

They Want Their Wives to Be." The results of the paper's survey are pretty much summed up in the sub-headline: "Men About to Be Graduated from America's Big Institutions Are Agreed That Mixing Housework and Office Work Is Bad for Mental Happiness." (The "Big Institutions" it mentioned were Yale, Harvard, Princeton, Williams, Dartmouth, West Point, and Annapolis.) A poll at Vassar in that same year showed most of the young women there in agreement with the graduating men: 90 percent of the women wished for marriage, while only 11 percent were planning careers. Three years later, after the women's movement had peaked, one Edward S. Martin may well have been expressing a certain widespread male attitude in his cynical acceptance of the Nineteenth Amendment: "women suffrage was good if only to have it over."

In 1926–27, *The Nation* printed a series of essays by a variety of feminists, a number of the pieces reflecting a sense of disillusionment that mirrored the then declining prospects of the women's movement. Inez Haynes Irwin, a suffragist, journalist, and novelist, recalled an overwhelming sense of frustration in her earlier years:

> I regretted bitterly that I had not been born a man. Like all young things I yearned for romance and adventure. It was not, however, a girl's kind of romance and adventure that I wanted, but a man's. . . . A profound horror of the woman's life filled me. Nothing terrified me so much as the thought of marriage and child-bearing. Marriages seemed to me, at least so far as women were concerned, the cruelest of traps.

Neysa, to be sure, rarely, if ever, thought in such dire terms. Yet much of her life was lived as if these *were* her premises. Although more than one observer has used the adjective "feminine" to characterize Neysa, many another has made it plain that she abrogated for herself the same full measure of freedom enjoyed by the men in her set.

Since the war, Neysa's set had been practicing, in word and deed, an activity that finally gained a name in 1923: "debunking." The Ku Klux Klan might be rising in Oklahoma, and William Z. Foster might be telling a New York rally that Christ was "the original Communist,"

9
▼

but round and about the Algonquin Hotel on 44th Street such fervent protestations were scoffed at. This set was radical only to the extent it kept up a gibing diatribe against a lingering Victorian morality, by then a much-battered antagonist, and in that it fostered, sometimes rather too much to its own self-satisfaction, a breakdown in traditional social and class distinctions. On the periphery of the group was a great romance of the decade, that of the once impoverished and now millionaire song-writer Isador Balin (Irving Berlin) and the beautiful, wealthy, unconventional young socialite he married, Ellin Mackay (whose revelatory piece, "Why We Go to Cabarets: A Post-Debutante Explains" was *The New Yorker*'s first "shocker," a symbolic and snobbish protest against the stodgy ways of high society by one of its younger, more restless members).

More toward the center of the group was the mutual devotion of Mackay's aunt, Alice Duer Miller, and Harpo Marx: the patrician romantic novelist came from one of the oldest and most prominent New York families (Gracie Mansion was her ancestral home), while the plebian clown came from a family that barely had time to establish itself in a New York tenement before he flunked out of the second grade. Alec Woollcott, the critic whose outsized personality often dominated group gatherings, hardly had a "class" background at all: he had grown up in the Phalanx, a Fourierist Utopian community in Red Bank, New Jersey, where he lived with nearly a hundred others in a huge old hotel that the group had converted to its communal ways. Beside the likes of these members, Neysa's background must have seemed rather too ordinary and middle class, and much in need of the romantic glossings she occasionally, if distractedly, gave it.

Needless to say, relationships within the group were usually frenetic, if not neurotic. At one point a Jungian psychoanalyst was called in to tell Woollcott what many of the group's amateur psychoanalysts had already discerned: namely, that Alec was in love with Harpo. ("But in a nice way," added Groucho some years later.) Obsessions ran high: if George Kaufman, with his phobias and gloomy insecurities, was "a mess," as Dorothy Parker proclaimed him, then Parker, with her alcoholism and regular, botched suicide attempts, must have been something more of a mess herself. It may be some measure of Neysa's sounder mental health that when she finally did decide to marry, she went about it in the extremely casual fashion of her set but was also sure to go far outside her set to choose a mate.

Jack Baragwanath was certainly an unliterary type himself, he was certainly no "wit" in the Algonquin sense of the term, and he certainly did not much care for some of Neysa's friends, most especially Woollcott. But he was two things most of the men at the Algonquin were not: he was kind and he was very handsome. His common sobriquet, in fact, was "Handsome Jack." Six feet tall, broad-shouldered and lean, he wore his dark hair slicked back and sported a thin mustache. His close resemblance to some of the dashing male leads of the period's films could not be missed.

Nor was Jack's background remotely similar to that of any of the Algonquin men. Born in 1887, the year before Neysa, he was the rebellious, rakish son of a ministerial family (with his grandfather, father, who had emigrated from Cornwall, and an uncle all Methodist clergymen) from upstate New York. Jack had studied geology and engineering at Columbia University from 1906 through 1910, then spent the following decade working in the roustabout world of the high-altitude mining camps of Equador and Peru, an experience that forever roughened his already hearty wit. In 1922 he was recently divorced, from a woman whose eventual disenchantment with his wandering, irregular life he could well understand, and completely free to indulge his strong attraction for the company of pretty women—in a New York City which had become more open, more exciting, and more daring in the years since he had known it as a collegian.

One evening an actress Jack had been seeing brought him to a party Irene Castle was giving for her husband—there he met Neysa McMein. Like most men, he was immediately and immensely taken with her. Jack's first impression of Neysa, as he recalled it in his autobiography, *A Good Time Was Had*, was that "she wasn't a beauty, she was just beautiful." But Neysa noticed Jack no more than to extend him one of her common, offhand invitations to visit her studio. Jack eventually went there, but was rather taken aback by her total disregard of him after she tendered him an enthusiastic greeting: she simply turned him over to her guests and returned to her work. When he saw several subsequent visitors treated in the same cavalier fashion, he knew himself to be no worse off than many another of her admirers, if not yet one of her favorites.

Over the following months he persisted with Neysa, sketching out, in the few quiet moments he could secure with her, his life story. He told her his father was a minister, that he had lived for years on the west coast of South America, and that he spoke Spanish. Neysa, no doubt half in jest, conflated and romanticized these details: soon she was introducing him around as the son of a minister to Washington from "one of those Latin American countries."

In his own circles Jack was known as a wit and raconteur; his stories were often crude, sometimes vulgar, but he told them with such mimetic style and joie de vivre that he dissipated most of their coarseness. In Neysa's circle, however, he initially felt intimidated and verbally over-matched: "Here was Neysa, the highest paid pretty-girl cover artist in the world, they said, and a woman who knew everybody brilliant in New York. Who was I? A kind of mining-camp hick, struggling along, barely able to make those well-known ends meet."

After months of scouting about for a permanent position, Jack found a very good one, inspecting potential properties for a mining company. The only catch was that he had to agree to undertake a trip to inspect some mines in Peru as his first assignment. He expectantly arranged what was to be a farewell dinner with Neysa, but he realized "she didn't give a damn" when he told her he would be dropping out of her life for several months. He sailed off disillusioned. Early in 1923, he was back in New York and renewed the relationship with Neysa. For a week they were together on a yachting cruise to Palm Beach, but still Jack felt he was not becoming an especial favorite. Then he went off to New Mexico, still convinced he rated no higher in Neysa's eyes than many another man. He was wrong.

While he was away this time, something important happened: Neysa's mother died. Belle Parker McMein had been almost completely paralyzed in a riding accident years before—although clearly in more mundane circumstances than the "riding to hounds" Neysa sometimes vaguely implied was the setting for the mishap. Ever since her father had died in 1918, Neysa had quietly been taking care of her mother in New York, seeing that she had constant nursing care and eventually moving her into a brownstone adjacent to the 57th Street studio. Here Belle's sickbed was put next to the window and the invalid propped up so she might have a view of the flow of foot and motor traffic on the busy street, a small diversion that provided her only relief from the tedium and constant pain. While Neysa recognized that her mother's death was a release for both of them, still it depressed her to think that all her immediate family was now gone. At this moment she turned to Jack Baragwanath, first for simple comfort, then for something more.

Neysa's spirits, as they usually did, soon returned to their full vigor. She planned a trip to Europe with a male entourage and lightly dismissed the several marriage proposals Jack was encouraged to make because of their new intimacy. Two nights before she was to sail, Jack proposed yet again. This time, though, he framed the offer in a way that appealed to Neysa's unconventional streak and romantic leanings: they could marry in secret now and directly go their separate ways. Jack himself was scheduled for a mining expedition to northwestern Quebec shortly and figured to be away until late June, about the time Neysa would be returning from Europe. Only then would they need to reveal the marriage. His father could perform the ceremony up in Peekskill, an hour's drive north of the city, and no one would be the wiser.

For once, Neysa was persistently logical. Why not wait until she returned to marry? Because he feared she might "fall for one of those lovely men you're going to travel with or some other elegant bastard you meet over there," Jack replied with gruff good humor. Besides, he added, being a married woman might encourage her to live up to her vows. Neysa laughingly replied that a marriage certificate would hardly create much of an inhibition for her. And then, more illogically, she agreed to marry Jack.

May 18, 1923, was a quiet day in the world. The New York papers reported that in yesterday's game Babe Ruth had hit his fifth home run of the season. (He would hit forty-one in all, eighteen shy of the record he had set two years earlier.) Statistics were released which indicated the cost of living had risen 59 percent since 1914; an expert, a male one, estimated that it now cost "$100 a year minimum to dress a woman" (presumably their husbands were to do the dressing); and a group of Democratic women, their clothing apparently taken care of, was laboring to bring the 1924 convention to New York City so as to convince a skeptical national public, then as now, that the city was not full of "ogres." (They succeeded in getting the convention, but probably much to their regret: held in the blazing heat of midsummer, it turned into a bitter two-week wrangle of party factions, with a compromise candidate, the unsuccessful John W. Davis, chosen only on the 103rd ballot.)

That day, Neysa and Jack motored up to Peekskill and were married in the early afternoon, Jack telling his rather startled parents that he had met Neysa at a church social. Since they knew of Neysa only vaguely through her magazine covers and not through the columns, gossip and otherwise, she populated, this white lie about Neysa spending her evenings in semi-ecclesiastical settings washed with them. Had the newspapers known of the wedding, they would have reported it in full measure, for Neysa's doings in 1923 were most certainly news, and this was the most significant of them in months.

Because Jack and Neysa had decided to keep the marriage a secret, Neysa was to receive another proposal—equally unconventional, if more decidedly ambiguous—within twenty-four hours. It came from Alec Woollcott.

As two of his best friends, Beatrice Kaufman and Joseph Hennessey, put it, Woollcott was "capricious, willful, spoiled and at times moody." He could also be, as his many enemies would willingly attest, acid, foul-mouthed, and bitchy. Yet the essays, sketches, reviews—and in later years, radio broadcasts—that made him such a popular figure were so cloyingly sentimental that he fully merited his dubbing of "Louisa May Woollcott." Rendered impotent—probably by a severe case of mumps in early manhood—Alec had fashioned a witty, cutting, and sometimes self-deprecating verbal sexual life as a kind of substitute for the physical one he could never have. Not quite admitting to his sexual incapacity, he nonetheless toyed with the oddness of his stunted sexuality, appalling more than one casual acquaintance with his seemingly heartfelt confession that he desperately wanted to be a mother. With so obviously a sexual creature as Neysa, he kept up a bantering, friendly, discreetly lewd sexual war of words. At times he could be mockingly apt: he once suggested that they write the story of their life together and call it *Under Separate Cover*. At other times, he could be jealous and petulant, acting, as one less than kind observer put it, "like a butterfly in heat."

The day before Neysa sailed found Alec in one of the latter moods. Since he had been in the hospital for a minor operation, Neysa had excluded him from plans for her upcoming European jaunt. Just about the hour Neysa was marrying Jack up in Peekskill, Alec found out about her trip. Immediately, he resolved to join her. He booked passage on the *Olympia* and rushed back to "412"—the 47th Street brownstone he shared, in his own high-handed way, with Harold Ross, his World War I army buddy and soon-to-be editor of *The New Yorker*; Ross's wife Jane Grant, feminist and budding writer; and Hawley Truax, an old classmate of Woollcott's at Hamilton College who would shortly become and long remain treasurer of *The New Yorker*. Between packing his suitcases, ferreting out his passport, and straightening out his more pressing writing commitments, Alec told Ross and Grant of his plan to surprise Neysa on the ship, adding that he might well ask her to marry him. They were more than dubious about the plan.

Jack did not accompany his new bride to the pier, professing a distaste for sentimental partings. Besides, had the photographers there seen the secretive newlyweds together, they might have suspected something was up. Alec, apparently, was able to slip aboard unnoticed, a notable feat considering his large, familiar bulk. In any case, Neysa did not discover him until she came on deck after the ship had cleared New York Harbor. Suddenly, there was a beaming Alec in a deck chair, a brand-new Parcheesi board on his lap and love, for the moment, in his heart.

It was high time he settled down, he told her; she should, indeed she must, marry him. His ill-timed avowal of love forced Neysa to reveal her one day's marriage. Alec undoubtedly was a bit piqued, for almost everything that upset his plans piqued Alec. And he was probably more than a little jealous. (Neysa would remain among his most sincere heterosexual attachments for the rest of his life.) But he must also have been somewhat relieved. Circumstances having obviated the very small chance that Neysa might accept his proposal, Alec could now enjoy his "manly" gesture without the accompanying sense that it had been spurned. For the remainder of the voyage, he and Neysa settled down to something about which they were most serious and unambivalent: game playing.

Landing at Cherbourg, Neysa and Alec, both of whom had been over to France nearly every summer since the war ended and knew the country well, made their way up to Paris, where two more of Neysa's entourage, Art Samuels and Jascha Heifetz, were waiting. Despite the many hours Samuels spent lounging around Neysa's studio—during the early 1920s he always seemed to be there when anyone else came to call—this handsome young man enjoyed a varied reputation as a wit, composer, editor, of *Harper's Bazaar* at this time, and clever advertising man. Heifetz, by 1923, was already a much-celebrated virtuoso. As an adolescent he had landed in the United States and brashly announced to reporters, "I've made my own living and supported my family from the time I was six years old," only to receive a taste of American wisecracking in the ready reply of one of them, "I suppose that up until then you were just a parasite." Several years later, Heifetz found his way to Neysa's studio and discovered a rare place where he could relax and take a crash course in the American idiom at the same time. He came whenever he could. Within a few days, Marc Connelly, whose string of successful play collaborations with George Kaufman had made him one of the early stars of the Round Table, had joined them—after dutifully accompanying his mother on a trip round England.

The Paris about which Neysa and her male companions sported had become a thoroughly Americanized piece of terrain by 1923. As Connelly recalled it in *Voices Offstage*, the atmosphere was comfortably familiar, particularly for American provincials seeking cosmopolitan flavor:

Paris in the summer of 1923 contained almost as many Americans as French. The Left Bank was swarming with the vanguard of young writers from the United States. Veterans of World War I were coming back to revisit familiar scenes. On the Rue Pigalle one heard more English than French, and such Gallic night spots as The Chicago Inn, Charley's Quick Lunch, and Bricktop's made the street cosy and homelike.

According to Connelly, very late one evening, while waiting to catch an early morning train to Biarritz, the group made its way to the Café du Père Tranquille for some of its famed onion soup. While waiting to be served, Heifetz asked if he might borrow the violinist's instrument before he put it away for the evening. Then, until dawn, Heifetz, who went unrecognized since his Parisian debut was still three months off, played Viennese waltzes, with the muffled sounds of a nearby market awakening for the day providing his "orchestral accompaniment." The restaurant staff and the few remaining patrons were enchanted—and the three-piece orchestra amazed—by the playing of the young Russian virtuoso.

Many of Heifetz's Russian countrymen and countrywomen were in evidence in the Paris of the 1920s, which could then claim to be the expatriate capital for half a dozen countries. With Janet Flanner, who had just settled into that long Parisian residence she was to chronicle as Genêt in her "Letter from Paris" for *The New Yorker*, and another friend, Neysa went to the premiere of Stravinsky's *Les Noces* by the Ballets Russes, perhaps the most legendary of the many legendary openings Paris saw in the 1920s. Since two of their seats were in the front of the orchestra and the third high up in the gallery, Neysa worked out an elaborate scheme for their rushing back and forth in relays, thinking it, in her American way, only fair that all three of them should get an equal share of the evening's great excitement close up. With her high spirits and beauty and eager, unpretentious manner, Neysa cut a noticeable figure on even so crowded a stage as Paris in 1923. Flanner long remembered how her beautiful Midwestern friend often outshone many of Paris's more cosmopolitan beauties that spring.

Neysa and her men—Ferdinand Touhey, who worked for the Paris office of the *World* had now joined the group—eventually set off from the capital for a driving tour south to Nice. Arriving in the small town of Mauléon just before nightfall, they were surprised to find no one at the hotel desk or, after further searching, anywhere in the hotel or, indeed, anywhere in the whole town. It began to look like the entire population had vanished on the instant, since all the buildings had been left unlocked and nothing had been put away. After an hour of conjectures and still no reappearance by the citizenry, they shrugged, checked themselves into the hotel, made themselves dinner, and went, a little trepidatiously, off to bed. At sunrise, they were awakened by a loud, brassy version of the "Marseillaise": it was the town band leading the weary populace home from the annual fair, which had gone on through the night in the nearby countryside.

At Bagnères-de-Luchon, the group's gambling mania, a prevalent one in the Algonquin set, overcame its members. The Gallic countryside was temporarily dismissed as the object of their contemplation while they spent hours sitting around a huge bed shooting craps. Neysa's luck turned from very sour to very sweet, to her soft, crooning delight. In the end she bested the men handily and walked off clutching two handfuls of bills, much to the puzzlement of the hotel's proprietor and its other patrons, who were left to speculate on just what strange, vivid things these traveling Americans were about.

When the group returned to Paris, Woollcott left it and sailed for home. Neysa, for some reason, gave Touhey the details of her marriage— or, more probably, gave him permission to print the more printable details of the story her traveling group had been chuckling over these past weeks. Then Neysa sailed for home herself. Jack, who had returned to New York earlier than expected because his mining expedition had very quickly proven fruitless, was suffering through the hottest June the city had seen since 1884. When news of his marriage to Neysa was wired from Paris, New York became even hotter for him.

On June 23, 1923, the New York papers, several with a sly delight, reported the wedding as the latest of Neysa's eccentric, carefree doings. Quipped one, "Miss McMein, it was thought, was wedded solely to her art—for the present at least." Another spoke of the joining of "the illustrator and engineer," implying a union, such as it was, of art and science. Several reporters journeyed up to Peekskill, where a befuddled Reverend Baragwanath, involved in the first newsworthy event of his hitherto quiet life, told them it was his impression that his son would soon be going off to join his new bride in Paris. (Actually she was already steaming home.) He added that Neysa was a "wonderful woman," using the adjective in its most literal sense: Neysa was certainly proving "full of wonders" for him.

The following day, the *World*, the central newspaper of the Algonquin group, carried a story speculating on the origins and development of the romance that led to this odd marriage, summarizing its conclusion in the headline: "Neysa McMein Won on Yachting Cruise, Is Belief." It also noted, probably more on target, that Neysa may have been inclined toward marriage out of a certain loneliness stemming from the recent death of her mother. If Jack, four decades after the event, exaggerated the degree of public laughter directed at him—recalling nonexistent headlines like "Famous Artist Marries. Spends Honeymoon with Four Other Guys," and, "Neysa McMein Secretly Wed. Lucky Bridegroom Sulks at Home"—it was probably because he confused the public smiles with the semi-public laughter, which was considerable.

For several weeks, Neysa's odd way with matrimony was the chief topic on which many of the town wits exercised themselves. FPA (Franklin Pierce Adams) reported, in the mock-Restoration prose of his "Conning Tower" column, "news come that Mistress Neysa hath been married a month now to Jack Baragwanath, and a fine lad he is, too, and all a great surprise to me." (FPA made a point of, and a living by, knowing just what his celebrated friends were up to most of the time.) The competition of the wits lasted long enough for Marc Connelly, one of Neysa's accomplices, to return to New York and ring in with his entry: "Marry McMein and See the World." But the palm went to Herbert Bayard Swope, then in the midst of his great executive editorship of the *World*, for his mock-aphorism: "A New Groom Sleeps Clean." Jack Baragwanath was much embarrassed, and not a little worried about what he had let himself in for with his second marriage.

Jack went to the pier to meet Neysa's ship; so did the reporters. Neysa fobbed off the latter with a few innocuous, lighthearted comments: "I thought McMein was bad enough, but I'll need to practice to get Baragwanath out in one breath." When the newly joined newlyweds were finally left alone, they were shy of one another. As they rode back in the taxi to Neysa's studio, where they were temporarily to live, the same unspoken questions must have occurred to both of them. Was their marriage just a piece of momentary foolery they would come to regret? Would it, could it succeed? And what would happen to that large measure of freedom to which they had both become so accustomed?

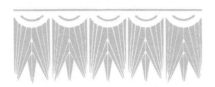

MARJORIE
AND
NEYSA

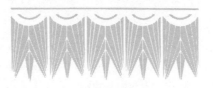

2

Marjorie Moran
McMein
of Quincy, Illinois

The person the reporters had hurried
to the pier to interview on her return
to New York in June 1923 represented
more of a triumph over prosaic and
adverse circumstances than they, or
even her new husband, suspected. The
vague, carefree, romantic aura that
hung about Neysa McMein was a matter of choice and will, ably assisted
by publicity. It was none of her birth-
right.

There was nothing remotely romantic or unusual about Neysa's family.
Her paternal grandfather, Hugh
McMein, was born in Scotland in 1825
and taken to New York as a boy. There,

in the late 1850s, he married Fannie Gallaher, an Irishwoman of sturdy Protestant stock who had come to the United States with her family as a twelve-year-old in 1849. Their first son, William, was born in 1860 and their second, Harry (who was to be Neysa's father), in 1863. Shortly after, the family moved to Quincy, Illinois, where a third and last son, George, was born in 1869.

Fannie was religious and Hugh drank—which seems to be the sum total of their noteworthy characteristics. Hugh's drunkenness, in fact, was something of a *cause célèbre* at Fannie's Vermont Street Baptist Church. The church records for November 1870—in tones more reminiscent of November 1670—indicate that Hugh's persistent inebriation merited a special committee of its own:

> The committee on Bro *Mc Mein* reported that they had interviewed him and had presented him with the *heinousness* of his crime of drunkenness and that he had promised to abstain from all intoxicating drinks for the future but the committee was credibly informed that he had not kept his promise.
>
> Bro Mc Mein being present stated his sorrow for his sins and begged the church to stay action on his case and he would prove to the church the sincerity of his resolve neither to touch or taste a drop of anything that would intoxicate.

A month later, the committee reported another, decisive lapse on Hugh's part: "Bro Mc Mein not having kept his solemn engagement the hand of fellowship is withdrawn from Bro Mc Mein." That may have ended matters with the church, but Hugh and Fannie dragged on for another decade, with Hugh drifting from one laborer's job to another: coal teamster, groom, hostler. They separated about 1880, with the twenty-year-old William, already well established as a printer on a city paper, the *Whig*, and launched on a career that would make him a classic provincial success, taking over the male leadership and chief support of the family.

The town to which Hugh and Fannie McMein had brought their infant sons during the Civil War years had been built on an old Indian camping ground, the only spot for 120 miles on the east side of the Mississippi where high bluffs struck directly down to the river. Founded in 1822, not far upriver from Mark Twain's Hannibal, and named after the current president, John Quincy Adams, the town had quickly thrived, and become rather notorious, as an important river port and shipping center. Despite its nearness to slavery, Quincy remained solidly Union for the duration of the Civil War and served as a key military outpost in the westernmost tip of Illinois.

By the opening of the war, Quincy had grown into the state's second largest settlement, next to Chicago. However, the railroad mania of the 1840s and 1850s, which fostered an enthusiastic civic commitment to the building of the Quincy and Chicago railroad, had necessarily set rather narrow limits on Quincy's future growth. When railroad links from the west were completed through to Chicago and the Atlantic seaboard in 1855, the commercial importance of the Mississippi River packets began to decline sharply. From being a bustling antebellum river port, through which goods flowed from the surrounding areas and to the east, postbellum Quincy became merely the terminus of one of many rail lines emanating from Chicago. Instead of seeing river packets gliding in and out of their busy port, Quincyans now saw trains back into their end-of-the-line station. It was not, in these postwar decades, that Quincy ceased to prosper and expand in the Northern economic boom fueled by the rapid development of American industry, but rather that it did so at a much slower rate, and in essentially a more provincial way, than before the war.

When John and Margaret Parker and their five children moved to Quincy from Kentucky in the 1870s, the family was most surely motivated by the greater economic opportunities in Illinois than in the Reconstruction South. And for nearly four decades afterwards John Parker did manage to earn a steady, if unspectacular, living in Quincy, running a second-hand furniture shop, a grocery, a restaurant. By the time that Belle, the second of his five children and his only daughter, married in 1887, the family had thoroughly integrated itself into the life of the community.

The marriage of Belle Parker and Harry McMein on April 15, 1887, was a quiet affair. On Harry's part, it was undoubtedly overshadowed by the marriage a year earlier of Harry's older brother, William, to Lydia E. Warfield, the daughter of one of Quincy's richest merchants and most visibly leading citizens. The modest Parker residence where Belle and Harry were married by the Trinity Methodist minister was no match for the scene of the McMein-Warfield nuptials: the brand-new Warfield mansion, designed in the Romanesque Revival style by Joseph Lyman Silsbee, and built at the head of Quincy's finest thoroughfare, a fourteen-block stretch of Maine Street which was lined with splendid elms whose branches formed a high, shady cathedral arch.

Harry, by all accounts, continued to live very much in the shadow of his much more successful older brother. William, after establishing himself at the *Whig*, managed to secure positions there for both his younger brothers. By the time he married Belle, Harry had been a printer, reporter, and night editor for the paper. He would continue to fill a variety of roles on the solidly Republican *Whig*—the region was an early bastion of the party and remained loyal as the party grew more conservative—until the turn of the century, when William's initiative would again provide for his younger brother. After buying out his partners at Volk, Jones & McMein, William formed the McMein Publishing Company, installed himself as president, and created for Harry a virtual, if hardly lavish, sinecure that he would hold until his death in 1918.

It was to the Vermont Street house where Fannie and her three sons had established themselves after their separation from Hugh that Harry brought his new bride in April 1887. Already his mother was severely ill—two months later, just short of her fiftieth birthday, she died. By then, Belle was already pregnant.

On January 25, 1888, Margary Edna McMein—who was to be the couple's only child—was born. The following year, Harry took out a mortgage on a house at 1652 Kentucky Street, in one of Quincy's most respectable sections and just two blocks off from William's grander house. Within the year, his father, apparently forgiven his familial transgressions, moved in. When Hugh died in 1894, his place was taken by Belle's recently widowed father, who remained in residence until he remarried some years later.

All in all, it was a family life made close more by financial exigencies than by positive choice: with these largish houses it was a considerable saving to take in an unattached parent. For her first dozen years, then, Marjorie—which is how her name soon came to be spelled—always had one grandfather or another about the house, although it was her maiden great aunt, Anna Gallaher, a long-time schoolteacher in Quincy, who was her chief (and perhaps only) inspirer in childhood circumstances that were often strained.

What strained them most directly was that, as the whole town knew, Harry was following all too closely in his father's none too steady footsteps. Like many heavy drinkers, Harry had a weakness for symbolic gestures, such as squandering the mortgage money. Yet one of the few stories Neysa McMein told Jack Baragwanath about her girlhood concerned a small, insignificant instance that shows Harry Moran McMein in his best light—and as the source of that enthusiasm for life that his daughter would develop so much more fully than he:

> Once when I was quite a little girl my father and I were going to the corner in Quincy to take a streetcar. Before we got there we saw the trolley coming and he grabbed my hand and said, "Come on, let's run!" I said, "We'll never make it—we'll miss it." "All right," he said, "let's miss it, trying!"

Often Harry's drinking and consequent irresponsibility was more a family trial than a family entertainment. Money was always tight and uncertain, and Harry was sometimes seen in the company of the town's less reputable women. In the face of her husband's growing alcoholism and unconcern, Belle withdrew into herself, becoming nervous and uncommunicative. Like her mother-in-law before her, she devoted much of her time and dwindling energies to the affairs of the Vermont Street Baptist Church.

Meanwhile, Marjorie, left more on her own than most of the children in the respectable part of town, developed into a pretty, bright young thing, with an evident talent for music and a liking, when family circumstances were peaceful and prosperous enough to support it, for dispensing cookies and social cheer to groups of neighborhood children, whom she would assemble on the porch of the Kentucky Street house. In worse times she would appear in hand-me-down clothes and could even be sullen and unfriendly. Whether or not Harry occasionally beat her, as rumor had it, Marjorie's childhood was sufficiently awful to cause some public alarm. Several times the Gardner family—whose fortune derived from the invention and manufacture of governors for steam engines—had to take in Marjorie, who was a classmate of daughter Marion, to live with them for a month or two. Marion's mother, it was (and still is) said in the Gardner family, "practically raised" Neysa McMein.

Just as Harry's life in Quincy was overshadowed by the success of his brother William, so Marjorie's must have been by that of William's daughter, Melvina. "Cousin Mell," who was almost exactly Marjorie's age, enjoyed all the privileges and prestige accorded a child of a leading citizen, a man known as a country club stalwart, a golf enthusiast, and, most importantly, an entrepreneur to whom many looked for jobs. These privileges included, as was usually the case for the sons and, less frequently, the daughters of Quincy's "aristocracy," the chance to go east for college. (Mell chose Vassar.) Marjorie must have been a little envious of her cousin's easier, less troubled life, but there is no indication that she was bitter. Marjorie had minor triumphs and major, if still vague, ambitions of her own.

In high school—where, coincidentally, actress Mary Astor's father was her German teacher—Marjorie worked against the unpropitious circumstances at home to make a success of herself. In the quaint, but still familiar, rites of adolescent passage, she succeeded. On March 14, 1906, the senior class of Quincy High School gave a literary evening. One Zens Smith, "robed in the costume of an Indian warrior and accompanied by a chorus of ten Indian maidens," sang the class song of his own composing, "Medicine Man." The chief piece of the evening was Goldsmith's *She Stoops to Conquer*, with Marjorie, as Kate Hardcastle, its chief attraction. The reviewer for the *Daily Herald* assured readers that the play was a "literary gem of the first water" and typed Marjorie the star of the evening. (It was to be her first, and last, favorable stage review.) Then he added, more prophetically than he could have known, "Kate 'stoops to conquer,' but Marjorie need never do so; her rich gold hair, pretty face and natural charms of manner forbid it." When her class graduated three months later, it was the largest the city's only secondary school had yet seen: a mere forty-one students (in a town big enough to support two daily newspapers).

Several months before that graduation day, in a McMein family council, Marjorie's immediate fate had been decided. Although she was inclined to make something of her musical talent, she accepted the verdict that the family's traditionally perilous financial situation necessitated a career with more immediate prospects for making her self-supporting. She would, in a highly utilitarian way, make do with another of her discernible, if still largely undeveloped, talents: her ability to draw. Her father agreed to help support her through a course in commercial art at the Art Institute in Chicago, if she agreed to work to make up the rest of her expenses. As it turned out, what with Harry's usual lapses, the Gardner family— which could well afford it—would also end up paying a share of the costs.

The young woman who went up to Chicago in September 1906 had a last reminder of the kind of life she was leaving behind forever, save for periodic visits. A few days before Marjorie went, Belle had suffered another attack of "nervous prostration," brought on, it was reported, by the mysterious "visits of a crank" to the house next door. When Belle inquired about his business there, he "threatened to kill her" and so sent her to her sickbed. When Marjorie left for Chicago, the police were still investigating.

The Chicago to which Marjorie McMein moved in 1906 was not, of course, entirely new to her, since Quincyans fairly regularly visited the metropolis, even though it was nearly 300 miles off by rail. Still, living in Chicago was a very different matter for someone used to the quieter, smaller ways of Quincy. Chicago in the early 1900s was a brawny, smoky, noisy city. Its skies were orange in the day and crimson in the night from the never-extinguished fires in the furnaces of the steel mills on the South Side; its air was rank from the mingling of animal smells in the stockyards. By 1906, Chicago's population was nearing 2 million—with immigrants now pouring in from Eastern Europe, as they had poured in from Germany, Ireland, and Scandinavia in earlier decades. For nearly a quarter century it had been America's second largest city, but still of a size that its citizens could travel beyond its limits without too much difficulty.

Despite its vigor and the ferment of important literary and artistic activity, Chicago was not yet fully "civilized" when compared with the cities of the Eastern seaboard. In all, it was a large, industrialized version of a frontier town, a metropolis whose most representative figure during the tumultuous period of phenomenal growth might well have been the bullish, picturesque, meat-packing baron, Philip D. Armour, a man totally devoid of interests outside his business, a man who liked to boast that he had found a use for every part of the pig but its squeal. Chicago was not, on the whole, the kind of place in which Marjorie McMein hoped to spend her life.

Nonetheless, she worked away dutifully at her commercial art course at the Institute in Grant Park. During these student years she must have entertained, as she occasionally did in later years, aspirations toward something grander than commercial art, although she was probably also simultaneously discovering her sure commercial instinct and potential. She learned that the strength of her talent was a fine, sometimes bold sense of color, and that its severest limitation was a lack of fiction and fancy. As with her life, so with her art: her gift was for ornamenting and embellishing the actual rather than for creating the original.

To help support herself during these years of study, Marjorie took a variety of odd jobs. She played the organ in a church and the piano in a 10-cent store. She also provided musical accompaniment for silent films in a nickelodeon. She wrote music for a vaudeville troupe, a job that evolved into writing "music for a comic opera" in later tellings. And when there was no call for her musical talents, she swept floors and did other manual labors. Her life, between the schooling and work, was busy—although she still found time to spend in the vaguely bohemian world of art students and aspiring artists. One of her friends, an Institute classmate with the odd name of Main Rousseau Bocher, was, like Neysa, destined for fame in New York, but by a much more circuitous route: the fashion designer, who ran his name together to create the "Mainbocher" label, established himself as one of the dominant figures in the Paris couture of the 1930s, but had to move his salon to New York when the Germans entered the city in 1940. For the next three decades, his dresses would represent the ultimate in stylish simplicity for New York society.

In 1911, in a symbolic move, Chicago's mayor, Carter Harrison II, closed the Everleigh Club, the city's most famous, highest-priced, and most luxurious brothel. Chicago was obviously trying to temper its image as a wide-open, brawling metropolis. (The gangsters of the 1920s and 1930s would do much to undercut such gestures toward respectability.) By 1911, Marjorie McMein had graduated from her commercial art course and was doing her bit as a respectable young woman: for $15 a week she was drawing pen-and-ink sketches of hats for Gage Brothers Millinery Company. But after the initial pleasure of seeing some of her sketches appear in the advertising pages, she grew bored with the routine work. Occasionally, it was true, she was asked to model hats—having become a tall, striking, green-eyed beauty—but the most exciting thing she could hope for, she knew, was a chance to do some not very demanding design work.

Marjorie wanted something more of life, and she realized that Chicago, which still tied her back to the life of Quincy, would never be the place where she would find it. She also began to feel that her real life—that exciting, somehow glamorous life for which she felt herself fated—was being unduly postponed. Like hundreds of other bright young artists from across the country (then and now), she yearned for New York, where a number of her friends from the Art Institute had already emigrated.

The opportunity to go there came in the form of an invitation—motivated, no doubt, more by her beauty than her histrionic talent—to join a vaudeville troupe heading for New York. On the way, Marjorie discovered two things from the succession of one-night stands in dreary, half-full halls, followed by nights in shabby hotel rooms and days on slow, drafty trains: that the life of the traveling player was not for her, and that she was not performer enough to sustain that life even if she had wanted it. It suited her just as well, then, that she was dismissed from the troupe the day after it landed in New York.

In later times, Neysa McMein very rarely spoke of her growing years—neither her daughter nor her stepson remembers her mentioning them even once—but when she did, she created conflicting impressions. To some, like Charles Brackett, she represented these years as a pleasant but insignificant prelude to the life she had created as "Neysa." To others, like Ruth Gordon, she gave the impression—true in the psychological but not the literal sense—that she "came from the wrong side of the tracks in Quincy" and was glad to be shuck of a largely distressing past. To still others, like Janet Flanner, she always remained a girl from small-town America despite her success in New York's glittering society.

Undoubtedly, there *were* some provincial things Neysa chose to preserve about herself, especially her endless capacity for delight and surprise in the ways of metropolitan life. Yet, she just as clearly had no nostalgia for the place of her birth. After 1918, she returned to Quincy but once: to bury her mother there in 1923. Whatever she chose to preserve of her provincial past, Neysa had internalized and used as counterpoint in the life she did lead. In this, she was at one with the cultural and literary spirit of her times, which saw Midwestern small-town existence as a prelude, often a drab one, to the excitement of Eastern big-city life, most specifically life in New York. Of that flowering of American fiction that began in the 1910s and reached its peak in the 1920s, Alfred Kazin has written in "The Background of Modern Literature":

> The symbolic novel of the period, at least in America,
> was against the small town—*Main Street; Winesburg,
> Ohio; Moon-Calf*—and embraced the excitement of
> the big city—*Manhattan Transfer, The Great Gatsby*.
> The symbolic heroine was the "emancipated" woman;

the symbolic crusade was against snoopers and vice-
leaguers and book-censors. The common characteristic
of the remarkable group of novelists who became famous
in the 1920s—Dreiser, Anderson, Lewis, Hemingway,
Willa Cather, Fitzgerald—is that they were all from the
Midwest, provincials seeking in the city a philosophy
from which to attack the old values. The symbolic issue
of the period was freedom.

Neysa McMein was certainly a real-life heroine who might well have
been cut from this fictional cloth.

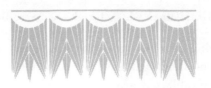

=3=

The Creation
of Neysa

Like Fitzgerald's Jay Gatsby, if not in
so grandiose a fashion, Neysa Mc-
Mein was very much a creature who
sprang from a "Platonic contemplation of herself." By her own admission, and as her vaudeville troupe soon
discovered, she could not "act for sour
apples," but that admission referred
strictly to stage performances; in her
life, she acted the part she had chosen
with ease and conviction. And in line
with the role she played, that of the
famous, beautiful, and carefree artist,
she edited past events to conform to
present images.

Around the year 1912 there is a

curious, but explicable, fold in Neysa's biography, with events and locales run together in contradictory ways. The reason for the confusion is simple: the perpetuation of a lie, not a very great one, about her age. From the time she came to New York onward, Neysa declared herself to be two years younger than she actually was (which is why virtually every printed source, taking her word for it, sets 1890 rather than 1888 as the year of her birth). It would be decades before those two years caught up with her. For the moment, twenty-two seemed to be exactly the right age for a young woman just landed in New York and about to make her fame and fortune.

The story of her early years in New York, as Neysa later told it, was simple, although it contained a few typically Neysean twists. According to her, she had come to New York in 1913, struggled for a few years, then changed her name from Marjorie to Neysa on the advice of the numerologist Asa Neith Cochran; shortly thereafter she began to experience her great, and unabated, success as a cover artist and illustrator. The story is also, at best, only half-true.

Certainly, Neysa was, by instinct *and* choice, credulous and impulsive—and so inclined to act on something as dubious as the advice of a numerologist. She loved fabulous revelations and would implicitly believe them rather than spoil her fun by an easy puncturing of such fancies. It is probably true that, as she told Jack Baragwanath, the original source for "Neysa" was a horse, an Arabian filly on a New Jersey gentleman's farm ("Homer Davenport's place"), where she had gone for a weekend visit shortly after coming to New York. However, the name change was by no means coincidental with her success, since the former had already been effected by July 1912. Early in that month, the Quincy papers reported Marjorie McMein's visit home from New York—dutiful, if ambivalent, about her parents and hometown, during that period she usually visited twice a year, in July and December—and noted that, in the artistic ways of big-city life and to the initial puzzlement of her friends, Marjorie had recently become "Neysa."

Symbolically, if not literally, Marjorie McMein had become Neysa at the moment she stepped from the train into the great hall of Pennsylvania Station and from there into the whirling life of New York City. For a new city and a new life there had to be a new identity. That it would be nearly four years before the city would take any notice of Neysa, the new and greater version of Marjorie McMein, was a matter that could easily be excised from later renderings of her early years in New York.

In July 1912, the Quincy papers also reported, no doubt on Marjorie-cum-Neysa's word, that within the month she would be returning to New York to reopen her studio there. That "studio" then, and for several more years, consisted of no more than a space for her easel by the window in the small apartment in the Lincoln Arcade (the present site of Lincoln Center) that she shared with a few other, equally struggling, young women. Here she drew the hundreds of sketches which she took on her weary, and generally unrewarding, rounds of the city's magazine offices. Her first sale made her wonder if she could afford a second: the Boston *Star* gave her 75 cents for a sketch which had taken over $7 in materials to produce. At the worst of financial times, she and her room-mates were restricted to a diet of popcorn, supplemented by large glasses of water to make it swell and fill their stomachs.

For Neysa, there were the usual sort of pick-up jobs that fell to struggling artists, actors, and writers. For 50 cents a night, just about enough to keep her in popcorn, Neysa worked at the Metropolitan Opera as an extra. It was the age of Caruso, Farrar, and Toscanini, so Neysa must have found the work musically sustaining, if not financially re-warding. (She remained a devotee of the opera, more for its music than its social status, all her life.) Once, an aspiring playwright, the fiancé of a friend from Chicago, Katherine Calvert, managed to get both young women small parts in a small play, but again Neysa proved more a decoration than a thespian. At twenty-six and admitting to twenty-four, Neysa was still without a career of any noticeable sort.

Despite the financial struggles and initial lack of recognition, Neysa had no regrets over coming to New York. It was every bit as exciting and grand, if even more overwhelming, than she had imagined in her provincial fantasies. Chicago was Quincy grown large and loud, but New York, just then emerging from the haze of its late Victorian moment, was genuinely fast and bright. And it was the jumping-off place for, and the only American city culturally tied to, the capitals of Europe. Charlie

Chaplin, who first came to New York at just this time (and who would later become a fast friend, and more, of Neysa's), recalled in his autobiography how the city then pulsated with a certain bold excitement that empitomized the sense of possibility then missing, at least for a product of London's tenements, in European life:

> . . . as I walked along Broadway it began to light up with myriads of coloured electric bulbs and sparkled like a brilliant jewel. And in the warm night my attitude changed and the meaning of America came to me: the tall skyscrapers, the brilliant, gay lights, the thrilling display of advertisements stirred me with hope and a sense of adventure. "This is it!" I said to myself. "This is where I belong."

Neysa, too, was caught up in this sense of possibility. If she was still waiting for fortune to turn her way, she was waiting gaily, sure that her significant life had already begun.

From time to time there were some minor successes with her art. The Butterick Company bought a sketch for $75, so she could say, at least, that her rate had increased a hundredfold. There was some advertising work. And when she had the money—it was by then 1914—Neysa enrolled in classes at the Art Students League, still intent on making more of her small but tangible artistic gifts. Here she worked on figure drawing (classes were still segregated by sex for nude sketching) and portraiture. The following year she managed to talk someone into letting her do a portrait of "Gyp the Blood," one of the gunmen about to be executed in the notorious Herman Rosenthal murder. It was the first of her portraits, and the start of a secondary career as a portraitist that would eventually, of necessity, displace her first during the last decade of her life.

Despite the struggle for work, Neysa was living her life with a determined joy. Her friends in those New York years before the war were chiefly, like herself, would-be practitioners of the visual arts, a number of them men and women she had known in her Chicago years. By her own proud admission, she "walked and rode [preferably on elephants] hundreds of miles in suffrage parades." She became an accomplished sportswoman, an agile player of tennis, badminton, and croquet. She took a ride with Count von Zeppelin in his "finest" dirigible (reportedly the first woman given that distinction). With another woman friend, she managed a motorboat trip along the Algerian coast, after which, rather daringly, the two women accompanied a band of Arabs on a camel ride several hundred miles inland. And she had a number of love affairs, preferably with men of independent mind and often with men of independent means.

In New York's more sophisticated and bohemian circles of the 1910s, sex had become an emblematic gesture in the name of that larger freedom many had come to the metropolis in search of. For a romantic young woman from provincial Illinois, sexual freedom was the most dramatic manifestation that her life was being lived at a bolder, more exciting pitch. It was, however, more than just her casual (and guiltless) attitude toward sex and her tall, lithe beauty that was gaining her something of a reputation as a siren. Somewhat apart from her sure sense of independence, there was about her a quality "warm, tender and sheltering," as one woman observer characterized her special attraction for men— particularly for successful men who nonetheless retained many of their insecurities. There was a softness in her manner and a calmness in her person which many men found very reassuring, even as many women puzzled at it. Neysa had become, in some instinctive way, both independent in the new manner and somewhat "feminine" in the old.

It was more by accident than design (or numerology) that Neysa found the key to her own commercial success. Struck by an elaborate display of pastels in the window of an art supply shop, she bought a small set and began working in this, for her, new medium. Immediately, she realized something: pastels made the most of her only real artistic gift, a flair for color. The pastels imparted to her sketches of young women a sense of spirit and vibrancy that had been missing. Within a few months she was regularly selling those sketches to the *Saturday Evening Post*, *The American Magazine*, and other large circulation periodicals. The "chicken scratch" signature of "McMein" was becoming a recognized and valuable commodity; for two decades it would continue to find ready buyers.

Back in Quincy, the locals were beginning to take some notice of, and not a little pride in, the success of "our Neysa." Her semi-annual visits home were regularly chronicled: Neysa went to this party, that house for dinner, gave her lighthearted opinions on art, the relationship of the sexes, et al. The latest appearances of her sketches and covers were duly noted, whether she happened to be in town or not. When she was "the subject of some valuable publicity in *McClure's* for this month," the town puffed out its collective chest a bit. When, in 1916, Neysa managed the purchase of an automobile, Quincy was watching—and approved this new sign of her success and increasing affluence. And when, several years later, she spoke to students at Quincy High School about her work, she was heralded as "one of its graduates who has truly made good." For the moment, Neysa was the biggest thing happening to Quincy in the larger world. (Mary Astor, née Lucile Langhanke, would soon be bigger.)

If Neysa made some impression on the mind of Quincy in these years, Quincy itself could still sometimes impinge directly on Neysa's New York existence. An old friend, Madah Weems Brady, fled Quincy, putting up—Mr. Brady termed it "hiding out"—at Neysa's Lincoln Arcade apartment. And when the former Mrs. Brady remarried in Missouri the following year, Neysa was part of the wedding party, cut the wedding cake, and found the ring. She still, herself, had six good years to go as a bachelor girl.

Another appearance, a more significant and lasting one, of Quincyans in Neysa's New York life was the arrival not long after the Brady affair of Ruth Gardner and her husband. Six years younger than Neysa, and the youngest of the three Gardner children, Ruth was a celebrated small-town beauty. In 1915, she had married Alfred Miller Botsford, like her a child of one of Quincy's leading families. Within the year they found themselves woefully bored with Midwestern life—Botsford had already spent four college years in the East, at Williams—so they took the first opportunity to hie themselves off to New York, he to try his luck on the stage and she to see how far her small-town beauty and social gifts would get her in a much larger, more competitive arena. Ruth immediately made contact with her sister Marion's great friend, and Neysa, just then making her way into the more exciting reaches of New York's literary-artistic set, was able to introduce Ruth and her husband to a number of her new and important friends. The young couple was launched.

In a very roundabout way, it was the reunion of the two Quincyans in New York that eventually led to the financing of *The New Yorker*. In one of those oddly intimate marital reshufflings that appear rather frequently in the Algonquin set, Ruth divorced Botsford and married his best friend from college, Raoul Fleischmann, of the yeast and whiskey family. Through Ruth's friendship with Neysa, Fleischmann was brought into the Algonquin crowd for its weekly poker game. Within a few years, one of the players, Harold Ross, found a much more productive place for Fleischmann's funds than the pot of a poker game: *The New Yorker*. Supporting the fledgling magazine through its first few years often seemed more of a gamble than even an inveterate gambler like Fleischmann—who would "rather gamble than eat" by one estimation—fancied, but publishing the magazine eventually proved the best bet he ever made.

Over the years, there was to be some rivalry between the two beauties: the more conventionally beautiful, blond Ruth, delicate and smart, and the more striking, tawny Neysa, with her, as one contemporary observer put it, "vivid handsomeness." In the end, though, the same New York set proved too small to absorb the two beauties from the same place in Illinois. As the years went by, and especially after Ruth divorced Fleischmann and drifted apart from the Algonquin set, the two women went their own social ways, only to meet again in their last years, when both were dying.

In the mid-1910s, it would have been difficult for Neysa, who was hardly a person for precise definitions anyway, to define just what specific sort of success, beyond the commercial, she was seeking. The kind of bright, gossipy, quasi-literary society of which she so naturally became a part after the war existed only in embryonic form before it. To the extent that the group had a center, that center was not a physical place at all: rather, it was FPA's "Conning Tower" column, then published in the *Tribune*. In 1917, Neysa decided it was high time she entered the lists of that society. She went to visit FPA.

Franklin Pierce Adams was, like Neysa, a Midwesterner (from Chicago in his case) who had come to New York in search of a smarter, more sophisticated life. Born in 1881, he had moved to New York in 1903 and had immediately begun to establish himself as a newspaperman. By 1909 he was well enough known to collaborate with O. Henry—on a quickly forgotten musical, *Lo!*—and by 1911 he had created, for the *New York Evening Mail*, his "Always in a Good Humor" column, which he renamed "The Conning Tower" when he moved it to the *Tribune* in 1914. From the first, the column was a forcing house for the kind of witty sophistication FPA had come to New York seeking and was now helping to define and exemplify.

In the column, Adams combined pungent observations on contemporary trends and events—he was the grandfather, or perhaps great-grandfather, of *The New Yorker* style of humor—with the contributions, chiefly light verse and aperçus, sent him by a willing, talented, and unpaid group of aspiring writers. Quaint and creaky as it now reads, the column did set new standards in American humor (legitimizing puns, for one thing) and helped start the career of any number of writers. Dorothy Parker's witty bow in FPA's direction—"he raised me from a couplet"—could have been made by a number of other writers who came to sit beside this "homely little man" at the Round Table in the decade following their first appearance in his column: Marc Connelly, Robert Benchley, George S. Kaufman (who invented the "S" as a means, he thought, of giving added distinction to his contributions to FPA's column). If FPA was, as several commentators have noted, more of a conductor than a writer, it was true that he beat a quick, light, and, for the time, witty tempo. By 1920, "FPA" was the best-known set of non-presidential initials in the country.

FPA enjoyed a reputation as, in the words of one of his contemporaries, "a facile artistic talent, a quick wit, and a brilliant personality." Nothing fostered this impression so much as his weekly chronicle, in what now

seems excruciating detail and unbearable mock-Restoration prose (Samuel Pepys's diary was his ostensible model), of his hourly doings as a
social and theatrical gadabout on the metropolitan scene. To be a regular
"character" in that chronicle was to be assured a certain vaguely mythic
notoriety. Neysa now felt herself ready to assume that role.

Putting aside whatever superstitious misgivings she had, Neysa, bearing a nosegay of sweet peas, descended on FPA at his *Tribune* office on
Friday, April 13, 1917. FPA could be easily swayed ("Compared with
me, a weather vane is Gibraltar"), and swayed by Neysa he was. For
the afternoon, these two transplanted Midwesterners "talked of Quincy
and Chicago and Literature and the war." Even then, Adams felt "re-
gretfull that she went away so soon." Although she might not have
realized it at the time, Neysa had made the essential contact that would
determine the shape of her life for the next decade—and beyond.

In the following weeks, Neysa appeared regularly in FPA's record of
his doings. He visits her apartment, reports she is ill, dines with her,
takes her to the Lambs' Gambol (where both find a rising humorist, Will
Rogers, the best of the evening's entertainment), and escorts her to a
lecture by an Arctic explorer (where only Neysa finds the penguins
accompanying it amusing). "Mistress Neysa" is pictured "very fair in a
blue dress"; after a separation of some months, FPA reports "her charm
no less than ever." Over the first years of their acquaintance, FPA was
discovering what he would later characterize as Neysa's chief, if most
curious, attraction—namely, that her ignorance of certain things could
be more enlightening than other people's knowledge of them. No doubt
he, and many another man, took a witty pleasure in informing her.

Neysa, for her part, took to being informed very gracefully, for she
was a good listener, though hardly a passive or uncritical one. Those
men, and occasionally women, who undertook the informal task of ed-
ucating her had to be up to the mark themselves. Despite a willed
casualness and vagueness, Neysa also maintained a stubbornly realistic
streak that allowed her to separate sense from nonsense. Janet Flanner,
who had a chance to observe Neysa close at hand just as she was
becoming famous as an artist and personality, stressed the element of
provincial canniness that her friend retained: She could be frank and

insightful, and she refused to accept second-hand information. Neysa was known, more than once, and making no pretense of clumsiness, to tip a bowl of soup into the lap of a dinner guest whose conversation was proving to be pretentious prattle. Although her Round Table friends never required such a demonstrative response, the group's fanciful, brittle, often cruel wit did sometimes need the counterbalance of Neysa's earthier, more zestful and direct style.

By 1917, many of the stalwarts of what was to become the Round Table group were already known to FPA, although still largely unknown to each other. For instance, the evening before Neysa had presented herself in his office, FPA had dined with Robert Benchley, but Neysa did not meet the advertising copywriter and aspiring humorist until several years later. In the interim, though, there was another matter most of the members of this yet-to-be-formed group had to attend to: World War I. FPA and a number of other future "Algonquin men" went off, in their high-spirited way, to fight and win the conflict. So did Neysa.

It was the war that was to give the final tap to the older, monolithic New York social world whose power and importance had been declining for the previous two decades, even as the witty world FPA was picturing (and creating) in his column was one of a number of alternates gaining in prestige and importance. By 1900, the solid power of the "Metropolitan 400," the inner circle of New York families which constituted the city's high society, was starting to break down, and the 1910s were a transition period to the postwar era in which elements of that society would mingle with and merge into "Café Society," and that with literary-artistic group-ings like the Algonquin.

Social life was becoming more public—Café Society, for one, brought together people who would not normally have visited each other's homes—and the number and variety of social arbiters was increasing noticeably. From the moment she landed herself in New York, Marjorie McMein had been, without fully knowing it, rehearsing herself for this coming social age. As one of her great partisans, Charles Brackett, had to admit, "talent hadn't been a preponderant part of the equipment" Neysa brought with her to New York. However, what artistic talent she did have she would combine deftly with her far greater talent, "a gift for people," to make her one of the social heroines of the age. Before the war, Neysa had become, in a minor way, what, in a major way, she was to be for two decades after it: a celebrity.

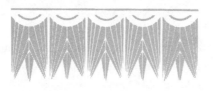

War and
Its Afterwit

When the war did finally pull in the Americans, Neysa was ready—and more than a little eager to see it first-hand. She volunteered herself to do a series of posters for the United States and France, promised the *Post* and *McClure's* some covers ("the dough-boy from life," as later reports always seemed to characterize these of her drawings), and enrolled herself as a troop entertainer under the auspices of the YMCA, not normally her kind of organization. In early June 1918, she sailed off for the front, on a troop ship darkened against the attack of German submarines. It was an eerie, ominous crossing, a silent and dark journey very much in contrast to the lightsome voyage she was to take to that same destination almost exactly five years later, on her "honeymoon."

Before leaving New York, Neysa and her two artist companions, Anita Packhurst and Jane Bulley, provided themselves with several new sets of what Neysa called "real New York clothes," quite certain that the doughboys would appreciate the sight of three pretty young American women dressed in something reminiscent of home rather than the heavy, shapeless, olive-colored YMCA uniform, with its massive, thick cape and helmet-size and helmet-weight tricorner hat. But even in her uniform, Neysa must have been a fetching figure for the young men long deprived of female companionship. Despite her thirty years, the determinedly youthful Neysa was still for them an emblem of the "American girl"—hearty, smart, enthusiastic, and beautiful—the soldiers desperately wanted to remember, and to believe they might live to see back home. With the soldiers, Neysa and her companions spoke "real home talk," and, as she would later do with men much more worldly and famous, Neysa exercised the rare art of listening, while deftly declining a number of impulsive marriage proposals.

The spare sets of clothing the women had brought with them proved more than just alternate costumes, for the doughboys would don them for dances and shows and improvised skits, thereby multiplying the "female" presence among them. As Neysa recalled, "Sometimes we'd dress 25 soldiers with bits of women [sic] finery and call them girls and then dance and dance with 2,000 men." As an entertainer, Neysa's pièce de résistance was a bit she did using Winsor McCay's "Gertie the Dinosaur," the first animated cartoon. While a rickety projector flashed the film on a bedsheet that served as a screen, Neysa provided an outlandish accompaniment on a portable organ (her nickelodeon experience standing her in good stead) and sang, uninhibitedly and wholeheartedly, snatches of particularly inappropriate popular songs. By all accounts the performance was, in that tense, dangerous locale, hilarious. It regularly brought down the house—or rather, the tent. Neysa had managed to reintroduce into that blasted landscape a much-needed sense of simple, silly American fun. Some measure of that moment in her life—and some indication of the notoriety she had by then attained as a cover artist—is this surviving bit of Kiplingesque doggerel done by one of her many soldierly admirers:

"Have you heard of the show at the Y tonight?"
Said Sergeant O'Grady to me.
"Why no" sez I, "an' whats at the Y?"
"Sure it's Neysa McMein" sez he.

"Neysa McMein, do you not know the name?"
Said Sergeant O'Grady to me.
"Not Neysa McMein, that lady of fame,
She has broken the hearts of a million of lovers
Who fell in love with the girls on the covers
Of the magazines way back home" sez he.

"She's a lady of fame, this Neysa McMein,
And she numbers her friends by the host;
She's the party that places
Those wonderful faces
On the Saturday Evening Post."

One of the things that obviously endeared Neysa to the troops was her decided preference for a bit of fun over the necessity to obey rules and remain as safe as possible under dangerous circumstances. Bill Flood, who headed up a balloon company stationed very near the front, invited Neysa to entertain his troops, cautioning her to keep the visit secret from superior officers, since his unit was nearer to the fighting than entertainers were officially allowed to go. Naturally she went, and obliged the troops by doing a large illustration, an American eagle strangling a German snake, on one of the balloons, which the Germans promptly shot down.

Although the war proved to be a crucial experience for many of the men in the Algonquin group—it was, for instance, the source of Heywood Broun's first book and of severe wounds to Robert Sherwood, as well as the introduction of a number of members to one another—Neysa actually experienced its severity more fully than some of the men. For her, the months in France were both "wonderful" and "terrible," as she admitted directly afterwards. For three weeks each month she was sketching and entertaining at the front, often less than a mile from the battle line. She was taken through Verdun, and during a massive evacuation of the wounded and dead she was in the Saint-Mihiel sector, where she was pressed into service aiding the nurses, assisting at the operating table, and offering some little comfort at the bedside of men with limbs blown off, faces mutilated, minds gone to shell shock. "The pain, the agony," she asserted, perhaps recalling her art, was too awful and grotesque "to picture." Around her, moving through the devastated landscape, her artist's eye saw nothing but figures in the most somber colors: the dark blue or olive drab of the soldiers' uniforms and the black dresses of the French women, their uniform of mourning.

Several times Neysa suffered through German bombings—the war was quite ferocious right up to its end in November—an experience she recounted in her flat but precise way to a reporter back in Quincy:

> Since I have lived through air bombing I never will be frightened at anything on earth. The terror of air raids cannot be imagined. They are heralded by the blowing of sirens and the ringing of church bells, and amid this din the lights are extinguished and then suddenly come the bombs, falling no one knows where. The noise they made is worse than that of the battles. The French immediately seek underground shelter—all over the cities places of safety are designated by signs—but the Americans prefer to stay above ground. When I was where there was a piano I rushed to it, and played as loudly as I could. The American boys in the hut would sit quietly in the dark. Once a building next to our hut was hit and totally demolished. Sometimes while riding on roads an enemy machine [presumably the newly devised tank], which is always known by its peculiar trill, would

come along and aim right at us. Trees were our only shelter.

Like many of the men, and a few of the women, who were to set the more hedonistic tone in American life the following decade, Neysa had some direct memory of the hellish world of trench warfare to make an indulgence in life's pleasures the sweeter—and the more imperative.

For a week each month, Neysa was back in Paris, which was relatively secure and safe by 1918. There she improvised a studio to do her posters and cover sketches. It was in Paris that Neysa, through FPA, met two of her later intimates, Sergeant Alexander Woollcott and Private Harold Ross. All three men were involved in writing and editing the *Stars and Stripes*, the newspaper of the American Expeditionary Forces. None of them was particularly committed to the war—they had just fallen into it and had found, in some measure, a way to fall out of it via the newspaper work. The paper, which was put out in an atmosphere lacking in military decorum and procedure but hardly wanting in liveliness, combined a modicum of war reportage with morale-building pieces (straight, corny, or tongue-in-cheek) and an occasional piece of satire or fancy. Not surprisingly, the paper was enormously successful, so much so that it proved to be self-supporting. Like Neysa herself, the trio that put it out had a fine sense of commercial values.

The collection of Adams, Woollcott, and Ross—particularly with the beautiful Neysa in tow—must have been one of the odder groups gamboling about wartime Paris. The spruce officer's uniform, with its Sam Browne belt, did little to disguise Adams's homeliness, and the squat Woollcott was already taking on that eunuch-like plumpness that gave him his distinctly owl-faced look. As for Ross, gangly and gat-toothed, "No one, not even his prejudiced mother, could deny that . . . [his] body was badly put together," according to Jane Grant, who first met him in France and found enough reason, despite his appearance, to marry him a few years later. In an odd way, though, all three men—and Neysa to a lesser extent—found that the war suited their talents, both artistic and social.

For Adams, Ross, and more particularly for Woollcott, it was a new, different theater for their wit and acerbic camaraderie, while also being a vouchsafe of their manhood. Years later, still gloating in the knowledge that he had served abroad while many others had not, Woollcott answered Groucho Marx's query as to whether he had ever "gotten laid" during all his war adventures with a single qualifying adverb, "Infinitesimally"—a reply that would have served equally well for a question on how much he had participated in the actual fighting. Ross, who was probably the only private in the AEF to carry a calling card (it gave the Adjutant General's office in Washington as his business address), was in an oblique way rehearsing the kind of editorial maneuvers that would lead to the creation of the sophisticated *New Yorker* seven years later. Perhaps most importantly, all three of these men, and Neysa as well, found that their capacity to enjoy themselves could survive unpropitious, even hazardous, circumstances. Peacetime New York would be a cinch after wartime Paris.

What ended the war for Neysa, just a month shy of the Armistice, was a cable announcing her father's death. Because the several letters reporting his worsening illness had failed to reach her, Neysa was taken by surprise by the news. Although Harry McMein's alcoholism had for years made his health, not to say his life, problematic, ironically what actually killed him, back home in peaceful Quincy, was Vincent's angina, a disease commonly termed "trench mouth" because of its frequency among the very soldiers Neysa encountered daily. Neysa cabled her invalid mother that she was coming home straightaway, and on the next day she embarked on a Red Cross ship sailing to New York. The ship carried hundreds of wounded soldiers, more than a few of them insane from the pain and trauma of their wounds. Again Neysa found herself pressed into nursing service, though there was little she could do. The ship made full steam and arrived in New York in just seven days. From there Neysa made that long train journey from New York to Chicago and then on to Quincy.

Quincy, like much of the rest of America, was still in the throes of a great patriotic fervor for this "war to end all wars"—although very worried about the young men it had sent off to fight it. Neysa was immediately besieged for information—and could say, yes, she had seen Jim Irwin and Ed Randall and Royal Jackson and some other Quincy men she knew. They were well and, of course, homesick. When pressed on what the men needed, she declared it was nothing extravagant, but rather something simple and reminiscent: "good homemade fudge."

For the moment, Neysa was the only voice of firsthand authority on the war in a town insatiable for news of it—and in need of some reassurance. Neysa promised an address, once she had straightened out family affairs. There was not, to be sure, much to straighten. Harry had left $1,000 in war bonds and no other estate, except the mortgaged house and lot on Kentucky Street. Neysa, it was obvious, would henceforth have to be the sole support of her invalid mother. She would have to take Belle McMein to New York, with a nurse to care for her on the way, and employ several nurses to give her round-the-clock care when she got her there. Neysa's recent prosperity—she was by now a regular and well-paid cover artist for the *Post* and an occasional illustrator for a number of other large-circulation magazines—made the proposition economically feasible, if not particularly convenient or even pleasant. Famous and beautiful "bachelor girls" were assumed not to be burdened with invalid parents, so their men made no allowances on that score. Besides, the fact that Belle Parker was almost as infirm now in mind as in body made the seeing of her, as well as the seeing to her care, all the more melancholy a proposition.

Another melancholy note in Neysa's return home—and a further sign of how quickly her familial past in Quincy was slipping away from her—was the death, very sudden and unexpected, of Harry's younger brother, George. He had been down from Davenport, Iowa, not far up the river from Quincy, for Harry's funeral and appeared to be in the best of health. A few days after his return home he was stricken with appendicitis and died directly following an operation. He was not yet fifty. Neysa arrived home in Quincy to news of this second death. It is, in fact, some wonder that her weakened mother did not perish in the virulent flu epidemic that was then raging and that would claim over a million American victims—far more than the war—before it ended.

The health board having agreed, the night before Neysa's scheduled

departure for New York was set for "daring, dauntless" Neysa—as one
report of the event characterized her—to address Quincy's citizenry on
her war experiences. Despite the 1,300 seats in the Empire Theater—
the town's largest—less than half those seeking admittance gained it.
Neysa's talk, as it turned out, was part of a larger victory celebration,
Germany having surrendered two days before. The evening was a major,
and emblematic, small-town event, the biggest public event of Quincy's
war years. Neysa spoke of all she had seen "over there": of the quiet
and grim French and English soldiers, dispirited and drained by years
of trench warfare; of the contrastingly raucous and devil-may-care American "boys," still plucky enough to wear flowers in their buttonholes as
they went "over the top"; of the black French colonial troops, whose
fierce songs "bring the shivers and carried men 19 million miles from
Quincy." Neysa described how she and her companions traveled the
gutted roads in a broken-down old Ford and how they "played everywhere—on manure wagons, in cow pastures, in barns and in dugouts."

In all, she confirmed what most in her audience, having lived the war
at third hand, already believed: that despite the sufferings and deaths,
the "world" war was a terribly exciting experience for Americans and
that they should be regretful for having missed it. As with her pretty-
girl covers, so too with her talk: Neysa had a finely developed sense of
what the general public wanted. As a lecturer she was a decided hit,
such a hit that she was invited to repeat her performance the following
evening. Even then, three hundred persons had to be turned away. Neysa
barely had time to savor her second night's triumph before she was off.
At midnight she, her mother, and a nurse boarded the "Eli" for Chicago.

World War I had been, all things considered, a tonic for American
society, a fierce yet relatively brief battle on foreign soil that left Americans feeling exhilarated and confident for having suffered and won
through that trial. As Alfred Kazin noted in *On Native Grounds*, both
the immediate and long-range effects of the war on Europe and America
could hardly have been more divergent:

In Europe the war had ended in a general impoverishment and exhaustion, in a despair which, when piled up with so many despairs through the twenties, was to lead into the final desperation of Fascism. . . . To millions of Americans, however, the world of 1920 seemed merely richer and more comfortable, if less naïve, than the world of 1914. . . . [There was] a growing sickness among men in Europe, a spiritual sickness as well as a social despair, that contrasted strangely with the gaiety and recklessness of society in America.

Neysa's Quincy talk on her war experiences had been, despite the horrors and deprivations it chronicled, a precursor of the national mood of gaiety and brightness that would have as one of its symbolic institutions the Algonquin Round Table. As George Abbott, who has lived through ten decades in this country, put it, the 1920s were unique for the general sense of lighthearted expectation they engendered: "Each morning we would wake up asking 'What fun shall we have today?' " Neysa, as it turned out, was commonly the one who provided the answer for her friends.

Before the Algonquin group could form, all its members had to find their way back to New York. By February 1919, FPA was again writing his column and fastidiously recording his hourly doings, including a reunion dinner which Neysa cooked for him. Woollcott, on the other hand, was dispatched to Germany with the Army of Occupation and did not return until much later in the year, after which he settled back into his job at the *Times* drama desk and prepared to reinflict his outsized person and personality on the public. Broun returned and began a host of writing activities, asserting in his pieces that peculiar blend of whimsy and progressive attitudes that would make him the best-known columnist of his time. Ross came back with a plan, soon enacted, for a magazine that would pick up where *Stars and Stripes* left off ("By the same bunch, for the same bunch, in the same spirit"). *Home Sector*, which was shortly bought up by and merged with the sagging *American Legion Weekly*, was to constitute, over the next five years, the last phase of Ross's editorial preparation for launching *The New Yorker*. In short, many of the men and women who came back from the war and who would form the whole, large Algonquin group found themselves moving into a world more receptive to their specialized, limited talents than the 1910s had been. FPA, Neysa, and to a lesser extent Woollcott—all of whom had experienced success in the prewar years—were the three "established" figures around whom the group could form.

Two political events of 1919, the ratification of the Eighteenth Amendment, instituting Prohibition, and the election of Warren G. Harding, were, by way of contraries, to help set the tenor of the reckless decade that was to begin the following year. Prohibition, particularly in a self-declared center of the new sophistication like New York, was both a sham and a scam. What liquor was not concocted in the city's bathtubs—including a much-employed one at Neysa's studio—was easily smuggled in by the rum runners that regularly plied the harbor. Prohibition did, however, change the nature of drinking, making it, for many, a more fierce thing and, for virtually all, an activity now undertaken in mixed company. With the male enclaves of the saloons gone, Americans did their drinking in the privacy of homes or the semi-privacy of speakeasies. Women, at least in the smarter sets, became boon companions on the drinking scene. Neysa, for one, learned to drink with men and to drink like a man—and she continued to do so for the rest of her life.

The sweeping election of the easy, ineffectual, handsome (and, as was later proved, philandering) Harding was as much a national turn away from politics, as represented by the unprecedented international involvement of the Wilson presidency, as it was a conservative political turn. To be sure, the heavily Republican make-up of Harding's Congress—59–37 in the Senate and 301–131 in the House—bespoke the preference for a quieter, more conservative political atmosphere, but it did not endorse conservative politics so much as it bespoke a weariness with politics per se. One of the freedoms the age sought was a freedom from politics.

Neysa, who always remained a registered (if often lapsed) Republican, was commissioned to do a sketch of Harding shortly after his election.

In a piece on the experience, she assured the readers of the *Ladies Home Journal*—Neysa regularly appeared as something of a sage in the women's magazines of the period—that Harding was, indeed, a kindly man, and far more handsome than even his photographs indicated. No doubt Neysa was at one with most of her readers in finding something reassuring in Harding's political quietude, in his seeming decency. "He had no knobs," said Charles Willis Thompson of the bafflingly vague and ill-informed Harding. Coolidge, "Silent Cal," who succeeded Harding in 1923, was, if anything, harder to grasp. From time to time the temperate political climate of the 1920s would be broken by events on the right (the rise of strong anti-immigrant sentiment in the early 1920s, the growth of the Klan to over 4 million members by mid-decade) and on the left (the Wall Street bombing of 1920, the furor over Sacco and Vanzetti); but for the most part politics in the 1920s, like Prohibition, was there to be disregarded as one chose.

In its own way, the Algonquin group was at the center of a social revolution, though ultimately a conservative one, that took place during the decade. As Alice Duer Miller, who became the eldest member of the Round Table set, noted, the war broke up the old social crowds in New York and allowed new ones to form, and she herself threw her patrician lot in with a younger group of writers and wits. New kinds of elites were forming: often less rich and less grand than the older elites, but also more numerous and more varied. Over the next two decades the members of the Algonquin group would go far, usually under self-propulsion, on the group's reputation as an intellectual elite. Neysa, who was very much one of them without being very much like any of them, went along for the ride. For the rest of her life she would be, to some extent, "in society."

For the early 1920s, there were two chief models for metropolitan sophistication, FPA's column and *Vanity Fair*, the magazine which Condé Nast had bought in 1913 and turned over, with chic, witty results, to Frank Crowninshield to edit. Both conveyed a sense of youthful irreverence for the pieties and inanities of American life, and both treated those persons and events they favored with extreme partiality. The two publications were the arbiters of that would-be sophisticated age—just as, by the decade's end, *The New Yorker*, broadening and perfecting the Round Table style, would establish itself as an arbiter of sophistication strong enough to survive the great shifts of fashion and history over the next six decades.

FPA's chronicle of his work and play now seems quaint and insignificant, but in his detailing of events like his visit to the Lardners' Greenwich, Connecticut, home, where Ring played the piano and Neysa wagered him $7.50 over the authorship of a song, or of his visit to the circus, where Neysa and Ellis Lardner "rode upon the elephants and looked more royal than any queens ever I saw," he was creating, small event by small event, a new kind of literary-artistic celebrity, one whose every action seemed meaningful, interesting, and worth recording.

Places too were "in"—like Texas Guinan's brassy, lively nightclub and, less to full public view, Polly Adler's well-appointed brothel, to which a number of the Algonquin men regularly repaired, and where the shy but lecherous George Kaufman maintained a charge account until he discovered the "freer" ways of some aspiring actresses. ("A lovely girl, I took an interest in her" became Kaufman's none-too-subtle way of alluding to these "theatrical" conquests.) Most visibly "in," though, as its adherents were constantly reminding the reading public, was the Algonquin Hotel with its Round Table.

Summations of the origin of the Round Table are legion and range from John Mason Brown's simple surmise ("an improvisation which turned into a habit") to Margaret Case Harriman's fanciful simile ("The Algonquin Round Table came to the Algonquin Hotel the way lightning strikes a tree, by accident and mutual attraction"). Suffice it to say here that the Algonquin was very nearly an inevitable place for these young writers and wits to gather: it was close to the newspaper offices and theatrical agencies of midtown Manhattan where many of them worked; the food was good, if a bit plain; the prices were relatively low; and they could not have been more welcome. The hotel's proprietor, Frank Case, had been courting and catering to theatrical folk for nearly two decades. John Drew and Lady Gregory had stayed there; the Barrymores were regular, faithful patrons; and Douglas Fairbanks was not only a long-term guest but also a welcome playmate for Case's daughter. Literary personages, particularly writers for and critics of the theater, were a natural extension of Case's clientele. If, at first, they could not afford to be big spenders, their ready and freely dispensed banter was payment enough.

Nearly forty years after the Round Table's demise, Marc Connelly could speak of it in his autobiography with a satisfaction not wholly devoid of smugness: "We all shared one another's love for bright talk, contempt for banality, and the dedication to the use of whatever talents we had to their best employment." Conversely, Dorothy Parker, in what was meant to be a scathing condemnation of the group from the newly established position on the left she declared in "The Seige of Madrid," betrayed more than a little self-loathing in her castigation: "The only group I have ever been affiliated with is that not especially brave little band that hid its nakedness of heart and mind under the out-of-date garment of a sense of humor. . . . I know that ridicule may be a shield, but it is not a weapon." To the Algonquin proprietor's adolescent daughter, however, the Round Table group appeared chiefly, and more realistically, as one of "hard-working young people who led busy and scattered lives." The Round Table members did, early on at least, work very hard: at the nearby newspapers, magazines, and agencies, at their writing, *and* at their wit. At times, the Round Table could seem almost as much a rough-and-tumble jockeying for verbal position as a free-and-easy flow of wit.

On any given day the group at the table numbered between ten and twelve—out of a possible thirty or so who showed up with some regularity. Alec Woollcott, acting, in Ross's well-turned phrase, like a "fat duchess with the emotions of a fish," usually provided a mocking bass line against which the quieter and often more deadly wits, like Kaufman and Parker, could play their sparkling obbligatos. Initiates were regularly brought to the board—and almost as regularly left it as victims of the group's flat jokes and insulting humor. Within a few months of its founding, the Round Table, through a vigorous if unofficial promotion by its members, became one of the things to see and hear in New York. Yet, as Anita

Loos's Lorelei noted in her incisively "dumb" manner in . . . *But Gentlemen Marry Brunettes*, the phenomenon of the Round Table was more than a little tautological:

> Well, I soon found out that the most literary envirament in New York is the Algonquin Hotel, where all the literary geniuses eat their luncheon. Because every literary genius who eats his luncheon at the Algonquin Hotel is always writing that that is the place where all the great literary geniuses eat their luncheon.

The California novelist Gertrude Atherton, who had been a regular guest at the hotel over the years, was a kindlier, if still critical, observer. In her 1923 novel, *Black Oxen*, she fictionalized the group as "The Sophisticates," the cream of contemporary "Youth." The witty bantering of the luncheon table she termed, rather as the group itself might have, "an excellent forcing-house for ideas and vocabulary," but she also managed to catch, from time to time, a sense of the group's almost desperate dependence on public notice: "Personal mention of any of the Sophisticates added a cubit to reputation. Three mentions made them household words. Neglect caused agonies and visions of extinction. Disparagement was preferable. By publicity shall ye know them."

Neysa, whose forte was not quick wit in any case, usually did not, except on the occasional Saturday, join the group at the Round Table. Her studio, up on 57th Street, was too far off from the Algonquin to make the hotel a practical place for daily luncheons. It would, however, be a rare afternoon when enough of the Round Table's sitters did not make it up to her studio to give her the luncheon conversation almost verbatim. For her part, Neysa balanced the group's overabundance of wit with, as one observer at close hand described it, "that ineluctable quality called charm." In the midst of high-flown fancy Neysa could often strike a note of droll simplicity—and she punctured more than one pretentious routine with some down-to-earth remark. For a group that was chiefly literary, Neysa also provided a vital link to other groups. As Jane Grant observed, "the paths of artists and writers did not often cross. It took Neysa to merge the groups after she met Aleck." It was, then,

58
▼

chiefly by her differences—of character, of profession, of habit of mind—
from most of the other members of the Algonquin group that Neysa
established her central place in it.

New York sophistication circa 1920 demanded, from most of its practitioners, a certain hardness, for metropolitan life was becoming all the
more anonymous and confining.* Dorothy Parker, who admitted to practicing the art of being "smarty," could rather mercilessly pin down the
metropolitan personages in her stories in one quick, and withering,
glance: "The young man in the chocolate-brown suit sat down at the
table, where the girl with the artificial camelia had been sitting for forty
minutes." Noel Coward, who was to be one of New York's, and Neysa's,
most constant visitors over the next three decades, recalled his impression of the city he visited for the first time in 1921: "it seemed in spite
of its hardness and irritating, noisy efficiency, a great and exciting
place." Neysa's particular way of surviving the onrush of New York life
was, by some mysterious means and often to the wonderment of her
typically high-strung friends, to maintain a calmness and imperturba-
bility even in the face of the worst chaos. As Coward himself, more than
once unnerved and dispirited by his own experiences with the New York
stage, attested several years after Neysa's death, "Never, in all the years
I knew and loved her, did I see her foolish or flurried or mistaken."
And Helen Hayes judged that Neysa, aside from her great and sometimes
inconsequential enthusiasms, maintained a streak of indifference that
allowed her to stand apart from the petty squabbles that often afflicted
and sometimes embittered members of the querulous Algonquin group.

One of the ways in which the Algonquin group most directly mirrored
the newer version of sophisticated urban life was precisely in that it was
itself hard, bright, and more than occasionally mean-spirited, as well
as, by way of compensation, sentimental. As Ruth Gordon, who came
to the group after it was well formed, put the matter: "Everybody in was
tough. Everybody could take it. And did. And everybody could give it

---

* Among other things, people were being packed in closer and closer: between 1913
and 1928 the average size of the new apartments built in the city went from 4.13 rooms
to 3.34 rooms, while the size of the buildings housing them doubled.

out." The young actress soon found that Neysa, for all her warmth and vagueness, could also inflict social wounds with the best of the Algonquin crowd. At a gathering of the group, Neysa pointed a finger toward Gordon and asked archly, "Who is *that*?" Naturally, Gordon was abashed and not a little terrified—to be "in" with this group was for many to exist, or at least to exist in any sense that mattered.

The Algonquin group was, if anything, as various in appearance as it was single-minded in its devotion to wit and adamant in its cliqueness. Those constant companions of the early 1920s—Sherwood (at 6'7"), Benchley (at 6'), and Parker (at 5')—resembled a "walking pipe organ" as they strolled down 44th Street from the *Life* offices to the hotel. On these walks Sherwood was often tormented by a group of midgets (from a show at the Hippodrome across the street), who would scurry about his feet and mock up at him, much to the amusement of Benchley and Parker. The long, lean, mournful-looking Kaufman was already a fair way toward earning his title as "the gloomy dean of Broadway." The gangly Ross now sported a dreadful crewcut, his hair standing up, like bristles, a full three inches. (Actress Ina Claire professed a strong desire to take off her shoes and walk across his ruglike head.) The slightly dowagerish, but ever gay and clever, Alice Miller—Neysa, in her whimsy, always called Alice "Butch"—added the suggestion of an earlier age through her somewhat old-fashioned dress and deportment. Most immediately striking, though, was Woollcott, who accentuated his already bizarre appearance with affectations of dress and conduct. Harpo Marx, who came to love the confounding Woollcott as much as Neysa did, recalled in *Harpo Speaks!* his first impression of Alec with the manic irreverence that made Harpo so central a figure in the Algonquin set:

> He looked like something that had gotten loose from
> Macy's Thanksgiving Day Parade. I couldn't help think-
> ing of Mons Herbert's old vaudeville act in which he
> blew up a rubber turkey . . . until music came out of
> its ass. . . . If Mons had blown up a plucked owl, put
> thick glasses and a mustache on it, and dressed it in

an opera cape and a wide black hat, this is what it would
have looked like.

Besides the regular members, there were always handfuls of pretty
and fashionably dressed actresses about the Round Table, and some of
them—like Ruth Gordon, Peggy Wood, Helen Hayes, Mary Brandon,
and Madeline Hurlock—married men in or attached to the group. But
most of the actresses came and went rapidly and almost always remained
on the periphery. Neysa quickly became the group's chief standard for
beautiful, healthy, gay, and sophisticated young American woman-
hood—a role she was inclined to play. Only Parker, very pretty in her
own petite way, could have challenged Neysa's position, but Dottie was
too neurotic, self-destructive, and acerbic to set any standard beyond
the considerable one she established for brilliant, spontaneous wit.

Imperturbable as Neysa was—as Edna Ferber pictured her, Neysa
could "say nothing, pleasantly"—she was not impervious. At the beginning of their relationship, with his typical enthusiasm for turning
people into projects of his own, Woollcott tried to take direction of her
affairs. Several sharp rebuffs made him realize that Neysa, for all her
seemingly lackadaisical ways, had a strong sense of what she did and
did not want to do. Of course, Woollcott, because his nature was con-
trolling—a point as evident in his writings as in his life—never completely foreswore his attempts to run Neysa's life, but after the first few
years of their acquaintance, the tyrant of the Round Table made Neysa
one of the few exceptions to his drive for total personal control. Neysa,
for her part, became one of Alec's strongest admirers and supporters,
even though several of the men closest to her despised him.

One of the ways Woollcott tried, early on, to shape Neysa's life was
romantically, since in his impotence he played at matching others in a
way he himself could never be matched. He hardly need have bothered:
in the early 1920s, Neysa, "that canny flirt," as one close woman friend
termed her, was more than ever besieged with suitors. Though she was
relatively discreet, Neysa had acquired a considerable reputation as a
"siren." Besides, as Helen Hayes recalls it, "there was a lot of hopping

from bed to bed in that crowd." There may have been—neither was saying—a brief affair with Robert Benchley, a temporary joining of probably the two best-loved and most affable members of the Round Table group in its early years. (Although Benchley's great affability may have derived from a more neurotic source than Neysa's: a great need to be loved stemming from the moment he heard the anguished cry of his mother on learning that his older brother had been killed in the Spanish-American War, "Oh, why couldn't it have been Robert?")

There certainly were affairs, if short-lived ones, with some of the younger artists and musicians, as well as with several of the prominent men who fell into the orbit of the group that swirled about Neysa's studio. Neysa, it was known, was available, although it took a fair amount of talent and wit to win her. Very much in the newer mode of the relationship between the sexes in the 1920s, Neysa was also something of a "pal" to men—if less in the style of the brash ingenue than in that of the successful, high-spirited woman of independent ways and means. One writer on the period characterized her as a sort of "role model for flappers," but actually she was more a role model for the flapper's older, more appealing sister.

That so much of the Algonquin wit has survived—better than its literature—is largely the result of the group's avid sociability. Between their incessant gatherings at the Table itself, in Neysa's studio, at the West 47th Street brownstone Ross, Grant, and Hawley Truax shared with Woollcott, and at Heywood Broun and Ruth Hale's West 85th Street house, a well-turned, and often well-rehearsed, witticism could become legendary in a day, classic in two, and immortal in three. Nor did it hurt that the witticisms were often scribbled down and printed within a day or two, with the group's many columnists taking turns playing Boswell to each other.

The extent to which that wit is deserving of immortality was, even in the heyday of the Round Table, a matter of dispute. Edna Ferber, an occasional participant but one of the group's loyalest and loudest trumpeters, spoke of the "hard-boiled crew; brilliant, wise, witty, generous and debunked" (this despite the regular "debunking" of her grandiose novels of the American scene by various group members). But the fact is that many of the best writers of the age were simply not drawn to the Round Table. Even Ring Lardner was only an occasional and almost completely silent participant in the poker games, although the group's legend would claim him foursquare. One of the age's very best writers, Edmund Wilson, went to the Round Table, found it distinctly wanting, and simply avoided it thereafter. As he recorded in his diary of the 1920s:

> I was sometimes invited to join them, but I did not find them particularly interesting. They all came from the suburbs and "provinces," and a sort of tone was set— mainly by Benchley, I think—deriving from a provincial upbringing of people who had been taught a certain kind of gentility, who had played the same games and who had read the same children's books—all of which they were now able to mock from a level of New York sophistication.

No doubt Wilson was correct—certainly literally, but also intellectually—about the "provincial" outlook that defined the Algonquin set. Many of its members were, like Neysa, from the Midwest: FPA from Chicago, Grant from Kansas, Ross from Colorado, Connelly and Kaufman from western Pennsylvania. Others were from provincial places closer in: Benchley from Worcester, Parker and Woollcott from New Jersey. Even Broun, from the Upper West Side, had a curiously naive and unsophisticated side: "He seemed ungraduated in the truest sense," observed his son, implying that Harvard may well have been prescient in never granting Heywood his degree. To all of them the achievement of a career connected, more or less, with the arts or with literature in the nation's intellectual capital seemed rather a marvelous and wondrous thing in itself.

Benchley, whom John Farrar Straus dubbed "the Santayana of the Algonquin" (and Wilson "the Scarsdale Aristotle"), was, in his way, the epitome of the group's provincial humor. To be sure, there is in Benchley's humor, even in the best of it, a friendliness and assuring normality. Pieces with titles like "The Menace of Buttered Toast," "Do Insects Think?," and "The Tortures of Week-End Visiting" deal, in their own deft manner, with things comfortably familiar to those readers in "Muncie or Quincy or above 125th Street," as Benchley himself, with a nod toward Neysa, delineated the hinterlands beyond the civilized world of which 44th Street was the main thoroughfare. In the Algonquin group, the sophisticated naiveté that was a staple of its humor did not always have to be feigned.

Several years before the Algonquin crowd formed and began perfecting and disseminating its particular brand of wit, Freud published his study, *Wit and Its Relation to the Unconscious*, a work which could have served as the group's primer. In Freudian terms, what was practiced at the Round Table was "tendency-wit," a type of humor that is as much social as verbal: "Tendency-wit usually requires three persons. Besides the one who makes the wit there is a second person, who is taken as the object of the hostile or sexual aggression, and a third person in whom the purpose of the wit to produce pleasure is fulfilled." A perfect miniature demonstration of Freud's point is Kaufman's remark when, after several hours of abysmal playing, his inept bridge partner announced that he needed a moment to go to the men's room: "Fine. This is the first time this afternoon I'll know what you have in your hand." The joke, we see, is very much better if we picture the other two players there to derive the pleasure in Kaufman's discomfiture of his partner.

If Neysa only occasionally played the part of Freud's "first person," the wit maker, she often deftly avoided being the second, the wit's victim, because she was so amply and evidently suited to be the third, the one who pleasures in the wit. A rare exception was Woollcott's gibe at her when she appeared at a party wearing a spectacular—and knowing her tastes, probably eccentric—new dress: "Why, Neysa, you're positively scrofulous with mica." The unaccustomed thrust produced a burst, likewise unaccustomed, of tears. Being a victim was no fun.

The pleasure the Algonquin group took in word play—like Kaufman's one-line review of an Italian tenor, "Guido Nazio was nazio guido"—was ultimately more a social pleasure than a purely comic one. Being clever, or "smarty," meant recognition from an audience that shared one's allusions and so could applaud one's dexterous rearrangements of a common parlance. Neysa was one of the most determinedly social of them all—and it was in the salon she offhandedly ran, and in her inventiveness with word games and party games, that she provided the Round Table with the extended circumstances it needed to function as more than just a group of lunch-hour wits.

As Connelly noted, almost everyone at the Round Table succeeded simultaneously—he might have added "very quickly" (if one dates their success from the founding of the Round Table). In 1921, there were seventy-six legitimate theaters in New York, and in those days costs were low. Any show that ran one hundred performances returned a profit and was a "hit." One of the group's earliest successes was *Dulcy*. Borrowing a character from FPA's column (a flighty, charming, and triumphantly ignorant woman named after Cervantes's Dulcinea), Kaufman and Connelly wrote their play in a month, and Neysa drew the program cover for them. It was one of the brightest hits of the season and established Lynn Fontanne, in the title role, as a star. As Kaufman's biographer Malcolm Goldstein has written, the success of the piece, like many of the early successes of the Algonquin crowd, induced a sense of euphoria and limitless possibility:

> To be young and talented and living in New York in the 1920s, with money to spend and the promise of more of it to come—this, the happy situation of Kaufman and Connelly after the opening of *Dulcy*, was the best life imaginable. Connelly thought it was as fantastic as a child's dream of pleasure in which the whole sky was filled with balloons and anyone could pull down as many as he wished.

A great attraction—as well as the ultimate limitation—of the Algonquin set is that for years its members continued to approach life and career with a certain childlike sense of expectation. It was, for instance, a lucky run of cards that helped Broun to purchase the 85th Street house, and it was an unlucky run that pushed him to sell it. Woollcott, with a quite accurate sense of his often petulantly childlike critical approach, simply divided one collection of his essays into two categories: "Enthusiasms" and "Resentments." Neysa devoted as much energy, and almost as much time, to inventing party games as she did to her art.

There was, to be sure, something almost magical about the way the Round Table members could assert themselves in their often inconsequential style and still prosper. The public was much in tune with their spirit of play—and quite amply rewarded the group's expressions of that playful spirit. As a result, within a few years many in the Algonquin group had money to spare—and often enough spare money with which to make more money. The 1920s were a boom time for the stock market, and anyone with some money to invest and a knowledgeable friend in the market, which is to say a majority of those in the Algonquin set by the mid-1920s, could steadily pile up considerable extra earnings. Under the circumstances, Neysa had probably the best friend possible: Bernard Baruch.

The financier-turned-statesman had a distinct fondness for theatrical and artistic types, people he found a pleasant diversion from the business and government personages with whom he spent his long working hours. Neysa and her studio were, not unexpectedly, much to his liking. Thinking she had no head for business—he was a bit off in this calculation—Baruch oversaw all of Neysa's investments. Thus, she started the steady accumulation of funds that would see her through most handsomely to the early 1940s. Although she was, for twenty years, one of the highest paid illustrators in the country, it was really the heady financial atmosphere of the 1920s that allowed her to parlay her substantial earnings into funds that made her, for a while, almost rich.

As Heywood Hale Broun, the child of two members of the Algonquin set, observed in *Whose Little Boy Are You?*, there was, in addition to the group's hardness, a strong streak of sympathy for one another. It was more than just jokes and witticisms that they shared between them: "The Algonks lent each other money, found doctors and psychiatrists for each other, and, best of all, listened to each other's troubles." At all this sort of swapping back and forth Neysa was a natural. Her resources, her studio, and, later, her home were always available to those whom she favored, and she favored a great many. What she offered most completely, though, was—according to those who received it—a kind of enlightenment beyond precise measure. What she received in return was the complete devotion of dozens of friends.

The easy success of Neysa and her friends was the cause of no little resentment on the part of unsympathetic observers of their iconoclastic ways and of the new brand of sophistication they devised and offered for public sale. One actor, who was irked enough by Broun's regularly scathing reviews of his performances to sue the journalist for libel, must have been made apoplectic by the outcome of the case: a judgment in Broun's favor, followed by Broun's next review, the one-line dismissal of "Not up to his usual standard." George M. Cohan sneered at the new standards of humor and conduct the group set, calling the luncheon gathering "a round table without a square man at it." The father of the actress Peggy Wood warned her that she was associating with a group of "first-rate second raters." S. N. Behrman, yet to make his first success as a playwright, wondered what, in the larger scheme of things, his acceptance on the part of Woollcott and his friends amounted to: "Knowing him, being part of his entourage was, in a sense, a symbol of arrival. But what else did it symbolize?" As even Anita Loos conceded, Neysa was the "reigning queen" of the Algonquin set—but it was clear that Neysa never quite realized the very limited extent of her domain. For the first half of the 1920s, neither she nor anyone else in the Algonquin inner circle was impelled to question the validity or importance of the fame they had so easily secured.

The 1920s was a commercial decade and the members of the Round Table, for all their libertine and iconoclastic ways, were representative of the age. They wrote—or drew—to sell. Irreverence was the most valuable literary commodity of that moment, and Parker, Kaufman, Connelly, Broun, and, in a more subdued way, Benchley did a bustling trade in it. Woollcott set up a particularly brisk trade in the treacly kind of irreverence in which he specialized. Given its commercial bent, it is not surprising that the group readily welcomed several businessmen, especially into its poker games. Insurance man Ray Ives was a particular intimate of Woollcott's and an original member of the Neshobe Club, the group that summered at a private island retreat in Vermont. Raoul Fleischmann put a fair part of his share of the family fortune into *The New Yorker*. Paul Hyde Bonner, who was doing extremely well with the Swiss silk firm of Stehli into which he had married, was also a regular member of the group, when he was not off in Paris surveying the latest fashions; how well he carried over the group's informal lessons in literary commercialism is evidenced by his emergence, nearly three decades after, as a popular novelist.

Neysa's work was even more commercially oriented than that of other "artists" in the Algonquin set—but then, she never pretended it to be otherwise. A kind of upward-looking hierarchy was established: just as Dorothy Parker envied Hemingway his "more serious" art, so Neysa granted the greater seriousness of the work of Woollcott, Kaufman, Benchley, and other writers in the set compared with her own. It was as if the small-town girl who came to conquer the big city needed her literary friends to be the geniuses they sometimes professed themselves to be and a willing public more than occasionally believed them to be. Nowhere did this view more obtain, under her own gentle prompting, than in that 57th Street studio which Neysa McMein managed to make the leading New York salon of its time.

5

A Very Modern Salon

The great years of Neysa's salon, 1920–23, coincided exactly with the great flourishing of the Round Table, which gradually declined to extinction between 1923 and 1930, although many of the close groupings it fostered would last another decade. From 1923 to 1926, Neysa's studio shared its position as the primary annex of the Round Table with "412," the Ross/Grant–Woollcott–Truax brownstone on West 47th Street. When Neysa was forced to move from her 57th Street studio—the building was being razed—her salon came to an end, although her subsequent studios would continue to be wandering-in places for the literati and other people of interest and note.

The significance of Neysa's salon in its time is evidenced by the fervor with which many of its habitués recalled it afterwards. Newspaperman Arthur Krock spoke of it as "a salon in the eighteenth-century French tradition but with the informality of the twentieth," an institution created and held together by Neysa's "greatness as a human being." Margaret Case Harriman termed it "one of the last intellectual salons in New York." Ruth Gordon, in *Myself Among Others*, said simply that in her time it was "the only salon in New York." And an unnamed "friend" of Neysa's was quoted, in a *Newsday* article on Neysa half a decade after her death, as asserting: "Neysa had the nearest thing to a salon this country has ever seen. . . . She might be in her smock and serve bad port but everyone came and everyone loved it."

What Neysa's salon offered for many was a full measure of that freedom which was so much heralded and sought, but not always found, in the "Jazz Age." In this respect, Neysa's salon was not just an annex to the Round Table; rather, it was the Table's countermeasure. If the keynote of the Round Table was a brash, challenging wit, the keynote of Neysa's salon was a benign, witty tolerance. At the luncheon table, philistine culture had to be confronted and leveled with every breath (by wits none too sure about their absolute divorce from that culture). But by late afternoon that philistine culture seemed to recede as a deadening, threatening presence—leaving Neysa's studio full of witty, charming people who could, for that moment, feel themselves accepted, their values understood, their talents appreciated. At Neysa's studio, things were decidedly freer and friendlier.

The studio itself was a large, airy, ugly room, with a legendary untidiness and miscellany about it. What made it homey and warm was the mismatched furniture and bric-à-brac brought in as gifts. Tapestries, sketches, bits torn from the day's newspapers hung, in no discernible pattern, all over the walls; chairs piled up in corners as the crowd ebbed this way and that; books tumbled from the makeshift bookcases and spread themselves around as guests consulted and declaimed from them. In all, as Neysa later recalled it, the place achieved "the look of a well-

used workshop." Some pieces in the mélange were even said to be
valuable, but Neysa suspected that on closer inspection everything she
owned would prove to be a fake—but it was no great matter to her or
to her guests. Fortunately for the likes of Gershwin and Heifetz and
Irving Berlin, the studio also contained a grand piano, although none
too rigorously maintained an instrument. Once, checking on the cause
of some startling, unexpected dissonances, Heifetz lifted its lid and
discovered a handful of caramel candies melted onto the strings.

Late afternoons at Neysa's were, for the Algonquin group anyway, just
one rite in a daily social ritual that had a certain relentless quality about
it. As an elderly Marc Connelly remembered the situation, "We hadn't
seen each other since lunchtime so it was good to get together and renew
old acquaintances and talk over old times, because we wouldn't meet
again until after dinner, unless we had dinner together, which was also
a frequent occasion." (It was hardly surprising that under such a daunting
regimen a number of the group's writers, Connelly included, soon began
to produce less and less.) On first meeting the group, the young Noel
Coward tried to puzzle out the matter by asking, "Don't these people
see anyone bloody else?" when he encountered the same group, virtually
intact, in three places in a single day. One answer was that, for the
most part, they did not see too much of anyone outside their large,
floating group—although there were goodly numbers of each other to
see, upwards of eighty if everyone even vaguely affiliated is counted.
Another answer, as Coward soon discovered, was that Neysa's studio
was most often the staging ground for the group's outside encounters.
The "Algonks" might hold sway at Neysa's—or on some days, they might
not—but they never completely dominated there as they could at the
Round Table. No one, least of all the hostess, could be quite sure who
would show up at the studio on any particular day, who might arrive to
enliven and shape the afternoon's doings.

Neysa's peculiar genius as a hostess, as many have attested, was that
she most gloriously did *not* preside. Any guest who showed up in daylight
hours would get the same democratic greeting: Neysa, disheveled, her
hair and smock streaked by the drizzle of the pastel dust, would emerge
enthusiastically from the chaos surrounding her easel, give the visitor

a rousing, sticky handshake, and entrust his or her amusement to whatever group was already there and making merry. Instantly, she returned
to her work—and kept at it steadily despite the convivial temptations
near at hand and a noise level one visitor estimated as "roughly that of
a busy steel plant." If a visitor left while she was still sketching, she
would pause only long enough to offer another hearty handshake, thank
the guest profusely for coming, and urge a return visit. Neysa's non-
chalant stance as a hostess offended a few, and at first it puzzled the
more direct Jack Baragwanath, but it captivated a great many more. On
any given afternoon between 1920 and 1926 a fair share of the talented,
witty, and interesting people in New York could be found in Neysa
McMein's studio.

Perched on her stool, her eyes fixed on her drawing, and looking the
more lovely for her physical disarray and air of detachment, Neysa very
much created the impression of, in Helen Hayes's apt metaphor, "a
tortoise shell cat who had gone to art school." No doubt there was
something uncannily feline about her—as if at her bidding the noisy,
surrounding world could impinge on her not at all, except at those
moments when she would pause from her work to toss a casual remark
its way. Anaïs Nin, who, as a young model, posed for Neysa, was one
of several persons who found the blasé attitude Neysa exercised in her
studio, her ultimate air of indifference, more a cause of vexation than
charm. As Nin recorded in an early diary:

> I met many celebrities there—F.P.A. and Heifetz. It
> was so enjoyable, so bright and lively, that when I was
> finished posing for her and she was about to pay me, I
> said to her: "It was so wonderful, posing for you, I hate
> to take the money for it." "Oh, they all say that," said
> Neysa McMein bluntly and ironically. And I felt a flush
> of anger at the way she took my remark.

Others, in the more fortunate position of guests, took Neysa's almost
impudent casualness in the manner she intended it: as an invitation to
do just as they pleased. Neysa always did.

It was obviously, if indirectly, part of Neysa's charm for the many

men who came to her studio to pay her court that they could see her
working, oblivious to their presence and making a good enough living
by that work to put her beyond any of the favors they could buy her.
More than anywhere else, in her studio Neysa was her own woman, who,
in Flanner's characterization, "was capable of doing anything and explaining none of it"—and who, thanks to the popularity of her work,
had the financial means to sustain the doing and foreswear the explaining.

Heywood Broun, a sharp if not always quick Algonquin wit, once defined
repartee as "what you wish you had said." Neysa's studio could provide
a stage whereon the wits could redeem a dull luncheon performance or
reinforce a smart luncheon triumph. One afternoon the crowd might be
buzzing about FPA's splendid response to "meretricious" in the homonym
game, "I Can Give You a Sentence": "A meretricious and a happy New
Year." Or they might be chuckling over Kaufman's ingenuous reply to
the request that Woollcott be summed up in a single word: "Improbable."
Conversely, they might be recounting Woollcott's devastation of the latest
actress or aspiring writer brought, trembling and hopeful, to the luncheon
board—or enjoying one of those rare moments when the tyrant of the
Round Table was himself discomforted, like the time he fondled a newly
published volume of his essays and sighed, "Ah, what is rarer than a
Woollcott first edition?" only to be brought up by FPA's "A Woollcott
second edition."

More usually, though, Neysa's salon was a place for relaxation, if
often of the frenetic sort, rather than for competition. The studio was
large enough to accommodate those games the Algonquin group played
with such manic devotion, large enough, in fact, to sustain, in an atmosphere of general hubbub, a variety of conflicting activities. Woollcott's description of a typical afternoon at the studio, in his celebratory
essay "Neysa McMein," exceeds by only a little the average reality of
the place:

> Over at the piano Jascha Heifetz and Arthur Samuels
> may be trying to find out what four hands can do in the

syncopation of a composition never thus desecrated before. Irving Berlin is encouraging them. Squatted un-
comfortably around an ottoman, Franklin P. Adams,
Marc Connelly and Dorothy Parker will be playing cold
hands to see who will buy the dinner that evening. At
the bookshelf Robert C. Benchley and Edna Ferber are
amusing themselves vastly by thoughtfully autographing
her set of Mark Twain for her. In the corner, some jet-
bedecked dowager from a statelier milieu is taking it
all in, immensely diverted. Chaplin or Chaliapin, Alice
Duer Miller or Wild Bill Donovan, Father Duffy or Mary
Pickford—any or all of them may be there. . . . If you
loiter in Neysa McMein's studio, the world will drift in
and out. . . . Standing at the easel itself, oblivious of
all the ructions, incredibly serene and intent on her
work, is the artist herself. She is beautiful, grave and
slightly soiled.

The very lack of a unified group purpose at Neysa's salon was for participants a signification, more important that we can perhaps now realize,
that they had escaped the kind of middle-class, rule-dominated house-
holds of their late Victorian childhood, and that they were at last doing
just as they pleased. As Ruth Gordon pictured Neysa's in *Myself Among
Others*, "People eddied around the studio and talked with each other or
to, or at, or about, then drifted off and were missed or not." The very
lack of connectedness and defined group purpose was, paradoxically,
the only thing some visitors had in common.

This disconnectedness was more than a social style—it was a style
of humor with the Algonquin set as well. For example, these sentences
on the opening pages of Donald Ogden Stewart's minor comic master-
piece, *Mr. and Mrs. Haddock Abroad* (1924), announce a work cast in
the high style of the comic non sequitur: "She slept very well at home,
though, mostly on her back and left side. Her mother's maiden name
had been Quetch." Neysa came to this sort of comic illogic more naturally, if not less enthusiastically, than most in her crowd: both her

upbringing and her habit of mind were much more miscellaneous and disconnected than average. When Alice Miller asked Neysa how she had gotten to know Pearl White, the silent film star, Neysa replied simply, "I've always known her"—an answer that was as evident to the respondent as it was acceptable to the questioner. A more melancholy instance of this cultivation of disconnectedness and illogic is Benchley's pronouncement that "anyone can do any amount of work, provided it isn't the work he is supposed to be doing"—this from a writer who failed to grow beyond the short comic sketches he so deftly produced and who ended up, in his own estimation, being "a public clown" before the Hollywood cameras.

The one activity at Neysa's that was not by any means pursued indirectly or discontinuously, save in the legal sense, was drinking. One of the many who came to drink whatever was brewing in Neysa's bathtub, Don Stewart, recalled in his autobiography that the early years of Prohibition were highly intoxicating in more than a literal sense: "This was part of the great excitement of being a New Yorker in those days. Prohibition also added immensely to the *joie de vivre* . . . you were defying that damned Puritanical law, and consummating a rebellious act of independence and self-affirmation against the power of the reformers and their spies . . . in 1922 drinking was still a happy high adventure."

In the bathroom at Neysa's was a still so enormous that using the toilet was very difficult and using the bathtub impossible. Here Neysa and her friends made wine, gin, and other alcoholic concoctions, once even brewing up "real altar wine" from a recipe one of Neysa's models inveigled from a priest. Connelly and Benchley, after his resounding fall from the wagon, were the chief technicians for the delicate and elaborate mechanism—and none too skillful technicians at that. One day there was a terrific explosion in the bathroom: the studio was left a purplish mess and Neysa had to go into hiding for several days until she was sure the much-beleaguered Prohibition agents had not added her name to the long list of bootleggers they were pursuing.

As her friend and sometime collaborator Jane Grant recognized, "Neysa was not above a little lion-hunting"—and for all the casual charm and indifference Neysa exhibited in "running" her salon, she was inclined to press her offhand invitations to visit it on certain worthies until they capitulated. When she learned that H. G. Wells had accepted her invitation, she spent some quiet hours reading up for the visit in his recently published (and immensely popular) *An Outline of History*— though it was undoubtedly Neysa's insinuating charm and the liveliness of the atmosphere she engendered around her, rather than her recently acquired historical grasp, that kept Wells coming back each day for the remainder of his New York visit.

To her studio Neysa often attracted people wholly outside, and sometimes even hostile toward, the Round Table set. FPA dropped in one evening and found "H. Mencken, the poet," whom he termed "a gentle old man and a merry." Although he was but a year older than Adams, Mencken was a member of an older, less trendy—but in many ways sturdier—literary generation than that represented by the Algonquin wits. He was also more of a genuine iconoclast than Neysa and her friends, ever with one eye on commercial success, were to be. Most of the time Mencken preferred to drink with a group of male cronies in a Hoboken speakeasy, but occasionally he made his way to Neysa's modern gathering place, to sample her charm and be lionized a bit.

Although she had a fair amount of competition from the pretty young actresses who regularly found their way to her salon—Margalo Gillmore, June Walker, Helen Hayes, Mary Kennedy, Mary Brandon, Tallulah Bankhead—Neysa had the great advantage, in her untidy manner, of epitomizing the lightsome, carefree tone of the assemblage. What particularly struck Heifetz on his first visit was that Neysa forgot, if she had ever intended it, to ask him to play. (Dutifully, he had come with his accompanist.) Instead, he was just allowed to sit and drink in the high-spirited, slangy, racy conversation that swirled about him. He came back as regularly as his schedule allowed and was soon dropping current phrases—like "Get the hook?"—himself.

It was at Neysa's studio that many unions of one sort or another were forged. Here one great friend of Neysa's, Janet Flanner, met another,

Jane Grant—and the resulting friendship led to a correspondence from France that Grant persuaded Flanner to make regular and persuaded Ross to publish as the fortnightly "Letter from Paris" in *The New Yorker*. (Flanner's pen name for the column, Genêt, was no more than Ross's mistaken notion of the French equivalent for "Janet.") And here in Neysa's studio, as later in her Long Island summer home, elements of "society" were united, for a few titillating hours, with "our roughneck crowd," as Connelly termed the Algonquin group. Members of each set must have liked what they saw, for in ensuing years a good number of the "roughnecks" would move into, or very close to, "society," even as "society" doted more on the writers, artists, and musicians whose talents were enviable and whose celebrity was intriguing. What Woollcott asserted in 1923—"If you loiter in Neysa McMein's studio, the world will drift in and out"—was true enough if that world was counted as no more than the area between the East and Hudson rivers and between Greenwich Village and 96th Street. For many in this world, including those who inhabited it vicariously through the columns, it was world enough.

Musical evenings were a regular, if normally informal, feature at Neysa's studio. Heifetz might start the proceedings by playing a jibing version of "The Japanese Sandman" (which he called "Just a Japanese Sandwich") on the piano, to be shouldered aside by Irving Berlin or Deems Taylor, each intent on adding his musical irreverences to the proceedings. Soon the musical amateurs joined in, for many in the Algonquin set were competent, if hardly startlingly good, musicians. Benchley played, in his own sweet way, the banjo mandolin and Dorothy Parker was counted a virtuoso on the triangle. FPA favored the lighter wind instruments: piccolo, flute, and harmonica. Neysa, when the professionals let her get near the keyboard, would improvise some raggedy blues in her best nickelodeon manner. When she was debarred from the piano, she would join in the rousing community sing that often threatened to drown out the noble voice of Paul Robeson or the pure voice of Grace Moore that might be leading the group. Occasionally, the professionals took matters wholly into their better-trained hands—as did Gershwin when, given just the slightest encouragement, he played, with Bill Daly on second piano, his *Rhapsody in Blue* and Concerto in F at Neysa's studio before either was premiered in public. Presumably, Neysa had the caramels removed from the piano for these events.

As Arthur Krock observed in his memoirs, Neysa's studio was unique for the sense of musical fun it promoted and for the droll way the whole crowd had of mocking the solemnities of performance:

> . . . it was the only place where in a single evening one might hear Sherwood's gravely ludicrous rendition of "When the Red, Red Robin Goes Bob, Bob, Bobbin' Along"; Heifetz burlesquing the graduating solo of a boy violinist; Father Duffy singing old Irish songs; and Ring Lardner spinning such of his fantastic tales as "The Tridget of Greva" with the impassivity of expression found only on the faces of cigar-store Indians.

If Neysa's place was its own kind of stage, it was certainly one on which the usual seriousness of the performing manner was irreverently treated.

Irreverence was, in fact, often the chief mode of expression in the Algonquin set. Parker named her canary "Onan," because he was "always spilling his seed upon the ground." Connelly and Kaufman soon acquired Benchley's knack of writing hilarious parodies of the most sententious advertising copy of the time. Forced to come up with a new one-line comment each week to describe the dreadful and insufferably long-running play *Abie's Irish Rose*, Benchley threw the competition open to his friends—who by consensus declared Harpo the winner for his "No worse than a bad cold."

One of the group's most thoroughly organized irreverences was its tongue-in-cheek stage review, *No Sirree!*, which was rehearsed in Neysa's large studio and given on Sunday evening, April 30, 1922, at the 49th Street Theater. The review—its title was a flat, Americanized allusion to *Chauve Souris*, the French review that was one of the hits of the 1921–22 season—was intended to satirize contemporary fashions, stage and otherwise, and to demonstrate for the many stage celebrities who were invited to sit in the audience just what the Algonquin crowd thought of present theatrical fare. Actress Laurette Taylor, who reviewed the evening for one of the newspapers, gently scored the amateurism of the piece and suggested its players "all leave the stage before they take it up." Oddly, though, the evening did prove the theatrical making— and to some extent the literary unmaking—of one member of the Round Table set. Robert Benchley's "Treasurer's Report," which had seemed uncertain and unfunny in rehearsal, proved to be the hit of the evening and Benchley a "natural" on the stage. A piece of meandering drollery, it was the hopelessly tangled and digressive report of a country club treasurer to the membership. It very much created the impression of an inept "suburban duffer," to cite Edmund Wilson's characterization of the central figure in Benchley's humor, being overmastered by the world. Irving Berlin, among others, was greatly amused by the skit and hired Benchley to recreate it for the *Music Box Revue* the following theatrical season. Thus began Benchley's transformation from writer into per- former, a transformation that increasingly cut him off from his wife and children—since he chose to stay in town overnight after performances— and eventually made him, once sound films came in, more a creature of Hollywood than of New York.

While Neysa was later to gain a more formal reputation as a hostess, although her best parties would always maintain a casual and informal air, in the days of the 57th Street salon it was often difficult to distinguish, for either Neysa or her guests, between large gatherings and "parties," between impromptu dinings in and "dinners." One night FPA showed up by invitation for dinner—which was at least enough of an occasion for him to don a new white flannel suit—and sat down to dine and chat with Connelly, Art Samuels, and Irene Castle. Other nights, though, people would just stay on from their late afternoon visiting; it was not uncommon for fifteen or twenty guests to sit down to an impromptu dinner at the studio, often with a draw of the cards or a roll of the dice deter- mining who would foot the bill for the food ordered in. Similarly, if the guests lingered into the evening, as they often did on weekends, the gathering would naturally evolve into a "party." In fact, during the first half of the 1920s, much of the Algonquin group's collective life seemed one big, floating party.

Among the odder events held at Neysa's studio was a fashion show featuring Woollcott's styles. With dictatorial aplomb, but also tongue-in-cheek, Alec had taken an active step in correcting the oft-noted fashion failings of his women friends by designing his own, and certainly peculiar, line of creations. Fortunately, he had the good sense to give humorous mock-French titles, like "Fawn's Bottom" and "I'll Say She Is," to his bizarre dresses.

One night in late 1922, FPA showed up at Neysa's studio to find a great crowd of eager participants engaged in a new pastime: ranking everyone they knew according to "personal allurements, as in a crowd of 100 men how many would be indifferent to this woman, as in a crowd of 100 women how many would be indifferent to that man." Quite expectedly, some "terrifick disagreements" arose, he reported in his diary, and not a few egos were deflated, including that of the bearish Heywood Broun, who was surprised to find himself rated much lower than he fancied he should have been.

One of the men ranked highest must have been Charlie MacArthur, whose smiling, curly-haired good looks and easy, bantering way with women made him a most attractive figure—and one admired, without envy, by men. Any number of women, including a thoroughly (almost suicidally) infatuated Dorothy Parker, were mad for Charlie; but it was at Neysa's studio that Charlie found the woman he was to love. It seemed, at the time, a highly unlikely and distinctly unsuitable choice for the high-spirited, urbane newspaperman and playwright.

By 1925, when she met Charlie, Helen Hayes was long on stage experience but short on life experience. As natural, charming, and smart as she was on stage, she was awkward and tongue-tied off stage, most particularly when confronted with the challenging wit and social niceties of the Algonquin circle. When she managed to say something, it was often the wrong thing—in a group that put a premium on saying the right thing (by its own strict, if idiosyncratic, standards). Charlie, who blithely ignored the inconvenience of already having a wife off somewhere, was surprisingly taken with the petite, beautiful Helen. "He saw the woman lurking in the girl," as she later put it, and he was determined, in his own fun-loving way, to bring the woman out.

Picking up a dish of peanuts, Charlie pressed them on the young actress, who accepted them with mumbled thanks. Then he added, just loudly enough for the romantic remark to be overheard and so gain lasting notoriety, "I wish they were emeralds." (Twenty years later, haunted to the point of tedium by repetitions of the remark, Charlie reversed the procedure: returning home from India, he dropped a bag of emeralds in Helen's lap, saying, "I wish they were peanuts.") They talked through the afternoon, with Helen marveling at her luck in having landed for the moment "the catch of all time." Afterwards, Charlie took her home in a hansom cab. He promised to call her, which he failed to do, leaving the thoroughly smitten young actress worried but still hopeful. Each night, just before the curtain rose, she would look out into the audience to see if Charlie had come. Finally, he did come and sent a note backstage asking to see her. After that there seemed no stopping the romance.

Of the whole Algonquin crowd, only Neysa saw the possibilities of the relationship and supported it. She warned Helen to brace herself for the storm: Beatrice Lillie, whom Charlie had been seeing before she left for England, would soon be back in New York and the scoffers would have at her with tales of Charlie's new love interest. In no time, he would be straightened out and the upstart young actress put in her place. In and around the Algonquin set, as Helen would supposedly learn, one did not do things that met with the group's general disapproval. Gradually, though, Helen, with support from Neysa and with the show of Charlie's very evident devotion, won the crowd over. When she and Charlie married three years later, Alec Woollcott was best man.

Charlie's romantic gesture with the peanuts was very much in keeping with a certain tone set, first and foremost by the hostess, in Neysa's salon. Margaret Harriman dubbed Neysa "the last romantic," and there always did remain about Neysa, despite her offhand manner, a sense of wide-eyed wonder at the success she had in gathering the famous and the talented under her roof. Woollcott, mindful of Neysa's provincial origins, wrote that the great charm of her salon was that it "made a small town of New York." He might have added that it was a town populated almost exclusively by bright, attractive, and rambunctious people.

Like any small town, "Algonquiana" had its own weekly rituals and observances. Probably the most significant of these was Thanatopsis, that is, the "Thanatopsis Pleasure and Inside Straight Club," alternately known as the "Thanatopsis Marching Club and Chowder Society," or by any of a number of other comic names. Each Saturday afternoon the group would assemble in a suite at the Algonquin to play poker—kibbitzing, singing, and making dreadful puns the while. Normally, the game lasted through to early Sunday morning, by which time the immediate fortunes of several players might have been altered radically, since the average table stake of $500 was considerable even for those in the group who were prospering.

The gathering's name, if not wholly appropriate ("Thanatopsis" means a meditation on death), was certainly derived from an indicative source, *Main Street*, Sinclair Lewis's dissection of Midwestern town life. None of the group's other activities, not at the Round Table and certainly not at Neysa's studio, showed quite so clearly the provincial bent of the group's sentiments and norms. For one thing, Thanatopsis was for all intents and purposes a male preserve. While Neysa, Bea Kaufman, Jane Grant, and a few other women were occasionally allowed into the game, they were never really welcomed. Their sitting in was always brief, after which they were again consigned to the outer circle of kibbitzers and hangers-on. The inner circle of players consisted of Algonquin stalwarts like FPA, Woollcott, Ross, Connelly, the usually unlucky Broun, and Kaufman, who was an outstanding card player; some of the less central members of the circle (Sherwood, Swope); and a few artistically inclined businessmen who also liked to gamble (Paul Bonner, Raoul Fleischmann, Gerald Brooks from Wall Street), and whose ample funds made them particularly welcome. A Rumanian prince came several times—his game was said to be "funny but not Bulgar"—and so did Scott Fitzgerald, along with Ring Lardner, who was a more regular attendee. Johnny Weaver, Peggy Wood's young husband, came and lost all the royalties on his popular book of vernacular poems, *In American*. Charlie Chaplin came once and reportedly bored everyone by talking endlessly about his blood pressure. Rich dupes were always welcome, even though a few of them turned out not to be dupes at all and left the table just a bit richer.

Although the money at risk ensured a certain degree of seriousness about the proceedings, the game was conducted in an atmosphere, sometimes strained, of humor and good fellowship. Every time a particular foolish play was made, the ensemble would rise and sing, to the tune from *Pinafore*, "He Remains a Goddamned F-o-o-ool." There were awful puns from the losers: "I've been trey-deuced"; "I shall fold my tens and slip silent away." The winners just smiled and looked to end the game early.

In a gesture showing uncharacteristic good sense and restraint, Woollcott announced his (and Broun's and Connelly's) withdrawal from Thanatopsis, insisting that it was prompted simply by the conclusion that poker was "a waste of time." For Woollcott, one of the less adroit poker players (he excelled at other games and was termed, by Alice Miller, "a cribbage pimp"), Thanatopsis must also have been a waste of money— and in 1923 Alec had not yet become so recognizable a public figure that he could command top dollar for his work. In justifying his resignation from the club, duly announced in "The Passing of Thanatopsis," Woollcott invoked the sensible example of Neysa's distancing herself from the game:

> . . . the only two women who have ever been tolerated in the game [did not] prove to be either so jolly or so good as we could have wished. Indeed, both Neysa McMein and Mrs. Raoul Fleischmann (known to the Middle Western press as "Quincy's talented daughter" and "Quincy's untalented daughter," respectively)—both of these fair visitors played shrewdly, pocketed their winnings, and refused ever to sit in the game again on the grounds that the stakes were too high.

When it came to money, as her career demonstrated, Neysa could be uncommonly level-headed and practical. Besides, Neysa loved to devise and play games more for sport and intellectual fun than money.

The Algonquin set conducted an absurdly high percentage of its activities by group. Benchley, Parker, and Don Stewart went so far as to open a joint bank account, much to their mutual financial confusion. Kaufman wrote all but one of his many plays with a collaborator. In the early 1920s, Europe, and particularly France, was taken as a group vacation ground: each summer various combinations of group members would form and re-form as they roved about the Continent. Because so many of them were connected, in one way or another, with the New York theater (which closed down for the summer in those pre-air conditioning days), they often had the full summer at their disposal for their travels. Neysa, who was always a quick worker, usually managed to get far enough ahead in her illustrating to join them for the better part of the summer. In 1920 she was in Paris with Alec and several other friends; later she went on to the Pyrenees with another assemblage. In 1922, she joined Alec, Edna Ferber, Don Stewart, Deems Taylor, and Jane Grant on a Woollcott-conducted tour of the battlefields in and around Château-Thierry—and, having seen more action than the doubtable ex-warrior, probably gently deflated some of his grander claims to military glory. One summer Neysa set off for France with a rich young woman acquaintance whose style of travel, complete with her own silk sheets, proved not much like Neysa's own haphazard style of wandering. For Neysa, the usual pitfalls and discomforts of foreign travel were of no great importance. On her first postwar trip abroad she lost most of her clothing as she went along and was forced to wash her single remaining undershirt as she rode in a gondola along the Grand Canal. From Venice, she just managed to finance her passage home, arriving with 38 cents in her pocket.

What Connelly asserted about the Algonquin crowd—"We all loved each other. We hated to be apart"—betrays, if only implicitly, that strain of insecurity that impelled its members to remain a clique. Apart from their own "in" set, they always stood the risk of being misunderstood, undervalued, unappreciated. Traveling in groups protected them, in large measure, from having to deal directly with the places (and social worlds) they encountered in their travels. It was just this insularity that Anita Loos mocked in . . . *But Gentlemen Marry Brunettes* through Lorelei's depiction of a typical group rehash of one of its trips:

> So then they all started to tell about a famous trip they
> took to Europe. And they had a marvellous time, be-

cause everywhere they went, they would sit in the hotel, and play cute games and tell reminiscences about the Algonquin. And I think it is wonderful to have so many internal resources that you never have to bother to go outside of yourself to see anything.

Loos's casual adjectival "famous" before "trip" was not without point: much of what the crowd did *was* famous, not least for that large readership which followed its regularly chronicled doings. If Woollcott and his friends possessed any genius, it was the genius for projecting a sense of "in-ness" to their readers: they made their own, often inconsequential, actions seem something of a sophisticated norm. The degree to which this whole rather self-satisfied, if lightly taken attitude of the Algonquin set permeated the literary atmosphere of New York in the 1920s and 1930s is evidenced by a rueful admission of Thornton Wilder to Helen Hayes: "I know I'm better than the whole Algonquin crowd, but I can't act it when I'm with them." American literary history certainly supports the accuracy of Wilder's estimation of his relative talents; but the very fact that he, and others, felt this way is evidence of the Round Table's lasting power as a socio-literary phenomenon.

Neysa was much more an inherently social creature—and, save for Harpo, a much less inherently literary one—than any other key member of the Algonquin group. Just as her salon drew in dozens of persons outside her particular set, so too the range of her acquaintances—even in those years, 1920–23, of intense Algonquin camaraderie—was much broader than that of most other members. Clearly, Neysa's life, both in and away from her salon, was very full. She may have had a fair number of lovers, but she had many more male admirers still. Often Neysa could be found in the company of, if not actually "dating," two men—a strategy which Jane Grant saw as Neysa's way of guarding against the ardor of overzealous admirers. One evening she might be off to a movie with FPA and the bon vivant Art Samuels. On another it would be the opera with Don Stewart and Max Eastman, the radical editor and writer.

That someone like Eastman, still then a devout leftist, could mingle easily with Neysa and friends—to say nothing of his going to the opera—

is indicative of a certain sense of personal freedom that was so cherished at the time that it overrode any doctrinaire concerns: people in the literary-artistic-intellectual world of New York in the 1920s were simply very tolerant of each other's differences. Besides, they almost all shared a love of fun and an expectation of excitement. Looking back on the period four decades later, Edmund Wilson reflected, "I find that I am a man of the twenties. I am still expecting something exciting: drinks, animated conversation, gaiety, brilliant writing, uninhibited exchange of ideas. . . . it was part of the *Zeitgeist*." Neysa too continued to maintain for the rest of her life that sense of expectation engendered, and so often and amply rewarded, by the 1920s.

Throughout the decade, and particularly within the sophisticated metropolitan set, a casual eccentricity was assiduously cultivated. Jack Baragwanath, who sometimes found the newer, gayer world of New York to which he returned after a decade in South America a little puzzling, recalled a dinner party at the studio of sculptress Sally Farnham, Neysa's neighbor in the 57th Street building, which epitomized the charmingly eccentric mood of postwar New York. To quiet the chatterings of her pet monkey, Sally handed him a crêpe suzette, which he immediately draped over his shoulders, the warm mantle giving him solace and silencing him immediately. Evidently it was the usual remedy, for no one else seemed to take any notice.

As she got to know him better, Neysa brought Jack to the nightly gathering that often proved to be the last stop in the Algonquin crowd's noon-to-midnight round of groupings and regroupings: the boisterous assemblage at Herbert Swope's enormous apartment on West 58th Street. (When the original sixteen rooms proved too small for entertaining on the scale he did, Swope bought the floor above and created a thirty-two-room duplex.) Starting around ten o'clock, people would drift in. Just short of midnight Swope himself, his long day's work of editing the *World* done ("Le Monde, c'est moi," he often boasted), would arrive, striding into the room like a tall, red-haired Roman emperor, brisk, and still, in one apt characterization, "as full of energy as a Gatling gun." Most evenings, the festivities included some of those word and information games at which Swope, with his photographic memory, excelled—and which Neysa played with an expert's delight.

One night at Swope's was highlighted by an all-out fiddling contest among five of the world's leading violinists: Heifetz, Paul Kochanski, Albert Spalding, Joseph Fuchs, and Efrem Zimbalist. Each was to play Paganini's showy, accelerating *Moto Perpetuo*, starting at the beginning again the moment he finished it. Connelly began the competition by firing a starting pistol and the violinists began sawing away. Fuchs, who managed to last twenty-one minutes, was the winner, although the distinction was a dubious one: none of the players was able to lift a bow again for days. Most evenings the goings-on at Swope's went on and on, into the early morning hours. Jack was learning that, no less than the high-altitude camps of Peru, New York in the 1920s took stamina.

Stamina was something Neysa then possessed in great abundance. Unlike many in the Algonquin crowd, whose productivity began to slacken as the pace of their social life began to dissipate their energies, Neysa apparently had no great difficulties in maintaining a steady output of cover sketches, illustrations, and advertisements throughout the decade. That she was able to work surrounded by near riot and that she did not regard her art with high seriousness were two great helps in maintaining that output.

Neysa was, as George Abbott put it, "by avocation a hostess"—and though it would be inaccurate to say her avocation dominated her vocation, it was precisely her steady working away at her vocation that gave her the means *and* independence to become the charming, lightsome hostess she wanted to be. It would not be inaccurate to say that for those who knew her, Neysa McMein's art was distinctly less important than her person and her presence. Her art is interesting chiefly because of the rest of her life.

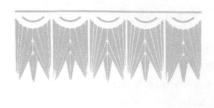

6

Neysa and the Pretty Girl

Neysa insisted that she could not draw even an egg without a model. Hers was, she freely admitted, a facile talent, remarkable only for its fine sense of color—an observation first made by Zuloaga, one of her teachers at the Art Institute. What Flanner wrote about the fictional Delia in *The Cubical City* was a drawing together of her scattered and shrewd observations of the Neysa McMein upon whom the artist Delia was based:

> . . . each blotch of color or tip of sultan's pimpled dome
> showed the deep volume of her physical talent and dem-
> onstrated her inability to draw. After years of success,
> Delia could not draw a bird or a milk pail without having
> the models set in a good north light. But she could have
> designed a palace in which no one could live and every-
> one would want to. She had a gift for inciting belief in
> unsubstantial elegance.

Through Neysa's work ran a strong romantic streak—of the popular
variety—a streak ultimately stronger and more significant than, but not
entirely divorced from, her talent. She was as an artist what she was as
a person: a great embellisher of the actual.

For all her shortcomings as a draughtswoman, Neysa was for over two
decades one of the most successful and highest paid illustrators in the
United States. From 1916 to 1923, she did nearly sixty covers for
the *Saturday Evening Post*, and from 1923 through 1937 she did *all* the
covers for the monthly *McCall's*. Throughout these two decades, she also
regularly drew for a number of other mass-circulation magazines, including the *Ladies Home Journal, Collier's, Woman's Home Companion*,
and *McClure's*. As Marc Connelly recalled it later, "Her fortune sprang
up like a beautiful flower and at one time you couldn't pick up a magazine
or see a magazine on a newsstand . . . that didn't have one of Neysa's
pretty girls on the cover; the most popular illustrator, probably, the
country ever saw." In any event, the "McMein girl" did become the
most recognizable, if not the most distinctive, female magazine type
since the "Gibson girl" of several decades earlier. Clearly Neysa had,
in her own fortunate and instinctive way, found the artistic means for
making the most of her talents and for allowing her to create works so
expressive of their period.

Neysa began her pretty-girl sketches in the mid-1910s and continued
them through the late 1930s, by which time her "pretty girls," aging
with, but not as rapidly as, their creator, had become "pretty women."
Still, Neysa's pretty girls remain quintessentially types of the 1920s.
These figures—athletic, attractive, smart, vivid, eager, and sometimes

a bit meditative—were charming and sophisticated without being coy or stuffy or remote. And they epitomized the new sort of young woman, a woman anxious to be, in the spirit of the times, a "pal" to men, if a disarmingly pretty and conventionally "feminine" one. Above all, the McMein girl gave the impression of being accessible. Typically she was dressed in an open-collar blouse or smock, instead of being bundled into a "costume" and set in a pose. Not as vapid and insistent as the "flapper," she was nonetheless expressive of the age's lighthearted, fun-loving spirit.

Edmund Wilson saw something slightly exotic about the type, referring in his diary to Neysa's "Americanized gypsy and Indian girls." Neysa herself modestly explained her art as purely imitative: "I just take a pretty girl and draw her the way she is." That "way" turned out to be much the same, year after year, cover after cover—and that sameness proved both the source of her popularity and the ultimate limitation of her range.

Although the McMein girl was not consciously developed as the antithesis of the Gibson girl, she certainly stands in something of an antithetical relationship to that earlier type. The Gibson girl was a buxom, pinch-waisted, broad-shouldered figure, her long hair up in a fulsome bun, a dress to her ankles, and a parasol often in her hand. If, as the editor of The Illustrator in America claims, the "Gibson girl, although aloof and refined, was everyone's 'ideal' sweetheart," then the national romance with the figure had a decided air of unreality about it. While not quite a caricature, the Gibson girl nonetheless had something of a cartoon aspect about her exaggerated hourglass figure—an aspect that, incidentally, made her a favorite target for the genteel humor of the 1890s. She was more an archetype than a type, a model on which the young women of the times could style themselves, but which they could never fully approximate. The McMein girl, by contrast, was a softer figure: in outline, in design, in manner. While she was strikingly pretty, her beauty was at least of the possible type. And her smart, casual air was something young women could attain, even if they were not pretty.

If the McMein girl was developed in opposition to any specific magazine type, it was the "baby doll" figure, insipid and sentimental, that was in vogue when Neysa began as a cover artist. Neysa's young women, by contrast, are sophisticated, self-possessed, and clearly, if just barely, adult. In 1917, a reporter wrote about the artist: "She knows that the public wants to see portrayed the high-bred, smart-looking American girl that one sees very often, but wishes to see oftener"—an indication of how quickly Neysa established herself as the creator of a distinct new type. The image of the McMein girl developed rapidly in Neysa's work for the *Saturday Evening Post*—and may well have contributed something to the great rise that the magazine, which was founded by Benjamin Franklin back in 1733, experienced during the 1910s and 1920s. While her first cover was a rather washy head of a vaguely attractive young woman, the sketch, perhaps because of the outdated bonnet the woman is wearing, has a distinctly old-fashioned look about it. But her second cover, less than two months later—a woman in a striped jacket, with an open-necked white blouse under it, wearing a broad-brimmed hat, and staring out at the viewer with a limpid gaze—already expresses many of the typical features of the classic McMein girl sketch, not excluding an often absurd hat (here a straw one with a large parrot on its crown). Soon Neysa's figures assumed a dependable regularity: the wide mouth, curved up at the ends; the prominent but not unattractive nose; the large eyes; the tawny coloring. Neysa may have looked at her models as she sketched, but she must also have paused to look in the mirror more than occasionally.

Three of her covers for 1917 added new elements to her style. Her May 26 cover, a woman in a light dress with a bright shawl across her arm, doing a piece of sewing atop a large sewing box embroidered with roses, gave greater range and play to Neysa's fine sense of color. In its color and its sense for the quietude of a domestic scene the sketch has echoes, faint echoes, of Mary Cassatt. Her August 11 cover, an aviatrix in profile, wearing a leather helmet and with the collar of her leather jacket turned up to her chin, is the first of Neysa's "heroines," shown here as part of the high adventure of flying. Her September 29 cover has the model in a posture that forecasts the style and mood of the 1920s. The woman, wearing an open-backed dress, is looking back half-seductively over her shoulder at the viewer—this was to become one of Neysa's favorite poses—her head framed by a large feathered fan: this is clearly a woman who, quite charmingly, does as she pleases.

As the *Post* covers demonstrate—or as any collection of Neysa's covers would—the McMein girl was first and foremost a variation on a single theme, and that theme was the artist herself. *All* her "pretty girls" resemble her; the question with each is only whether the resemblance is more or less exact. The sketch of Anaïs Nin (July 8, 1922), for example, definitely falls among the "lesser" resemblances—but one would still find it hard to guess who the subject was after her "Neysafication." If Alec Woollcott could write, "Each girl of hers was a real girl, salty with actuality," it was not perhaps because he saw Neysa as a realist, but only because he saw herself in each of her sketches.

When she moved over to *McCall's* in 1923 as its sole cover artist—she had done a few covers for them previously—Neysa had to blend her pretty-girl style with both thematic assignments and sketches of real persons. *McCall's* intended that Neysa produce her covers in series, the first being the "twelve most beautiful women in America." The opening cover in this series (Mary Pickford, March 1923) is rather good, strongly suggesting the innocent sexuality of "America's sweetheart." The rest of the covers alternate between actresses (like Winifred Lenihan, Ethel Barrymore), society women (like Mrs. Lydig Hoyt, Mrs. Angier Biddle Duke), and the dancer Irene Castle. The cover of Julia Hoyt, in which the contrast between the subject's deep red dress and glossy black hair shows Neysa's color sense at its best, makes it clear why Julia Hoyt was generally considered the leading society beauty of her day.

The 1924 series was "Types of American Beauty Drawn by Neysa McMein," a set that shows the more contrived side of Neysa's art. Most of the sketches lean heavily on clichés about nationality: "The Italian-American Girl" has dark, gypsy-like looks; the "French-American Girl" has severely arched eyebrows and overly rouged cheeks; the "Spanish-American Girl" is done with an elaborate mantilla and fan. Yet, in spite of the allusions to national characteristics, most of the subjects are prettified according to the kind of Anglo-American norm upon which Neysa's "pretty girl" was based. Only the "Indian-American Girl"—

perhaps because the model, Te Ata, daughter of a Chickasaw chief, had attained some notoriety—expresses more than a trace of racial individuality. However, this individuality is almost smothered under her heavy makeup (eyeliner, bright lipstick) and distractingly colorful war bonnet. It certainly says something about the times and the magazine for which Neysa was drawing, if not directly about Neysa, that the list did not include the "Afro-American Girl," although it went as far afield as the "Eskimo-American Girl" and the "Australian-American Girl" to round out its dozen types of American beauty. Despite the excitement then being generated by the Harlem Renaissance, and despite the fact that there were then some celebrated beauties in the black community, obviously the idea of a black woman as an American beauty did not then resonate with the editors or readers of women's magazines like *McCall's*.

Other series, such as "Twelve Milestones in a Woman's Life," while restricted by the vision of woman's place in the world as seen by *McCall's*, allowed Neysa's talents better scope. For instance, "Captaining the Team"—an adolescent in a dramatically red uniform, a bright white soccer ball beside her—shows the McMein girl at her attractive best: healthy, athletic, eager, and vividly pretty. Another series, the "Heroines of Great Love-Stories"—each cover accompanied a story within the issue, although Neysa did not do the inside illustrations—shows Neysa for the creature of her moment she very much was. It is rather disarming, but not necessarily unpleasant, to see Cleopatra as a McMein girl, and disconcerting, because we have so many portraits and photographs of her in our mind's eye, to find Queen Victoria tall and lithe. And Mary Stuart is shown wearing a hat that looks suspiciously like one of Neysa's own.

Neysa's series on the "Famous Heroines of Fiction" is more faithful to its sources, but also more rote. "Little Nell," for instance, is almost insufferably guileless. (One recalls Wilde's quip that a person would have to have a heart of stone not to laugh at the death of Little Nell.) Her "Alice in Wonderland," though, manages to turn the McMein girl features to very good effect: with her cupid bow lips and efficient prettiness, Neysa's Alice does capture the pouting, almost insolent, strength of that very self-assured young miss.

Although Neysa might not have been, as *McCall's* claimed, "the foremost pastel portraitist in the country . . . the poster genius of America," she might well have been the one whose work profited the most from working in that medium. While many of her covers do not sustain close aesthetic scrutiny, their often fine use of color makes them what cover sketches need first and foremost to be: eminently noticeable. Neysa was, at the very least, a good *cover* artist. Had she not discovered pastels, and thereby learned to exploit her gift for color so effectively, she would probably have had little artistic or commercial success.

About what success she did achieve, Neysa was always ambivalent. When the matter was put to her directly, she tended to be self-effacing; "I'm not a bit conceited about my work. I know it has nothing to do with real painting, but I am sincere in what I do. I put the best I have into every one of my covers." According to her stepson, Neysa "never complained" about being "just an illustrator." And while she worked quickly and surely (and hard), she seemed to take little interest in her sketches once they were finished. As Woollcott noted, she "often allowed her pastels to be reproduced by thrifty processes that drain them of half their color and more than half their character"—which is to say, she did little to ensure that they retained their only truly distinctive quality.

On the other hand, Neysa did impress many as being highly ambitious. Jane Grant, who knew her as long and as well as anyone, judged that "beneath her apparent casualness" there was a "deep-seated desire for success." Not only did Neysa develop an allied career as an oil portraitist, but she regularly returned for classes at the Art Students League to work on the requisite skills to sustain it. In a minor way, she also speculated on the theory of her art. In 1923, she published a piece, "The Woman Who Is a Design," based in large part on what she discovered in choosing and drawing the "twelve most beautiful women in America" for *McCall's*. With perhaps more bravado than her ability as a draughtswoman would warrant, she declared: "Once in a long time, say once a month, which is a long time in a crowded, hurrying life, I see a woman who is a design. . . . A design resolves itself into lines. It is independent of color. It has nothing to do with warmth. It is a blend of lines brought to completeness. It is the consumation [*sic*] of linear excellence. It is perfection in flesh or in marble." To the list of more celebrated beauties she denominated as "designs," Neysa added another, rather unexpected, name: Dorothy Parker. Men, too, according to Neysa, could be designs: Rudolph Valentino certainly, and even someone like the fighter Benny Leonard, whose "feints and moves are perfection." Being a male design was, apparently, more a matter of doing than, as with a female design, of being.

More directly to the point concerning the kind of sketches she did, Neysa wrote about American women: "They have admirable stance . . . stance is firmness of foundation plus freedom of movement. The American woman has freedom of motion, flowing, perhaps, from the fine center of her free soul. . . . I admire strength in a woman. It is a quality with which women are becoming more and more endowed. Freedom and athletics are bringing it about." In her canny, if undemonstrative, way, Neysa here manages not only to point to the underlying quality with which she conceived the McMein girl, but also to justify her own "free" lifestyle. That she should, just several months into her marriage, lay such stress on freedom was a forecast, if one was needed, that her marriage, were it to continue at all, would certainly continue in the breezy, open way it had begun.

Although she worked hard at it, Neysa never ceased to have fun making a living. When an early portrait commission took her to Chicago to paint a society woman, Neysa insisted on having her "maid" accompany her— and promptly signed up her then impoverished friend, Janet Flanner, for a free trip. The designation proved fortuitous: the commission turned out to be for a portrait of her subject, not in her usual grand surroundings, but rather as a simple milkmaid. Flanner earned her keep by spending hours posing for Neysa in their hotel room, holding a wastepaper basket by a corset string, until Neysa got the pose just right.

No small incentive to the men invited to Neysa's studio before the afternoon rush was the possibility of seeing a pretty woman posing in the nude for the artist. George Abbott once arrived early for a luncheon date and found a robust model calmly posing nude as Neysa calmly drew her. George, delighted by his immersion in artistic bohemia, kept sneaking glances at the model as he let his supposedly disinterested glance wander round the studio and out the window. At lunchtime, the model put on her smock, Neysa took off hers, and the three sat to their repast, with George marveling at the nonchalance of it all. Later, seeing the artistic result of the session, he would wonder how Neysa had turned this short-legged, curvaceous model into yet another of her lithe, tallish pretty girls. Neysa, who was too much aware of the power and draw of sexuality to be oblivious to its effects, must have taken some sly delight in such teasing visits, in playing so overtly on male pretenses toward sophisticated sexual attitudes, at least with those of her men friends who, like Abbott, were so strongly, so physically attracted to women.

When it came to her art, Neysa had at least one fanciful, enthusiastic, and clearly partisan, proponent: Alec Woollcott. By 1923, he was writing of the development of her art "from mere decoration to the greater exactions and greater satisfactions of authentic portraiture," insisting he had "been carried beyond my depth" by her latest work. If Neysa felt astonishment over the artistic development that Woollcott ascribed to her, it was probably more financial than aesthetic: she was astonished at the fees it commanded, although not at all afraid to push those fees yet higher for a ready magazine market.

As an illustrator, Neysa was a thorough professional. Her deshabille might have been something of an affectation to set off her beauty, but there was no pretense about her short, rugged fingernails—they were the unglamorous feature of someone who worked with her hands. Neysa belonged to the usual sort of professional organizations for someone in her position, like the Society of Illustrators and the Authors and Artists Guild of America, and she took a strong interest in improving the position of illustrators in relation to the magazines for which they drew. Like many in the Algonquin crowd, she accepted a wide variety of commissions, and managed, despite her often daunting social schedule, to meet her many deadlines without great difficulties, although, as she once wrote, she always had to get "a hell of a lot of work done" before she went off on of one her many extended jaunts.

Neysa never forgot, although she might have wished it otherwise, that her training was in "commercial" art. Like so many in the Algonquin set, she was first and foremost aware of herself as an artist with a product to sell. What Benchley ruefully, if half-jokingly, admitted—"It took me fifteen years to discover that I had no talent for writing, but I couldn't give it up because by then I was too famous"—was the kind of admission Neysa would never quite have had to make, for she had hedged her "artistic" bet from the beginning by always treating her work as a commercial product. In a sense, she was one of the most honest members of the Algonquin set, since her commercialism was always out in the open.

Although she was lighthearted, if dedicated, in creating her work, Neysa was quite serious and straightforward when it came to getting paid for it. Janet Flanner judged her something of a genius in selling her wares, an artist with the cool nerve to refuse substantial offers in expectation of even more substantial ones. And her friends knew that she was anything but cavalier when it came to overseeing her income. In the 1930s, she helped lead a successful court battle against a 2 percent tax New York City had begun to collect on illustrators' sales of reproduction rights to magazines—and she collected a $1,432 refund as a result. Neysa never pinched pennies, but she kept an eye on them.

For years, her $1,000-a-cover fee from *McCall's* provided the base of her income, but that left Neysa ample free time to do other kinds of work as well: illustrations, posters, advertisements. (*McCall's* specified only that she should do no other covers.) For twenty years, Neysa never had to scare up work, since it came to her. Unlike many of the women in the Algonquin crowd, a good number of whom were actresses or who, like Bea Kaufman, were chiefly dependent on their husband's income, Neysa was self-supporting. In this respect, she resembled the men in her set much more than the women.

Despite her training in the regular patterns of commercial art, Neysa always maintained an undisciplined element in her work. Woollcott wrote about her "doing instinctively the things it takes the plodders so many years to learn," but in fact what Neysa did best was the sort of thing that could not be learned. Flanner, in *The Cubical City*, was closer to the mark in picturing Neysa's/Delia's talent as the ability "of imagining color and line in magnificent unschooled unions and she turned out her expensive visions with the energy of an immigrant." Although the figure has its aesthetic shortcomings—for one thing, Neysa drew hands poorly and often out of scale—the McMein girl was difficult to imitate. She was as much Neysa's own as Neysa was a large part of her.

For two decades, Neysa was an artist whose opinions were sought along with her work. Back in 1921, the *World* not only had her do a sketch of the prizefighter Georges Carpentier, but also solicited her impression of this athlete who had recently become the new darling of the literati (including George Bernard Shaw, as well as the likes of Heywood Broun). Neysa dutifully added her fantastical bit of praise: "Michelangelo would have fainted for joy with the beauty of his profile, which is almost pure Greek." Looking for some sign that the Frenchman could defeat the bigger, stronger Dempsey, she waxed eloquent, if un-anatomical, over his legs, with their "hundred little muscles there is absolutely no accounting for." Whether accounted for or not, the muscles did not save him. Neysa was among the 90,000 at a Jersey City arena who saw Carpentier roundly beaten by the American champion.

Even when she was *not* doing it, Neysa's work could make a certain kind of news. In September 1926, *The New Yorker* retailed, in that half-gossipy style it was then perfecting, a mishap in *McCall's* latest plan for a series of cover sketches, of the most beautiful girl at each of the more important women's colleges. When Neysa was given the name and telephone number of the first "girl," she called to invite the coed to New York to sit, only to get a pleasantly puzzled response: was the artist sure she had seen the subject's photograph and was the artist still sure she wanted the subject to sit? It seems the magazine had somehow mixed the name of the most beautiful young woman at Bryn Mawr with that of an alumni official, class of 1900. *McCall's,* so *The New Yorker* assured its readers tongue-in-cheek, had taken the mishap as a sign and foresworn the women's college plan, with the result that its "new cover series will instead depict New York's cutest babies from the largest apartment houses—starting with the artist's own."

There was one kind of work she did about which Neysa, of necessity, had to remain anonymous: advertising. The 1920s saw a great growth in the advertising industry—to the extent that the twenties might rightly be considered the first period of modern advertising—and Neysa, particularly during the first half of the decade, did many advertising sketches. Woollcott, who would later, quite profitably, get into the endorsement game, wrote how "she will cheerfully draw for a department store, or a soap maker." No doubt what made her most cheerful about the work was the fees it garnered.

Neysa drew ads for Palm Oil Shampoo and Lucky Strike and Wallace Silver and Scranton Lace Curtains—and for dozens of other products which could, in one way or another, use an attractive woman in their advertising and were willing to pay a fair sum to get her there. Although these figures in the advertisements bear a resemblance to Neysa's pretty girls, they are typically less distinctive and were composed with an even softer focus than the McMein girl. More handsome than pretty, they might be cousins, if not older sisters, to the figures in Neysa's pretty-girl sketches. A 1925 ad for Cadillac—a chic woman in furs standing next to the automobile—is all softness and warmth, quite successfully suggesting the image of comfort and luxury the automaker was trying to project. Given her commercial instincts, it is no surprise that Neysa, within the limited range of female figures she could draw, was able to turn out successful advertising sketches.

Neysa drew the original sketch of "Betty Crocker," for decades (and long past Neysa's time) one of the prime domestic images of American advertising. Over the years, according to her daughter, Neysa was so often required to update this highly successful figure—to reflect changes in fashion, hairstyle, and domestic imagery—that she eventually came to see "Betty Crocker" as her nemesis, a creature who refused to stay drawn.

The June 1924 *McCall's*, which had Neysa's sketch of the "Indian-American Girl" on the cover, also had on the back inside cover one of Neysa's advertising sketches, a bride holding calla lilies and offering, at the behest of Colgate Ribbon Dental Cream, an almost absurdly white and wide smile. That Neysa's drawings should stand like a parenthesis around the issue is indicative, since the relation of her pretty-girl covers to the contents of each issue, particularly its advertising contents, is symbolic and significant. In the years she drew for it, *McCall's* was filled with dozens of advertisements for products that promised healthier skin, whiter teeth, shinier hair—to say nothing of the ads, enough to suggest a minor American plague was under way, for products meant to cure "halitosis." In short, much of the magazine's advertising "text" was a lesson on how to become like the fetchingly attractive (and clearly sweet-breathed) young woman on its cover. The McMein girl was, from the point of view *McCall's* established, a unifying image for each month's issue.

Until the late 1930s, when she was forced to take it up as her main profession, Neysa had a secondary career in oil portraiture. This work was, by and large, the focus of what higher artistic aspirations she had. Many of her portraits, if not distinguished, are more than competent. Her first oil, of Janet Flanner, won second prize in a Philadelphia competition; and a number of her other portraits drew favorable notices, typically at the "honorable mention" level.

Many of her portrait commissions, particularly after her career as cover artist ended, came through friendships. She painted Heifetz, Chaplin, Irving Berlin, Madeline Sherwood, Father Duffy, Ralph Barton, Bea Lillie, and many other of her friends and acquaintances, even Count von Zeppelin (he of the airship). Her last commission was for a portrait of the daughter of Walt Disney, whom she had befriended very early in his career. Other commissions—Joan Payson, Mrs. Cornelius Vanderbilt—came from that segment of "society" with which Neysa was, particularly through her summer life on the North Shore of Long Island, vaguely associated. Still others, public figures of one sort or another, came to sit for her because she was herself a public figure: Herbert Hoover, Charles Evans Hughes, and Jack Dempsey (apparently forgiven his devastation of Carpentier). When some of these portraits, along with some of her cover sketches, were shown at a one-woman alumni show at the Art Institute, they demonstrated Neysa McMein to be, whatever limitations she had, a student who had made good use of her Institute training.

If any of her oil portraits merits permanence, it is probably her 1923 oil of Dorothy Parker. The subject sits demurely, her thin arms folded in her lap. Parker's plain dress and the simple monochrome background pull the visual attention to the face, with its direct, absorbed gaze. The portrait captures the vulnerable, frail side of Parker's personality, along with the acute intelligence that was her strength. It also reminds us what a petite, attractive woman Dorothy Parker was before the dissipation and neurosis began to take their toll—and before recriminations and quarrels, including one with Neysa, made Parker into something of a scold.

As most of Neysa's portraits demonstrate, it was not for lack of skill that so many of her cover sketches ended up looking like much the same woman. If anything, her oil portraits tend to reproduce a photographic likeness of her subjects, stressing, if idealizing, their distinguishing features. In the last two years of her work at *McCall's*, perhaps as a result of all the work in oils she had by then done, there is a definite shift in Neysa's style. Her series of covers of famous American women in 1937, for example, evidences both a greater individuality in the figures (particularly when compared with the series of America's most beautiful women in 1923) and a new spareness, almost leanness, in both the figures and the composition as a whole. Although made attractive, Edna St. Vincent Millay, Amelia Earhart, Dorothy Thompson, even Helen Hayes, are not rendered extraordinarily pretty or glamorous. These are portraits of women who, more than anything, work—and work well—at their chosen trade.

After leaving *McCall's*, Neysa did four cover sketches for the *Saturday Evening Post* (March 1938–January 1939), and in these the new spareness and cleanness in her style is even more evident. Although the ages of the figures vary between perhaps twenty-two and thirty, none of the four is by any means one of Neysa's "pretty girls." There is a certain hardness in the beauty of all four, and three of the four have a little insolence in their gaze. All are drawn in brisker, more definitive lines, a difference particularly evident in their faces, but also in the crisper cut of their clothing. It may be that Neysa had just taken early notice of the angular, almost sterile theme that was to dominate women's fashions (and makeup) in the 1940s—or it may be that after more than two decades of turning up one variation after another on the same soft pretty girl, Neysa was finally ready to attempt some new style.

In either case, she might have become one of the more popular cover artists of the 1940s—if most of the popular magazines still needed artists to draw to contemporary fashion. But they did not: by then they had, at lesser cost, four-color photographs for their covers.

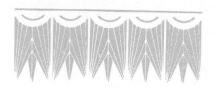

NEYSA
AND
JACK

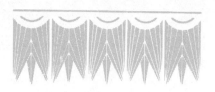

Living a Life with
Handsome Jack

Neysa was, as her closest friends realized, sometimes embarrassed when it came to subtler expressions of emotion—and such was probably never more the case than in the summer of 1923, after the artist returned from France and attempted to make a life with the man she had so impulsively married six weeks before. Jack Baragwanath, for his part, was full of doubts about their hastily chosen union—and he knew that Neysa shared these doubts. Still, he appreciated her reticence in expressing them. "She never let me know for a moment what her inner feelings were. I sensed them only vaguely. Outwardly she began to be quite gay and certainly good-humored," he wrote nearly forty years later.

Neysa, as usual, preferred to plunge ahead despite any misgivings. It was she who found them a place to live, a four-room apartment on Central Park South, just down from the Plaza Hotel and with a view out over the Park. And it was she who, with a degree of enthusiasm that Jack found surprising, set about decorating and furnishing it. Only gradually did he realize the reason for her enthusiasm: this was really the first home of her own that Neysa had ever had. Of course, she had no intention of giving up her career for domesticity. It would be a busy and varied married life, or none at all.

Socially, the balance between Neysa and her new husband was decidedly lopsided in her favor. Jack was still a relative newcomer in New York, and many of his friends and acquaintances there were semi-transients from the South American minefields, persons likely to vanish from the scene on very short notice. Neysa, on the contrary, was a long-term and very popular resident of the city's literary-artistic-musical community. If Neysa had suddenly, in her mid-thirties, to adjust to being married, Jack had, just as suddenly, to adjust to leading a vigorous social life among people who were not, by and large, of his own choosing. The adjustment, as he later put it, was not "altogether easy."

From the first, Neysa and Jack kept up the rigorous social schedule that Neysa had maintained ever since she had established, ever so casually, her studio-salon as an important social institution. Several nights a week they gave small dinner parties, and Jack got to see close at hand Neysa's ability to bring together and inspire people who stimulated each other. At one of the first dinners, Vincent Youmans played a song he had just finished. When Grace Moore arrived, she sang it, to yet better effect. Even Jack, who took a certain bullish pride in being unmusical, realized that "Tea for Two" was memorable and would be immensely popular.

Not long after, another of Neysa's musical friends, Irving Berlin—Neysa, among others, helped Berlin, who composed his songs using only the black keys, to transpose them—came to dine with *his* new song, "Always." By this time, Jack was beginning to feel more at ease with

106
▼

Neysa's celebrated friends, and was prompted to offer his own ribald parody of Irving's new composition:

> Not in rumble seats,
> Not in taxicabs,
> Not in telephone booths,
> BUT HALLWAYS.

Jack was, if dexterously, introducing something of the hearty mining-camp mentality into the metropolitan scene—and he was discovering those of Neysa's friends who appreciated his more direct, more earthy brand of humor. The number, if not great, was greater than he might have expected. Among Neysa's friends, Jack was starting to make friends of his own. One of them, William Rhinelander Stewart, who was only a casual acquaintance of Neysa's, was to be a boon companion of Jack's for a quarter century.

Neysa never put pressure on Jack to like, or even accept, any of her many friends. In fact, when she realized his detestation of Woollcott, the only one of her friends whom Jack found he actively disliked, she encouraged him to confront Alec and challenge the mocking, gibing taunts with which Alec tried to keep Jack, and other men connected with his favorite women, in place. And Jack did challenge Alec, albeit with not much more success than most who tried to slow, if not derail, the driving engine of Alec's insulting wit. In return for Neysa's encouragement in the enterprise, Jack freely admitted that Alec could, on his best behavior, be charming and ingratiating—and perfectly conceded Neysa's right to be one of those devoted to Alec.

When it suited both of them, Neysa and Jack would do things together in public. The September after their marriage, they went to Madison Square Garden to see the Dempsey-Firpo fight. Here Neysa surprised her new husband by "yelling like a stevedore and actually crying like a frantic baby" as Dempsey was knocked out of the ring, then came bounding back (with a little help from the ringside reporters) to finish off the "Bull of the Pampas" in the second round. After the uproar and mayhem—so well suggested in George Bellows's painting *Dempsey and*

Firpo—the Algonquin crowd repaired to the "412" brownstone, where Gene Tunney obligingly served as doorkeeper for a boisterous party which many tried to crash.

Several years later, in 1925, Neysa and Jack went to a classically disastrous dinner party at Edna Ferber's Central Park West apartment. The ostensible purpose of the gathering was to get a grand view of a total eclipse of the sun, but its practical result was the wreckage of a fair number of Ferber's prized objets d'art. For some, perhaps solar, reason, all the guests suddenly turned uncannily clumsy. A soup plate was overturned onto the tablecloth and floor; a rock-crystal liqueur glass slipped from a guest's hand and smashed. Woollcott, like the drunk he most definitely was not, then dropped his wineglass, leaving a horrid crimson stain on Ferber's exquisite rug.

To quiet the giggly hysteria that was spreading, Ferber suggested a party game, to which her fidgety guests rather gloomily agreed. At one point in the game, Jack and Edna were partners and were sent off into another room, but no sooner had they sat to confer than they heard a resounding crash from the drawing room. "I only hope it isn't my big oxblood vase," said the novelist, with a resigned sigh. It was—Harpo had swept it off the piano and was now desperately, if uselessly, trying to gather up the fragments. At this point, Neysa signaled to Jack that they should leave, but in his eagerness to do so, he kicked over a nest of Chinese lacquer tables, smashing his foot through their glass tops. Neysa pulled him away and they fled, barely managing to hold in their laughter until they were beyond earshot of the hapless Ferber.

As for their marriage, Neysa and Jack were finding themselves in very pleasant, if not always explicitly stated, agreement. Both were, in their different ways, free spirits: however pleasant their marriage might prove (and was proving), marriage could never be for them the central, defining element in their social life. Still, the two were determined to make their oddly begun union work.

And it did work, although in a manner that shocked some people—and created envy on the part of a few conventionally married folk. Neysa had made it apparent from the first that she had no intention of ceasing to see and go out with her many men friends, a plan to which Jack, with his strong attraction to women, was most amenable, since it would leave him equally free. Besides, among Neysa's regular enthusiasms, Jack found the opera a bore and the theater of only passing interest, and so was relieved that she could always call on one of a cache of more than willing male escorts to accompany her to these places. Parties, on the other hand, were something in which they both delighted, and so as often as not they went to them together. As Jack made more of his own friends, he and Neysa entertained less at home, or rather, they entertained less as a couple. "Their" dinner parties tended to be ones given by Neysa, with Jack usually tendered an offhand invitation to attend if he was not going to be dining out with one or another of his friends, male or female. Within a few years of their marriage, Neysa and Jack, by mutual accord, were leading essentially separate social lives. By then they were leading essentially separate sexual lives as well.

If relationships within the Algonquin set were noticeably freer in any one way, it was between the sexes. In their set, Neysa and Jack represented the full, logical development of the undemanding, independent relationship that obtained within many of the group's couples. For instance, the group's senior couple, Alice Duer and Henry Wise Miller, were people who inhabited different social worlds, who had essentially different sets of friends (although Henry would sometimes sit in at Thanatopsis), and who very rarely did much of anything, including dining, together. Even when under the same roof, Henry and Alice would communicate in writing "whenever a matter required a written report," as the staid Henry put it in what is, for all the separate ways between them it chronicles, a very fond memoir of his wife, *All Our Lives*.

Among the group's younger couples, it was, not surprisingly, Broun and Hale who, at the latter's insistence, made a totally free and undemanding relationship an explicit part of their marriage compact. They need not go everywhere together, or entertain always as a couple, or even have the same set of friends. The most overt demonstration of their separateness was that they inhabited different floors of their brownstone, although Heywood's monumental untidiness might have made Ruth's decision not to share a bedroom with him as much practical as ideological. Should either, they agreed, become unhappy or find a more suitable mate, their marriage could be dissolved on request, with no recriminations. "In later years," as the only child of their union has observed in *Whose Little Boy Are You?*, "they were dutifully to have the extramarital affairs that the twenties demanded as proof of emancipation, but the point of such affairs was supposed to be their casualness." In those days, sexual freedom was still taken seriously, even as it was taken lightly.

Neysa and Jack were able to have much the same kind of open relationship as Ruth and Heywood, without ever having to spell the matter out so explicitly, without ever having to make their equality and sexual independence so demonstrably a public thing. Neysa was more one for working through sympathies than agreements. The most that Neysa would say on the issue was that many marriages failed because the partners saw entirely too much of each other. Certainly she and Jack had more than enough friends to keep them busy outside of their marriage, and so they should feel no special obligation or make any particular effort to be together.

Jack, in looking back on their marital arrangement, credited Neysa's "wisdom" in insisting, if ever so gently, that they should lead somewhat separate lives. That "wisdom" in large part consisted of recognizing the possible: when it came to judging people's characters, Neysa was shrewder than Jack, and she obviously saw him as an inveterate ladies' man, as someone incapable of giving all his loyalty to home and hearth. Although she had no inclination toward a more regular domestic arrangement herself, she also realized that living with Jack Baragwanath pretty much precluded that possibility anyway.

After Neysa's death, Jack wrote of their quarter-century union, "There could be no doubt that our marriage had been decidedly successful." But he had also to admit that their relationship, by conventional standards, "was as much a deep friendship as a marriage." And it is this notion of the possibility of marriage partners being "friends" that typifies the kind of anti-Victorian sentiment which was the bonding agent of many marriages in the Algonquin group. These were partners who could afford, both financially and psychologically, to allow each other a freedom in marriage undreamt of by their parents. But like their parents, they *did* marry—living together was then an arrangement favored only by those much more radical or much poorer than the ambitious young types in the Algonquin set—and it was only within the convention of marriage that they tried to establish their unconventionality.

There is evidence too that for all their "advanced" marital ways, sex was still a difficult issue for many of them. It is quite probable, for instance, that when Bea and George Kaufman married—he was nearing thirty—both were virgins. In any case, their lack of sexual experience must have contributed to George's inability to have intercourse with Bea after her miscarriage early in their marriage, and so helped start him on a twenty-year sexual binge that eventually led to the public disgrace of being branded a lecher and adulterer in the Mary Astor divorce trial. Bea, in the meanwhile, made her own, quite full sexual life, although something of its substitute character is seen in the fact that a majority of the men in it bore a distinct resemblance to George.

With Neysa and Jack, the matter was not so extreme, although it had its small oddities. For one, Jack had a whole host of stories, some of them rather crude, in which he found himself in a compromising position with an attractive woman but, through some circumstance or another, never had sex—usually in spite of the woman's insistence. Neysa, too, tended to maneuver round an actual admission of her sexual liaisons: she would hint much but confirm little. Besides, with her liking for "homosexuals and neuters," as her daughter put it, Neysa spent a fair amount of her time with men who could be no more than good friends. Still, it is clear that both were able to acknowledge, tolerate, and absorb into their marriage a degree of infidelity.

Something of Neysa's attitude toward Jack as a lover can be seen in a story she once told Helen Hayes. One lazy summer afternoon, as they lay on a raft off the beach at Irving Berlin's North Shore house, Neysa recounted, and doubtless embellished, her tale of a passionate, tragic love affair with an aviator. He was, she assured the young actress, the true "love of her life." But when Helen began to commiserate with Neysa all too innocently and effusively for her great loss, the older and more worldly wise woman cut her off with a gentle rebuff: "For God's sake, Helen, it wasn't *that* bad—we'd been sleeping together for years."

A Victorian Englishwoman is reported to have had a simple formula for getting through sexual intercourse with her husband: "I just lie on my back and think of England." No doubt many of her American counterparts employed a like, if not so patriotic, formula—and it was this kind of sexual passivity, which she first saw embodied in her mother, that Neysa had determined, early on, to reject. She despised virginity and celibacy, seeing them as strictly negative virtues and as ways of keeping women all too easily in their place. If she was somewhat reticent about her sexuality, Neysa was nonetheless the sole agent in defining its limits.

In this, she was very much a part of the "New Morality" that a psychoanalyst, Beatrice Hinkle, delineated in a controversial 1924 piece in *The Nation*:

> . . . the upheaval in sex morals particularly affects the feminine world and by many people can scarcely be considered calmly enough for an examination. . . . It can be said that in the general disintegration of old standards, women are the active agents in the field of sexual morality and men the passive, almost bewildered accessories to the overthrow of their long and firmly organized control of women's sexual conduct. . . . Women are for the first time demanding to live the forbidden experience directly and draw conclusions on this basis.

Among the conclusions Neysa drew was that she liked being "one of the boys" and enjoying the sexual freedom traditionally accorded men. What she probably did not realize, though, was how much of a social change her sort of life represented from that of most American women in earlier generations. As much as anyone in her period, Neysa McMein exemplified the shift in emphasis from female bonding, induced by male sexual dominance, to women's reliance on heterosexual relations. There were, to put it simply, more men in her life than women—and the men counted more.

If Jack could accept this situation calmly, and there is no reason to believe he did not, his acceptance was not without self-interest: the New Morality also ensured a fair number of young women who had no qualms about dating this handsome and so loosely married man. That Jack typically chose pretty, but empty-headed and dependent, young women for his busy round of extramarital activities is some indication that away from home he preferred the less than fully equal sexual relationship that obtained there.

Still, Jack and Neysa had a relationship that was free of the kind of neurotic mood swings and uncertainties that beset many who tried to adjust to the new sexual freedom. It was the neuroses resulting from this new sexual arrangement that Dorothy Parker so cruelly depicted in her stories and poems. "I wonder why they hate you, as soon as they are sure of you," thinks the distraught woman in "A Telephone Call," trying, in desperation, to convince herself that "he" will ring up any moment, and knowing he will not. At best, for Parker, modern-day heterosexual relations were conditioned by an inevitable treachery and duplicity. In "Unfortunate Coincidence," she wrote how:

> By the time you swear you're his,
> Shivering and sighing,
> And he vows his passion is
> Infinite, undying—
> Lady, make a note of this:
> One of you is lying.

If Jack and Neysa—along with several other Algonquin couples— were an example of the benefits of a freer sexuality, Parker, in both her life and work, provided a disturbing countercheck. Casual attitudes toward sex could, without much of a turn, become chaotic, destructive ones. It was with a certain bitter self-mockery that Parker once quipped that the party game of "ducking for apples" was, but for its initial letter, the story of her life.

By all accounts, Neysa and Jack never argued about lifestyles, never upbraided each other for having different friends, interests, and attitudes, never quibbled over sexual liaisons. That they respected each other's differences—perhaps too uncritically in some ways—was a result of the genuine tolerance they shared. Often this easy tolerance hid the real affection they felt for one another. Jack's son, pondering the relationship between his father and stepmother, always remained puzzled about its nature and confessed frankly that he never came to understand it. Their daughter, who saw the relationship at closer hand, categorized it as a joining of "art and science," which, if anything, hints that the two necessarily had to operate upon different, incompatible principles and premises.

Even within their set and among their peers, opinions on their marriage differed. Howard Dietz saw Neysa and Jack as leading "libertarian lives." Ring Lardner, according to his biographer, Jonathan Yardley, "was willing to wink at peculiarities of behavior in some women he liked— Neysa McMein, a well-known artist of the time, was widely rumored to have had many prominent lovers—so long as they brought style, wit and class to the friendship." Most of Neysa and Jack's friends, however, thought their marriage unconventional but not illogical or, within their group, atypical. And George Abbott, who knew both parties probably as well as anyone, thought the marriage very sensible and possibly prophetic. As he judged it from the 1960s,

> Perhaps the unconventional marriage of Jack and Neysa will be a model for the marriage of the future. I can only state the facts: whatever their early relationship had been, by the time I came to know them it had developed into companionship. There was no pretense of passion, they were only loving friends, but I do not believe there was ever a home in which there was more love, more consideration, more humor and more joy.

There were, to be sure, conventional aspects to the marriage of Neysa McMein and Jack Baragwanath as well. It is very probably true—as that child herself believes—that the idea of Neysa having a child was essentially Neysa's, and that Jack, as he had done in his previous marriage, accommodated himself to the choice to please his wife. In any case, in the flush times of 1924, both Neysa and Jack were doing very well financially, and so the thought of having a child was eased by the notion they could afford to have it brought up by paid help. The child would not, they knew, much alter their busy social schedules.

Attitudes toward parenthood in the Algonquin set were generally off-hand, cool, sometimes even hostile. When Mary Brandon, Robert Sherwood's first wife, finally gave birth to the baby she had been chattering about for months, Dorothy Parker telegraphed her: "We knew you had it in you." Benchley's humorous pieces often scored the burden of child rearing ("In America, there are two classes of travel—first class and with children"), and indicated just why he ended up leaving his wife to bear that burden in suburban exile while he flourished as a wit about town. Even Woollcott, whose embarrassing confessions of his desire to be a mother were prompted by some genuine feeling, was much more maternal in theory than fact: four decades after his death, Woollcott is still recalled by many who experienced his treatment directly as a peevish adult who treated children abominably.

Neysa, for her part, accomplished the act of motherhood with as much calm grace as she ran her salon and did a number of other things. It was during a particular lucky run at roulette at a friend's house that Neysa suddenly left the table and told Jack they had better change their subsequent plans for the evening—it was time to go to the hospital. Their daughter, Joan, was born just a few days after Christmas 1924.

Neysa proved a fond but hardly doting mother. In an age when a certain lack of affection was considered progressive, Neysa was somewhat less than progressive. Spared most of the difficulties of actually taking care of Joan, Neysa could take a quite democratic interest in her development. After the disheartening experience of looking in on her mute, invalid mother over those five years, looking in on Joan, pretty and bright, was a positive delight. According to Marc Connelly, by the time Joan was about four, "Neysa used to look on her as a fellow adult" and hold long discussions and arguments with her. What with Neysa's disconnectedness and illogical leaps, Joan was probably able to uphold her end of these conversations well enough.

The direct benefits of Jack's second foray into fatherhood were, at best, negligible. Having determined that Neysa was "wrapped up in our little daughter, Joan," Jack went on with his life in much the same manner he had done before the child's birth, leaving Neysa's obvious affection to provide most of the intermittent doses of parental attention the child would get. Not compromising his independence for his wife, Jack was hardly about to do so for his child. Although he was perfectly pleasant with Joan, Jack was also distant—and that distance would, in time, produce the certain coolness, if not resentment, that some discerned in Joan's relationship with her father.

Despite his determinedly "male" cast of mind, Jack's vague disinterest in his children was gender-blind. For the first five years of his marriage, Jack very rarely saw his son, evidently secure in the knowledge that his ex-wife and her husband had ample means, both personal and financial, to see to Albert Kingsmill Baragwanath's upbringing. That upbringing was, in fact, proving rather old-fashioned: in the staid ways of upper-class nineteenth-century life that still held sway in that family, the child was turned over to the servants and lived a life apart from his parents, with but few friends of his own age. Except on rare occasions, he ate with the servants, went to bed early, and had, as he later realized, "a lonely upbringing, but I didn't know any better." Although it superficially resembled his stepsister's upbringing, in that it was the servants who did most of the tending, childhood for King (as he was then called) was part of a much more prim, regular, and respectable kind of family life than Joan's. His mother, who was certainly not born to this class, took on its mores and even assumed, after her mother-in-law's death, the airs of the family *grande dame*. In this world, Jack and Neysa's world was considered decidedly "fast" and more than a little scandalous.

Neysa apparently rested content in Jack's decision not to bring his son much into their lives, although, as might be expected, it was she rather than his father who proved the more sympathetic and engaging "parent" once they did begin to see him on a regular basis. What brought King into their lives on a regular basis was a piece of male vanity. Christopher Blackman Miller, King's stepfather, when the boy was about twelve, approached Jack about adopting him legally and giving him his name. The proposal infuriated Jack, and he rejected it out of hand—

but it did influence him to regularize his relationship with his son, if only in his own casual fashion. During King's adolescent years, father and son would have a yearly day out together: a fancy lunch, with awkward talk of school and future plans, followed by the matinee performance of some musical for which George Abbott had given Jack tickets. As soon as King was safely deposited in his seat, Jack would leave, only to return at the end of the performance to reclaim the rather bewildered teenager. (Whether Jack actually went off for a sexual liaison during the interval is unknown, but not improbable.) The effect of these "afternoons together" was rather one-sided: King was certainly learning about the kind of man his father was, if Jack was learning little more than that his son could attend a Broadway show on his own. Still, this sort of cavalier behavior and his dashing style made Jack something of a hero to an adolescent still awkwardly struggling with social niceties; the son grew to admire his father without quite loving him.

Because he was seven years older than Joan, King could not, when he first came to visit Jack and Neysa, be a regular playmate for their daughter. The result was that Neysa had to devote some of her time to entertaining the boy, which she did in offhand and charming ways. She invented endless word games and inveigled Jack into playing them too. She let King look on as she sketched, and casually mentioned her famous and talented friends to him. But most of all, she treated him more like an adult than he had ever been treated before: there was about their conversation an exciting frankness and directness, not excluding, as he grew older, a realistic discussion of his relationship with "girls." When King got home, his mother would often quiz him minutely on activities at her ex-husband's household, convinced, quite rightly, that a full account would give her a vicarious look into what was a different way of life, more exciting and celebrated, than her own.

Among the things that King's mother might have glimpsed about this "modern" couple was their essential economic independence from one another. Both had fairly substantial incomes; Jack probably, on average, made more money, but he also spent it more freely and invested it less wisely than Neysa. In any case, each had more than enough to support a separate lifestyle as well as to contribute a roughly equal share to their joint maintenance. After they built their first summer home, there was a tacit division of expenditures: the maintenance of their Manhattan apartment (and its servants) would be basically his, the maintenance of the summer home (which included several additional servants) would be basically hers. The general management of both homes, though, fell of necessity to Neysa, the slightly more domestic of the two. Neysa ran a light ship—or rather, two light ships—and the servants much appreciated her carefree attitude toward things like housekeeping and daily meals, as well as her democratic ability to sympathize with them over personal problems.

The division of expenses between Neysa and Jack was by no means a fixed, immutable thing. When Jack by his own admission "took quite a battering in the Crash" and found himself suddenly $40,000 in debt, Neysa told him simply, "Don't worry about it. I've got plenty [of money] for both of us," and took over his share of the expenses until his fortunes rebounded, which, luckily for them, they soon did. Throughout the 1930s, both Neysa and Jack were among those who lived in the economic afterglow of the boom 1920s. Neysa's work was still in great demand, at the same high prices, and if she was doing fewer advertisements and illustrations than before, in those economically depressed times the money she was making was worth more than ever. As for Jack, he was well established as a mining engineer at a time, directly after the resounding collapse of a stock market built on paper values, when the mining of precious (and other) metals seemed more desirable than ever. Jack did not want for work at substantial rates. It is not surprising then to find Neysa and Jack in December 1931, at the very nadir of the Depression, attending a society party at the Tide Club, with the proceeds ($5 admission, $1 a drink) going to the unemployed. Through the decade, Neysa and Jack remained very much among the "haves" in a society where there were more "have nots" than ever.

To understand Neysa's life apart from Jack, it is probably necessary to understand something of Jack's apart from her. According to George Abbott, Jack had a strong liking for "pretty nitwit girls," and often could

Neysa had an enigmatic smile for shipboard photographers on her return from her honeymoon. UPI/BETTMANN.

Neysa with four of the men who accompanied her on her honeymoon to France. Her husband was off in Quebec at the time. ESTATE OF MARC CONNELLY/DRAMATISTS GUILD TRUSTEE.

Neysa and Jascha Heifetz.

Neysa, Alexander Woollcott, Heifetz, and Ferdinand Touhey.

Woollcott, Heifetz, Neysa, and Marc Connelly.

Touhey, Neysa, Heifetz, and Woollcott.

Neysa loved large and eccentric hats—and often put them on her models. JANE GRANT COLLECTION, UNIVERSITY OF OREGON LIBRARY.

Neysa marching in a suffrage parade in 1917. COURTESY OF NATIONAL ARCHIVES (TIMES PHOTO SERVICE).

Alec Woollcott, for all his oddities, eccentricities, and pettiness, was one of the men Neysa loved best. CULVER PICTURES.

Unlike many of her literary and artistic friends, Neysa did not support FDR—but she found Wendell Willkie much to her vaguely liberal liking and campaigned for him in 1940. A. K. BARAGWANATH.

Neysa, Noel Coward, and Alec Woollcott on Neshobe. The three were devoted to each other. RICHARD CARVER WOOD.

It was in Neysa's studio that the shy young Helen Hayes first met Charlie MacArthur, when he passed her a dish of peanuts and sighed, "I wish they were emeralds." AP/WIDE WORLD PHOTOS.

Jane Grant and Harold Ross on the back porch at "412," the brownstone they shared with Woollcott and Hawley Truax, a classmate of Alec's from Hamilton College who was enlisted as treasurer for Ross's budding enterprise, *The New Yorker.* JANE GRANT COLLECTION, UNIVERSITY OF OREGON LIBRARY.

Marc Connelly and Robert Benchley in the flush of their early success in the 1920s, when anything seemed possible to the Algonquin crowd. ESTATE OF MARC CONNELLY/DRAMATISTS GUILD TRUSTEE.

FPA (Franklin Pierce Adams) was the most influential literary-artistic gossip columnist of his time. Many an Algonquinite, Neysa included, first became a celebrity through his column. INTERNATIONAL MUSEUM OF PHOTOGRAPHY AT GEORGE EASTMAN HOUSE.

THE GUFFEY—BIOGRAPHY OF A BOSS, NEW STYLE

J. P. Marquand—Alice Duer Miller—Horatio Winslow—Floyd W. Parsons
Nina Wilcox Putnam—Augustus Thomas—Eleanor Franklin Egan

GEORGE WESTON — FREDERICK ORIN BARTLETT — W. L. GEORGE
ISAAC F. MARCOSSON — IR₋₋ ₋ S. COBB — GEORGE KIB₋₋ TURNER

Beginning
Trimmed With Red—By Wallace Irwin

"I just take a pretty girl and draw her the way she is," wrote Neysa about her enormously popular cover sketches. The pretty girl who posed for the July 8, 1922, cover was a young Anaïs Nin. REPRINTED FROM *THE SATURDAY EVENING POST* © 1938, 1922, 1921, 1919, THE CURTIS PUBLISHING CO.

In the 1930s, Alec began dispensing his opinions over the air as well as in print. PERMISSION OF CBS, INC.

"She is beautiful, grave and slightly soiled," wrote Woollcott of Neysa at her easel, where she worked calmly amidst the usual frivolity. UPI/BETTMANN.

Jack Baragwanath and friend. In his photo album, where artistically photographed nudes from "Freedom Week" appeared across the page from family Christmas scenes, Jack labeled this picture "Palm Beach (Night Work)." A. K. BARAGWANATH.

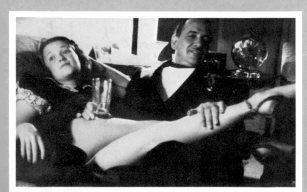

Neysa and daughter Joan, Christmas 1926. According to Marc Connelly, Neysa started treating Joan like an adult, holding long debates with her, by the time she was four. JOAN LEECH.

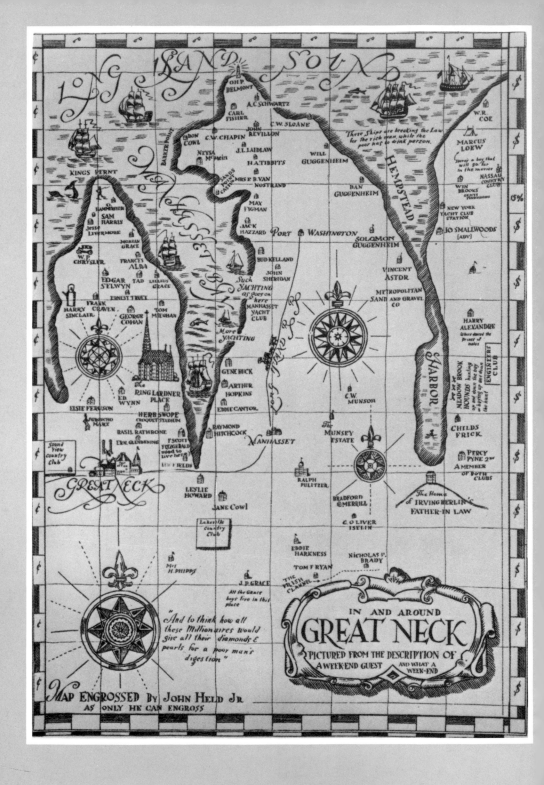

Neysa lived among the rich and celebrated: John Held's North Shore map for *The New Yorker* in 1927. DRAWING BY JOHN HELD, JR.; © 1927, 1955; THE NEW YORKER MAGAZINE INC.

The second house at Sands Point
as viewed from the front—or the
back. Neysa and Jack could never
agree which was which.
A. K. BARAGWANATH.

Arlene Francis at Sands
Point. She starred in *All
That Glitters*, the play Neysa
conceived, Jack wrote, and
George Abbott produced
and directed in 1938. It
flopped. A. K. BARAGWANATH.

Bernard Baruch at Sands Point. He
was Neysa's financial advisor until
Jack came along. A. K. BARAGWANATH.

Jack at croquet, an activity he described as
"a tough, acrimonious sport which was
played bitterly." RICHARD CARVER WOOD.

Averell Harriman was among the most
fanatical of the North Shore croquet devotees. He often took his mallet with him on
his diplomatic travels around the world.
RICHARD CARVER WOOD.

The clubhouse on Neshobe, where, according to one observer, a "bravura disorder" obtained. COURTESY OF PAUL H. BONNER, JR.

The comfortable stone house Woollcott built on the island in the mid-1930s, as it looks today. BRIAN GALLAGHER.

Alexander Woollcott, Neysa, Alfred Lunt, Bea Kaufman, and Harpo Marx—on Neshobe, the private island that served for two decades as the northernmost outpost of the Algonquin crowd. RICHARD CARVER WOOD.

Alec often insisted that island visitors join him for an early morning swim in the still chilly Lake Bomoseen. RICHARD CARVER WOOD.

On his home court, the bumpy irregular ground of Neshobe, Woollcott was virtually unbeatable at croquet. RICHARD CARVER WOOD.

Neysa on the dock at Neshobe in the late 1930s. JOAN LEECH.

be seen dating them around New York. His "nom de restaurant" for such activities was more a joke, a gibe at those men whose wives were so unprogressive as to frown on their dating, than a disguise: "Barry Warner." He was, as even his young daughter came to realize, "a real ladies' man . . . [with] lots of women" in his life. Much more often than Neysa, he made use of their "open marriage" for explicitly sexual encounters.

Many of his acquaintances attest to Jack's highly successful way with women: bluff, hearty, a little teasing, and more than a little suggestive. And he found a sufficient number of younger women who were impressed by his dashing good looks, now translated into a very handsome middle-aged style, worldly wisdom, and direct, ribald wit. Like Neysa, he had an abhorrence of stuffiness. If, as occasionally happened, he found himself trapped next to some dour, upright woman at dinner, he would, after a time, stare at her with mock solemnity and say archly, "Madam, please remove your hand from my knee." Jack made no pretense that he was not something of a philanderer, if a "licensed" one. Several men who knew him when they themselves were adolescents attest to how vibrant a personality "Handsome Jack" was in his long prime, how noticeably attractive he was to women, and how he epitomized those qualities most male adolescents idolize in an adult because of their lack in themselves: ease, self-confidence, and a bantering, ingratiating way with the opposite sex.

Among the young women Jack occasionally dated—and, with Neysa's approval, sometimes brought out to their summer home—was a chorus girl, Louise Hovick, who confessed to him that when out of Broadway work she had sometimes worked as a stripper in burlesque. She swore Jack to secrecy on the matter and even refused to tell him the name under which she appeared. It was some measure of the kind of life he led that Jack should eventually discover it for himself—by seeing Louise perform at a burlesque show one evening. Jack checked his program and found her stage name. It was "Gypsy Rose Lee."

In the 1930s, Jack learned to draw in a minor way, and while he was never any great success at it, his drawings of nudes, a number of them done for Christmas cards to his more understanding friends, give evidence of the kind of girl he favored. Jack's "girls" are slim, long-limbed, with pert breasts and very pretty faces. They are, in fact, very much what Neysa's "pretty girls" would look like if disrobed and set in coy sexual poses. They are also, quite apparently, young women who are open to the kind of favors someone like Jack could buy them. One of them sits, wearing only a pair of pumps, amidst a host of gift boxes bearing the names of her male admirers, looking lovingly at a bracelet on her wrist, with the conspicuous tag "from Jack" dangling from it. Below the sketch is Jack's unmistakable, if only vaguely seasonal, message:

> Baragwanath, the bard, by way of this card
> Sends you all the best of the season
> But *you* get a rhyme for wasting his time
> While baby was open to reason.

That the sort of young women Jack favored strongly resembled the pretty girls his wife drew had, in at least one instance, more than just symbolic significance. One afternoon Neysa was having great difficulty maintaining the attention of a model who kept fidgeting and looking at the clock. It turned out that the model had a heavy date that evening and was anxious to get home to prepare for it. The date was with Jack.

Most of the sexual hijinks engaged in by Jack and his male friends now seem tame indeed. One of the incidents that most amused him was a trick played on Herbert Swope at the Astoria Studios. Under the illusion that he was making a short, serious speech to test the effectiveness of the new medium of sound film, Swope agreed to go before the cameras. Just after the elegantly dressed editor located himself far downstage and began his speech (about the future of the Democratic Party), six naked girls tiptoed onto the stage and formed a line behind him. There they stood throughout the speech. Just before Swope came to his finely modulated conclusion, they tiptoed off. When, two days later, Swope saw the results and had to suffer the laughter of a carefully chosen audience of cronies, he was fit to be tied. Although the idea for the gag was actually Harpo's, through it Jack had some measure of revenge for Swope's mock headline, "A New Groom Sleeps Clean."

Neysa, as one of her friends put it, might have liked and depended on coincidences and other small acts of God to help shape her life, but Jack tended to be more direct and active in pursuing his pleasures. Although he loved to be with pretty women, and played the role of "Handsome Jack" to the hilt with them, his real world was a world of men, even if the men in it spent a good deal of their time talking about women. This minister's son, born in the late Victorian age and raised in an atmosphere of quiet piety, never quite got over the rebellious thrill of recounting and embellishing his sexual adventures.

Jack's world of men was also a world that dealt more centrally and more continuously with power than Neysa's. Although Bernard Baruch was a friend of Neysa's for some years before Jack appeared on the scene, he and Jack eventually became closer than he and Neysa had ever been. The mining engineer was impressed by the intelligence, aristocratic looks, and surprisingly ready laugh of the financial doyen. He was also surprised, and pleased, by Baruch's thorough grasp of mining, gained through a number of successful investments. Jack greatly enjoyed talking over the subject hours on end with him. The kind of elegantly rough fellowship that obtained at Baruch's extensive South Carolina estate, Hobcaw Barony—the mixture of luxurious accommodations, splendid cuisine, and almost compulsory hunting—perfectly suited Jack's tastes and conformed to his male-oriented image of what counted as significant. Jack found he liked being a friend to the powerful, and, in fact, his last two decades would be shaped by his friendship with one of the most powerful, William Paley.

It was in the late 1920s that Jack joined forces with the energetic, handsome Harold Talbot to form a small mining company. Together with a third partner, they developed a rather daring scheme for a gold-mining operation in the interior of New Guinea. Talbot, who knew a good deal about airplanes, was convinced that the "Junker," newly developed by the Germans, would have sufficient power to get the necessary heavy machinery over the mountains to the remote interior and to haul the ore out. It did, and the mine prospered greatly, thanks also to the low-paid help provided by the natives who managed the transition from a Stone Age society to a mechanical one with surprising efficiency. Together with a tin mine in Siam and a small, but "mighty," gold mine in Alaska, the partnership prospered throughout the 1930s and enabled Jack to cover his losses from the Crash within a few years.

Through Talbot, Jack also came to know other influential businessmen, like the automaker Walter Chrysler, and the banker Jules Bache. From them, he received favors small and large. When he heard Jack grumbling that the engine in his new Chrysler Airflow was knocking badly, Chrysler walked out of the North Shore cocktail party he was giving, rolled up his sleeves, and fiddled with the engine until it was ticking like a watch. When Talbot suggested to Bache that he should have a real mining man on the board of his mining conglomerate, Bache appointed Jack, and kept him on it for a decade, at a sizable annual fee. While most Americans were experiencing the rough financial going of the Depression, Jack Baragwanath seemed to be prospering more easily than ever.

A story Jack often told at the time is emblematic of the ease with which he and a number of his male cronies were then making their economic way: when an enthusiastic third party cornered Jack and Harpo and told them they *must* invest in a property he had uncovered, a mine in the Southwest so rich that you just had to bend over and pick the nuggets up, Harpo mockingly demurred with "Jesus . . . you mean we have to bend down?" Ironically, it would be the coming of World War II, which brought economic recovery of a sort to many Americans, that closed down much of the mining activity in underdeveloped countries to Americans and so reduced Jack from being an entrepreneur to merely a salaried, if well-salaried, employee again.

Jack's favorite definition of a mine was one borrowed from Mark Twain: "A hole in the ground owned by a damned liar." As the definition suggests, Jack always maintained about him something of the aura of the rough, racy, and adventurous life of mining—and it was this aura, played to the hilt in his stories, that made him a welcome companion to many men and a dashing figure for many young women. It was also a quality that Neysa, after a while, found was only of moderate interest.

After 1936, Jack was commonly spoken of in passing references as "an engineer and writer of adventure stories," the latter part of the tag coming from a series of mining-camp sketches he published in *Cosmopolitan* and collected together as *Pay Streak*, which Doubleday put out. Very much in keeping with the rowdy spirit of *Pay Streak*, Jack arranged one of his typically elaborate practical jokes around its publication. At Nelson Doubleday's suggestion, Jack wrote phony dedications—some suggestive, others positively lewd, and almost all highly insulting—to a score or so "friends." These Doubleday had printed, with the appropriate dedication bound into the complimentary copy sent to each supposed dedicatee. The one to Ina Claire, with whom Jack had been carrying on "a good-natured vendetta" for years, read: "To my dear friend, Ina Claire, in memory of that one glorious night in Atlantic City." She was furious, and swore that she wouldn't so much as have walked across the street with Jack Baragwanath. Even the usually unperturbable Harpo was distressed by his dedication—"To good old Harpo Marx whose face always reminds me of something seen years ago above a dashboard"—and pointed out to Jack that he had a public image, if a zany one, to maintain. It was, though, one of the most straightforward dedications, that to Edna Ferber (Jack knew enough not to be lewd with her), which caused the most trouble. Ferber, touched by Jack's supposed dedication, had been showing her copy of the book round and felt humiliated when the ruse was revealed. She did not speak to him again for years.

There was no doubt that Jack had the capacity to be offensive, and Neysa sometimes found his penchant for adolescent humor, things like joke presents and off-color remarks, annoying. Yet she had a number of things in common with him also. For one, Jack's broad humor reflected the earthier, more direct style that Neysa contributed to her sophisticated set. For another, Jack's political views were more in tune with Neysa's than those of many of her more progressive friends: both she and Jack were fairly conservative politically, with Neysa a member of that now nearly extinct species, "liberal Republicans," and Jack a middle-of-the-road Republican. For a third, they were both avid and skilled games players—often they would sit over a game board for an hour or two before going their separate ways for the evening. Theirs was, if something less than a full-time marriage, something more than a mere marriage of convenience.

In the homes they shared, Jack and Neysa favored comfort over elegance. As for interior decoration, Neysa never progressed much beyond the haphazard and miscellaneous style of her salon days, and Jack found the results of leaving the outfitting of their home to her quite acceptable and unpretentious. Besides, it would have been difficult to maintain any high style with the animals—a sheepdog and several cats, one with seven toes on each foot—they had wandering about the premises.

It did, though, take them a few years to find an in-town residence that suited their needs and largely separate ways. Their original apartment on Central Park South, with its four "boxlike rooms" (as Jack described them), had proven too small even before the baby was born. In 1925 they moved to a larger apartment on East 64th Street, and three years later to an even larger one at 1 West 67th Street, just off the Park, in the famed Hotel des Artistes, to which Neysa had relocated her studio in 1926. In 1933, they moved their residence just across the street, to 2 West 67th—and finally, in 1940, to a duplex apartment on East 66th Street, an apartment in which Jack continued to live for a decade after his wife's death. That all these moves took place within an area of just a few square miles indicates just how precise (even narrow) a vision of their metropolitan existence Neysa and Jack shared.

Often Jack returned to one or another of these homes to find that still "Neysa exercised some strange magnetic pull on people." Out on the terrace might be a miscellaneous grouping of "Wild Bill" Donovan, Frank Buck and his wife, Clifton Webb, Bernard Baruch, and Gary Cooper, the last accompanied by a handful of pretty girls that, like an unknowing Pied Piper, he had brought trailing along behind him. About just how these people arrived there—only for Sunday dinners were guests formally invited—Neysa was, not without reason, vague, for she was not quite sure herself. Long after her salon ceased to exist, Neysa managed to keep interesting people dropping in on her by making them so evidently welcome when they did.

Although they often traveled off in different directions, Neysa and Jack usually managed one or two joint trips a year. During the 1930s, one of the events they almost always attended together was the outsized Thanksgiving weekend house party Averell Harriman annually gave at his mountaintop mansion up the Hudson, Arden House. Harriman, who preferred not to see most of his business associates outside working hours, granted Woollcott dictatorial control of the guest list, and Alec took to the task with fervor. Here, from Wednesday through Monday, thirty or forty guests—from Algonquin stalwarts like Broun, Alice Miller, and Neysa through less central members of the group like Helen Hayes, Charlie MacArthur, and Oscar Levant, to an occasional outsider, like Hemingway, or a special friend of the Harrimans, like publisher Donald Klopfer—frolicked about the hundred-room mansion, often in the giddy confusion of some parlor game like "Murder." At Neysa's suggestion (or, some say, Alec's) the large "organ room," which was really a chapel, was turned to the more profane use of serving as a badminton court, its fifty-foot ceiling providing ample room for the game. After badminton, the crowd could adjourn to the bowling alley in the basement, or go shooting or even skiing, since there was usually a thick coat of snow on Mount Orama—Harriman's father had had the top of the mountain sliced off so he could put his mansion on it—by late November. One winter, to satisfy the croquet fanatics, of which he was one, Harriman had a platoon of servants shovel the whole large lawn so the guests might play through the weekend. Another game—less formal, but more complex— was speculating on the exact extent of the wealth represented by the mansion, with its almost uncountable furnishings, silverware, paintings, and so on.

One thing, though, the guests could not do was to enjoy a series of superb meals. Neysa's old friend Marie Harriman, Sonny Whitney's former wife, was notoriously disinterested in overseeing the kitchen. According to one report, she was not even able to find it when put to the task by some guests in search of a late night snack. The food at

Arden House, as one regular visitor recently and simply put it, "was lousy." By way of compensation, though, the liquor flowed freely, and more than one guest was found wandering vaguely through the far reaches of the mansion in a light alcoholic haze.

For Neysa and Jack, it was the games and the company, in that order, which drew them to Arden House. Although Neysa had the larger reputation as a games player (and inventor of games), many thought Jack to be an even better player. (Cleveland Amory, who certainly knows whereof he judges in this regard, once declared Jack to be the best player in the country.) For avidity, there was little to choose between the two. As for the company, Neysa found herself very pleasantly among, and playing games with, old friends, many of whom she was now seeing less regularly throughout the year than she had in the 1920s. And Jack found it no great burden to put up with the likes of Alec Woollcott in such spacious surroundings, especially with amusing people like Charlie MacArthur about. Like many in their large set, Neysa and Jack found the yearly gatherings at Arden House perhaps the most thoroughgoing survival of that fun-loving, high-spirited attitude of the 1920s. At least for the more privileged, the party had not yet ended.

When Jack
Was Away

While Jack was away or with one of his "pretty nitwit girls," Neysa did not want for male attention. She could regularly be seen dining around New York with the likes of Cole Porter and Otto Kahn and Clifton Webb. She was the favorite New York date for several celebrated men, among them Noel Coward and Charlie Chaplin, who periodically visited the city. She also had many more regular, if less celebrated, men friends. And then there was always Alec Woollcott. Neysa's life had not, all things considered, changed overmuch since she was a famous bachelor girl.

There was a "deep, if unimportant impulse to coquetry in her nature," judged one of Neysa's more perceptive male admirers. Neysa was, by instinct more than design, a woman who drew men to her. As Helen Hayes put it, "Oh, she was a siren, but she didn't resemble a siren in the usual way." About Neysa there always remained an air of softness and effortlessness, and unlike the more usual and adamant kind of siren, she did not tally up her conquests for public view. Still, there was in her manner a casual seductiveness, even suggestiveness, that Charles Brackett in *Entirely Surrounded* well captures by having his version of Parker complain, half in scorn and half in wonder, about his version of Neysa: "That voice of hers with the squeak of a bed in every inflection!"

And it does seem, indeed, that Neysa's easy sexuality was something of a minor fixation for Parker. John Keats, Dorothy Parker's biographer, reports that one of the wit's favorite stories concerned a nervous male friend "scheduled" to begin an extramarital affair with Neysa, but very uncertain about how he should proceed in this, his first piece of marital infidelity. Dottie assured him that all the preparation he needed was a quick trip to the drugstore for the necessary precautionary equipment. When he still hesitated, protesting that this *was* the first time he would ever be unfaithful, Dottie sent him off to the rendezvous with an ironic assurance: "Don't worry. I'm sure it won't be the last." Whether or not the story is true—Keats hints that it might have been invented, or at least sculpted, for the sake of the punchline—its supposed veracity rests, in significant part, on Neysa being recognized as someone who *could* have played her assigned role. Whereas Parker would, typically, have a brief, inevitably unsatisfactory, affair with someone like Lardner, or Ruth Gordon a much more serious but also highly unsatisfactory one with Jed Harris, the brilliant upstart producer, Neysa exhibited a strain of casual indifference that always kept her romantically safe.

In a 1925 article, when she was nearly twice twenty herself, Neysa proclaimed that a woman was most attractive at the age of twenty. Fortunately, she could then, and for a number of years thereafter, still bear the implicit comparison with her quite young standard. Until she was in her mid-forties, Neysa was thought by many men to be a startling beauty—and a most approachable and fun-loving one at that. Even after, she was described, especially by younger men much infatuated with her carefree style and still sensuous charm, as extraordinarily, compellingly attractive. It is telling that Brackett, when he drew Neysa in his roman à clef about the Algonquin set, should choose to make her fifteen years younger than she then was, while everyone else was depicted as roughly his or her own age: effectively Neysa seemed thirty-one, even if she was chronologically forty-six.

The response Neysa drew from women was much more varied than that she drew from men. We might justifiably assume some nascent lesbian romantic leaning in Flanner's admiration of Neysa's blithe ways and sure beauty. And we can see an obvious note of wish-fulfillment in what the ultra-plain "Ferb" recorded in her diary about Neysa's attractiveness being a benign triumph of style over substance: "On Sunday I drove to Neysa's with Irving Berlin. . . . She is very plain, almost ugly—but with great poise and intelligence. . . . I like her so much." Like Ferber, other women tried to puzzle out the precise secret of Neysa's appeal for men, but there was perhaps less of a puzzle than some postulated. Neysa was a beautiful woman who, simply and engagingly, preferred the company of men and made that preference appreciably clear to them.

That this preference encompassed much more than anything explicitly sexual is demonstrated in her long relationship with Alec Woollcott. About his sexual capacity, or rather lack thereof, Alec could be mordantly humorous. Once, during a North Shore weekend, he came down from his room very late for breakfast, rubbing his hands with glee, and announced to the crowd, "Well, I've just had my orgasm for the season." At a party publisher-writer George Oppenheimer was giving in honor of Rebecca West, Alec rushed in, literally threw himself at her feet, embraced them fervently, then rose and proclaimed matter-of-factly, "That's my sex life for 1933." Neysa, like others, found such performances highly, oddly humorous—it was good to see this "high priest of rudeness," as humorist Corey Ford denominated him, be as cruel to himself on occasion as he was to others on a regular basis. In a group that took a demonstrable, active interest in matters sexual, Alec was indeed the odd man out.

Still, Alec constituted Neysa's longest and most constant "extramarital" relationship. As Alec himself put it, they always managed to "get under each other's skins" in a way that kept them together, more or less, for a quarter century. Woollcott's first biographer, Samuel Hopkins Adams, insists that Alec was "never cured" of Neysa, that he continued to love her in his own erratic fashion until his death. (One could say much the same about his relationships with Ruth Gordon, Bea Kaufman, and perhaps even Alice Miller.) However, because of his stunted sexuality, there was often an unconsummated quality about Alec's quasi-sexual relationships, never more so than in the case of Neysa, who was the most overtly sensuous of all the women to whom he was close. Throughout their relationship the two often played at a coy sexual game based on, or at least allowed by, Alec's near eunuchhood. When both were nearing fifty, Neysa would still be writing to him that "I will fly to your arms" and signing the letter "Miss Pink."

Often Neysa was Alec's companion for opening nights. The tall, beautiful Neysa, usually dressed oddly or eccentrically, and the obese, plain Alec, in his dandified cloak and hat, made for a queer-looking couple. It is very doubtful that on such occasions Alec solicited Neysa's theatrical opinions—or that he even gave her sufficient chance to voice them, for Alec's great forte was monologue, not repartee, and Neysa was, apart from his large radio audience, among the most admiring and indulgent of his listeners.

From time to time, but less frequently than with some other of his good and true friends, Alec would become overbearing and there would have to be, at Neysa's insistence, a trial separation of some weeks or months. One of these, a six-month split, came in an argument over Sacco and Vanzetti. Alec was absolutely, high-handedly sure of their complete innocence and would brook none of the hesitations or doubts raised by the more politically cautious Neysa. Another separation came during the last months of his life, over a painful piece of selfish indulgence on Alec's part, and left these two oddly matched friends estranged at the time of his death.

Although Alec could be occasionally vicious with Neysa—such as the time he snipped that her dress "looked like it had been dipped in gumwash"—the very fact that he was nasty to her *only* occasionally is some indication of his real affection. More usually he was, in his highly sentimental way, extremely kind to and solicitous of her. And woe to anyone who attacked her in his presence, for the attacker would very probably receive the full measure of Alec's venomous tongue. Alec also experienced a fierce, impotent jealousy whenever he saw Neysa—or any of the women he was close to—attracting other men. His typical reaction, as George Abbott still vividly and rather bitterly recalled four decades after Alec's death, was to belittle and embarrass those men in public. Another, different measure of Alec's devotion was that he acknowledged Neysa's feline sensuality in naming his cat "Black Neysa."

Neysa, in return, was one of Alec's most loyal and steadfast supporters, although she was realistic enough to acknowledge that Alec was typically more amusing and witty than right in many of his petty battles. Through her long-term relationship with Alec, Neysa also ensured, though without calculation, that she would remain before the public as a personality as well as an artist, for Alec treated his great friends very much as resources which needed regularly to be publicized so others might enjoy them. To hear Alec tell of it, Neysa McMein was little short of a great artist— and much more fun than one.

Among Neysa's periodic male visitors, none was more important than Noel Coward. Of all the Algonquin set, it was Neysa he "loved more than any of them." For him she was "another of my very dear ones," a friend who always seemed full of a beautiful serenity in a life filled with trials and disappointments that often threatened to dwarf his considerable, if effervescent, triumphs. One of the jokes between them was that whenever she received word that Noel was coming to New York, Neysa would immediately cancel any and all engagements, with the simple excuse that "Beauty is coming to town" and that she must make ready. Like children, Neysa and Noel would "play games and laugh" and generally make light of the greater pieties that drove most people. Once, following a lunch at "21," they decided to send a joke telegram to the Lunts. Noel wrote out the message and then, as a further twist, signed it "Mayor LaGuardia." The woman behind the counter objected that it was improper to sign a telegram with the name of "any well-known person," so Noel crossed out LaGuardia's name and entered his own. Again she objected, repeating the rule, but when Noel proved his right to his own well-known identity, she declared, "In that case you can sign it 'Mayor LaGuardia.' " To Neysa, if not to Noel, the final verdict seemed logical enough.

Through Noel, Neysa became something of a regular visitor in the Anglo-American theatrical community. The kind of easy intimacy she enjoyed with it is indicated by the start of her offhand account in "Games I Like to Play" of how the parlor game "Psychology" was invented:

> There were only a few of us sitting around the fire one winter afternoon late, when the sun was going down and we were just in the mood for coffee and confidences. It was at Kit Cornell's isolated little house in the country. Noel Coward and I were enjoying a snack of coffee and sandwiches, and a good deal of conversation as well. We got to discussing ourselves and other people, folks in general, and folks in particular. Somebody wondered whether or not we really were telling the truth most of the time, and how we should go about it to find out how brave or self-reliant a friend might be. We arrived at a discussion of courage.

It was, however, more than just theatrical interests, or even a personal attraction to one another, that bound Neysa and Noel. Both were, in a very crucial way and long past the decade, persons shaped by the norms of "sophistication" that they helped establish and exemplify in the 1920s. As the British literary critic David Daiches has judged of Coward, "Writer, actor, composer, sentimentalist and wit, satirist of England and emotional patriot, Noel Coward represents in a most illuminating way the trend of sophisticated thought and response from 1920 onward." As the years went by, Noel came to depend on Neysa for a degree of solace from the pressures this once precocious darling of the Anglo-American theatrical world was experiencing as the price of his success. By the late 1930s, he was already complaining about a kind of social vampirism that was the high price of his theatrical celebrity:

People, I decided, were the danger. People were greedy
and predatory, and if you gave them the chance, they
would steal unscrupulously the heart and soul out of
you without really wanting to or even meaning to. A
little extra personality; a publicised name; a little entertainment value above average; and there they were,
snatching and grabbing, clamorous in their demands,
draining your strength to add a little fuel to their social
bonfires.

As a result, he whittled down the number of his New York acquaintances
and took greater inspiration from what he termed Neysa's "unique talent
for living." Particularly after World War II, when Noel was tired and
out of favor, did he come to depend on his friendship with Neysa, and
a few others, to bolster him in a personally dispiriting and depressing
time. As he wrote of her, giving ample evidence of that sentimental
streak Daiches mentions, "Neysa was one of the rare people in the world
whose genius for friendship could pierce through all facades, surmount
all defences, and find its way immediately and unerringly to the secret
heart." Neysa, who could be just as sentimental as Noel, was as single-
minded in her devotion to him. Even in the last years of her life, when
she herself began to weary, she always managed to find the good-humored
energy to bring Noel out of his doldrums.

Despite Neysa and Jack's laissez-faire marriage arrangement, Jack
did confess to being jealous of one of Neysa's regular men friends from
out of town, Charlie Chaplin. Considering Chaplin's well-earned sexual
reputation, Jack probably had cause. When in town for his brief, but
fairly frequent, visits, Charlie would monopolize Neysa's evenings, often
every one of them. Unlike some of her Algonquin friends, who found
Chaplin distinctly boring because his wit was not verbal, Neysa "adored"
Charlie. As a visual artist, if one of a very different sort, Neysa could
more readily understand and appreciate the nature of Chaplin's comedic
genius and would roar with hearty, delighted laughter at the intricacy
of his visual wit. She also found him charming and bright as a person.
Eventually, Jack came to admit the comedian was "an entertaining and

attractive man," if not the sort of fellow with whom he typically made a fast friendship.

Another, and very different, enthusiasm of Neysa's was the great Russian basso Feodor Chaliapin, who had acquired the habit of dropping in at Neysa's studio whenever he was in town to sing at the Metropolitan Opera. Legendary as Boris Godunov—his performances at the Met in 1922 caused a sensation and helped establish the hitherto neglected Russian repertory in America—this giant of a man, more than six and a half feet tall, also fancied himself a lover of legendary proportions. In a slapdash mixture of English and French, he regaled "Nayza" with tales of his early life, his career, his travels round the world's opera houses, and his long string of love affairs. In his boisterous Russian way, he bragged that he was "le meilleur, meilleur homme" in the world, never sick a day in his life, except for having "la gonorrhea tout le temps." It was, he concluded, as permanent a part of him as his voice. When Neysa inquired whether this affliction did not necessarily curtail his "affaires de coeur," he insisted that it did not, that the women whom he bedded took their infection as "une marque qu'elles ont couché avec le grand Chaliapin." Neysa was inclined to doubt it.

It was not always just for herself, but for the world she called into play around her, that some men found Neysa so attractive. Thinking back to the period before Neysa married, Flanner recalled how a rich acquaintance of Neysa's gave weekend parties at his house on the Palisades just so she would come and bring a group of friends with her. And certainly for the men who came to her salon, it was no small part of her attractiveness that all the talented and witty people who gathered there were, by their very attendance at Neysa's, attesting to the power of her person to bring them so amusingly together.

With time, though, some of Neysa's amusing friends did turn into bores. One of these was Pearl White, the silent film star, who had sadly declined into a premature alcoholic dotage. One evening in the mid-1930s she appeared, unannounced, at a dinner party Neysa was giving. Neysa protested that she could squeeze Pearl in, but that there was no room for her male escort—to which Pearl responded that it made no matter, for the man was merely a piano player and needed only to be shown to the Steinway and supplied with periodic drinks. With Pearl already sloppy drunk, the dinner, in Jack's retelling of it, proved a disaster: she dropped one shrimp down the outside of her dress, and another inside it. When Clifton Webb pointed out to her that "you have one cunning little shrimp inside your gown," she just said "the hell with it," and called for another Scotch. When the meal finally, and torturously, ended, Pearl announced abruptly that she had to go, then immediately collapsed on the floor. The piano player had to be conscripted to haul her out. The next afternoon Neysa received a bouquet of roses and a sort of apology; it read: "Neysa dear, I never had such a wonderful time. Love, Pearl." A few years later the actress, not yet fifty, died in Cairo.

Neysa's free, easy social acceptances had something of a prophetic cast. Her passing friend Otto Kahn, who experienced the social ambiguities of great success in the America of his time, liked to quote Disraeli's definition of a "kike" as "a Jewish gentleman who has just left the room"—and it is not without point that a goodly number of Neysa's friends, particularly her men friends, were Jews. At a social moment when anti-Semitism was a lingering, covert, but still very powerful force, Neysa was part of that newer element of "society" which automatically accepted Jews into its ranks and which insisted, if only implicitly, that talent and intelligence rather than breeding and pedigree were the primary qualifications. At the same time, this was a set which tended, in its striving for social equality, to homogenize its members. Just as Neysa herself became, for all the Midwestern residues, a creature of New York smartness, so other members gave over the ethnic and regional differences of their various upbringings. As George Kaufman's daughter remembered it, the world of her childhood was "more WASP than anything else," full of a notion of correct form that contrasted strangely with the rather iconoclastic premises upon which her parents and their friends had built their lives and made their reputation. These were people who wanted, at some deep level, to succeed in the terms of a white, Anglo-Saxon Protestant paradigm of success, even as they were helping to reshape and broaden that paradigm. It is significant in this regard that Neysa, for all the many men in her life, should only marry one of them—and that he should be about as pureblooded and recently transported an Anglo-Saxon as one could reasonably expect to find in the United States.

Despite an association with a wide-ranging and diverse collection of men, Neysa was not without certain regular ties to members of her own sex. For one thing, she was part of several female cliques that formed in her large set. One was for the express, if ultimately futile, purpose of opposing the petty tyrannies of Alec Woollcott: she and Alice Miller and other women victims of Alec's sometimes chauvinistic authoritarianism would put to themselves the simple, but baffling, question, "Why do we stand him?" They never did find the answer, but complaining to each other helped.

There were also more regular gatherings of women. For a while, Neysa ran a none too rigorous bridge party at her place in the Hotel des Artistes on West 67th Street. The other members were Alice Miller, Mrs. Crosby Gaige, and Ruth Gordon. The last remembers, apropos of the atmosphere, one afternoon when Neysa forewarned the players that her cook, Rose, had baked a cake and that they should treat the effort with due respect. When Rose, led by Neysa, came in bearing the confection, the others broke into what proved to be too demonstrable applause. Rose slipped, the cake went sailing and landed, upside down, beneath Neysa's easel. While Rose tearfully protested that her effort was ruined, Neysa calmly insisted that it could simply be sliced and served from its present inverted position—and proceeded to do so.

When she went to the teas that Alice Miller, still something of the blueblood, gave, Neysa received full recompense for her own rather inconsistent ways as a hostess. Alice, whose elegant carriage belied her innate clumsiness, would tip items off the tea tray and spill tea into guests' laps with regularity. All in all, it was a rather funny reflection of the changing social scene: Alice Miller, née Alice Duer, serving, none too smoothly, a group of social upstarts whose various talents and celebrity would have counted as nothing in society in the previous generation.

Neysa also functioned, if very unofficially, as part of Harold Ross's women's advisory panel. Together with the likes of Bea Kaufman, Alice Miller, and a few others, Neysa gave of her periodic wisdom, and some-times of her good common sense, to the eccentric editor of *The New Yorker*. And the man who complained, only half in jest, "I live like a hunted animal," and who protested, less than half in jest, "I don't want you to think I'm not incoherent," was regularly in need of the kind of kidding, earthy assessments Neysa and the others could bring to bear. Over the years, she helped remind Ross of the rather fun-loving and lighthearted spirit upon which *The New Yorker* was founded, the spirit which it derived from the atmosphere of the Algonquin set in the 1920s.

In the spirit of the provincial striving for metropolitan sophistication and smartness that the artist from Illinois shared with the editor from Colorado, Neysa, in several descriptions she wrote of the games she invented, would offhandedly but consciously drop the names of the various members of the English nobility with whom she had played them: Lady Ribbendale, Lord Amherst, and the Duke of Marlborough (the last impersonating a murderer). These were unstuffy nobles who, Neysa assured her readers, much enjoyed their spot of fun. The girl from western Illinois took it all in with a bit of wonder, even as the successfully transplanted Midwesterner was not surprised by who flowed in and out of the rather fabulous life in the artistic reaches of New York society.

At the same time, Neysa was a full participant in the very democratic American social whirl of her New York moment. No better instance of this insistently egalitarian attitude can be found than the parties Herbert Swope threw at his North Shore mansion—parties that, somewhat vul-garized, served as Fitzgerald's chief model for Gatsby's parties. With a fine, expensive sense of cuisine, Swope would have sumptuous food brought in from all corners of the metropolitan world and lay a lavish board. About the guests, he was somewhat less discriminating: some would come uninvited and some of the invited would linger on as per-manent guests, as Ruth Gordon did, more or less, for several years. Here lords and gangsters might rub elbows and exchange whatever pleas-antries they had in common. As Swope's biographer E. J. Kahn has said, "Age or social standing meant little at the Swopes'." What counted most was an evident, amusing vitality, a vividness akin to the spirit the host himself so amply evidenced.

All these people led, as the newspapers reminded the general public, romantic lives exciting beyond exact calculation, if not beyond regular reportage. Moss Hart, who was nearly a full generation younger than the Algonquin group of which he eventually became a semi-regular member, recalled in *Act One* his first encounter with this glittering set and its famous friends, a set about which he had been reading day in and day out throughout the 1920s. After a long, hard day's work up in George Kaufman's study, the fledgling playwright descended to what George had absent-mindedly informed him was "Beatrice having a few people for tea." The few proved to be many, and the many all proved to be rather fabulous personages, already long and fondly known to the young writer:

> The room was alive with people and I recognized every single one of them. It seemed to my dumfounded eyes as if one of those double-page murals of the great figures of the theater and literary world that *Vanity Fair* was always running had suddenly come to life.
>
> Everyone I had ever read about or hero-worshipped from afar seemed to be contained within my awestruck gaze, from Ethel Barrymore and Harpo Marx to Heywood Broun and Edna Ferber, from Helen Hayes and George Gershwin to F.P.A. and Alexander Woollcott—as though some guardian angel of the stage-struck had waved a wand and assembled a galaxy luminous enough to make the most insatiable hero-worshipper's hair stand on end. . . . Neysa McMein—it was unmistakably she—called to Mr. Kaufman, and he turned away, mercifully releasing me from any more introductions.

Not surprisingly, Moss Hart was somewhat distressed, even a bit frightened, by this first encounter, made the more terrifying by Woollcott's flat insult over an innocuous quasi-literary remark. Like other late entrants into the group, Moss had, over the ensuing months, to take his hazing and suffer the not inconsiderable agonies of committing a faux pas or two. Helen Hayes, who had won through the same trial a few years earlier, wrote about her great relief when, thanks to the good graces of George Gershwin, an already painful episode during her Algonquin "tryout" did not turn out much the worse for her. During a Christmas celebration at Neysa's one year, everyone was, in their characteristic way, "sparkling again," and Helen determined to assert herself as best she could by passing round an enormous box of chocolates. In her eagerness, she dropped the box, sending the guests to their knees in search of candies that had tumbled and rolled every which way, while, in despair, she slumped into a nearby sofa. When the guests were called in for dinner, Gershwin politely offered the forlorn actress his arm, but held her up until the rest of the guests had passed out of the room, then deftly removed several chocolate creams from the back of her dress. Much less fixable, though, were the large, unmistakably chocolate stains Helen's careless sitting had put on the ivory moiré sofa. After a moment's pondering, George simply shrugged, turned the cushion over, fluffed it up, and took the appreciative Helen in to eat.

In town, Neysa and her friends had a regular round of places they frequented, places that were, for the most part, outside the orbit of Jack and his friends. Besides the Algonquin and their homes and Neysa's studio, these included Moriarty's and "21" and "Bleeck's" ("Jack Bleeck's Artists and Writers," which adjoined the *Tribune* building on 40th Street). The theaters were also, of necessity, among their regular haunts, particularly in the earlier days. Neysa rarely missed the opening of the plays which her friends wrote or in which they were starring—and that number alone made for a busy theatrical schedule.

Sometimes during the period, early fall through late spring, in which this world flourished, its Algonquin members would break away for a day or two, but in ways that were more removed in place than spirit. One bright October morning in the mid-1920s, Neysa, Alice Miller, Ruth Gordon, Ellin Mackay, and Alec Woollcott embarked from Penn Station, in their own drawing room (at Alec's insistence, despite the brief journey), for Philadelphia. Their goal was a matinee performance of *Animal Crackers*, and their purpose was no less than to preview the

Marx Brothers farce with which several of the group's members were associated. The visiting Algonquinites pronounced the work of their fellows more than good, dined, and made their short railroad way back to Manhattan.

About this same time, Neysa also went to Philadelphia by rail in another private party. For the trip to the 1926 Dempsey-Tunney fight, Herbert Swope rented a private railroad car for himself and his male friends. In special recognition of her pugilistic enthusiasms, Neysa was permitted to join the party as its only woman. The group was going to see how their one-time doorkeeper would fare against a more formidable opponent than the cheery drunks he had kept at bay for them. Tunney did very well, well enough to take Dempsey's heavyweight crown in a ten-round decision. The whole excursion, full of strong wit and good fellowship, was one of Neysa's most complete playings at being "one of the boys"—although she was mindful of, and pleased by, the share of masculine attention that came her way.

Throughout the 1920s and 1930s Neysa was often on hand to celebrate the triumphs, of one sort or another, of her friends. She was one of the gayest and happiest revelers at the party celebrating the fantastically successful opening of Marc Connelly's *Green Pastures* in 1930. A decade later she was giving a party for the cast of *Pal Joey*, which George Abbott had so brilliantly directed. "Big crowds are such fun, I can never resist them," Neysa once said—and she always seemed to know where big crowds of her sort were to be found, which more than occasionally was on her own premises. Her stepson remembers how much, at least from an artistic and theatrical perspective, she seemed to know about what was going on "in town, who was doing what," mounting a new show, or quarreling, or up to some new adventure, romantic or otherwise. In the 1920s Neysa had found her social niche, and from then on she occupied it with alert interest.

Among the largish crowds that Neysa enjoyed were those she assembled for her weekly Sunday evening dinners, the only event in her loosely run household that had any sort of regularity. For these dinners she usually arranged a simple but often rather elegant meal, for she was a good cook and knew how to oversee a kitchen. Often, though, these meals proved to be mere adjuncts to the real fare of the evening, one or another of the group's elaborate and beloved parlor games. At Neysa's, it seemed only proper, and pleasantly necessary, to conclude the weekend on a note of play, even the intricate and absorbing kind of play many of these games entailed. As the years went by, these Sunday evening suppers of Neysa's became something of an institution, and even earned the occasional reference in the columns of the newer chroniclers of the social scene, such as Elsa Maxwell, who had come to replace the older ones like FPA (whose column petered out in the mid-1930s, after a quarter-century run).

Not all of Neysa's life apart from Jack, however, was a matter of socializing. There was, of course, the busy professional side. From time to time Neysa would be called on for a radio broadcast—her favored topic was, not unexpectedly, the types of American beauty. She also dabbled in writing of one sort or another, particularly in the last decade of her life, perhaps buoyed by the notion that the literary gifts of her witty friends might somehow have rubbed off on her—and, in a small way, they did. Her baker's dozen film reviews for *McCall's* in 1932–33 are cast in her own breezy, rather undistinguished style, but the pieces are not without flashes of Algonquin verve and wit. About one of Cecil B. DeMille's typically overblown epics, Neysa quipped: "The little boy who, after seeing a Roman spectacle, complained that there was one poor lion who didn't get a Christian ought to be hustled right down to see *The Sign of the Cross*, Mr. DeMille's latest opus." She was also witty in scoring typical examples of Hollywood miscasting, as for *Strange Interlude*: "Even the handsome Clark Gable, with unruly white hair, slightly resembled an ancient Pekingnese." About Hollywood's usual conventions and clichés Neysa reacted with an amused, tongue-in-cheek tolerance, born of her long fondness for the improbabilities of the screen: *Shanghai Express* was the story of "a glamorous lady [played by Marlene Dietrich] with the most impractical set of traveling clothes I have ever seen." And when she saw something she admired, like the trick photography for *King Kong*, she said so straight out and cited it as an achievement. As a film reviewer, Neysa was, like Benchley as an actor, something of a natural. Based on this limited set of examples, it might

141
▼

even be hazarded that in some respects Neysa had a finer critical sense than a few of her more literary friends, like Alec Woollcott, who practiced criticism as a regular trade.

Neysa's New York life, pitched between the worlds of commercial art, literary wit, and theatrical doings, was very much of a piece with the light, sharp spirit of metropolitan fashion which Harold Ross captured in his now famous (because uncannily accurate) prospectus for a magazine to mirror the smarter style of a New York which, in the mid-1920s, was more prosperous, lively, and varied than ever before, especially for its more successful citizens:

> THE NEW YORKER will be a reflection in word and picture of metropolitan life. It will be human. Its general tenor will be one of gaiety, wit and satire, but it will be more than a jester. It will not be what is commonly called sophisticated, in that it will assume a reasonable degree of enlightenment on the part of its readers. It will hate bunk.

Later in that prospectus Ross asserted that the magazine would not be "edited for the old lady from Dubuque"—nor, for that matter, as Neysa might have added, for the old lady from Quincy. Neysa knew just the kind of life she had, comfortably and forever, left behind out there in the Midwest. Neysa had chosen, and found the necessary financial resources to lead, the amusingly insular metropolitan life *The New Yorker* depicted. To the extent that the composite metropolitan life that emerged from *The New Yorker*'s pages was (and is) a fiction, it was a fiction more closely approximated than not by Neysa McMein.

The figure that Neysa cut on the metropolitan scene, and to a slightly lesser extent on the North Shore scene, was an essentially singular one. Although people identified her with Jack Baragwanath (and he with her), Neysa's personality hardly entailed her identification as part of a couple. To most who knew her, Neysa related to her marriage as merely one of her present circumstances, more or less important as the case might be.

Her personality, like most, had its quirks and excesses. One of its quirks was her impassioned concern for animals, her instantly "streaming eyes," as Thornton Wilder put it, at the thought that some animal might have to bear the degree of misfortune that regularly troubled the human species. Neysa was an adamant champion of any horse—and there were still a great many used in trade in the New York streets in those days—she saw being mistreated. Not only would she tongue-lash and threaten the owner, but she would also, if necessary, haul him into court to put a stop to the harsh treatment. She could be equally aggressive in other circumstances. Once, strolling through Central Park with a woman friend, she encountered an exhibitionist, whom she quickly sent flying with a well-directed rock thrown at the offender's offending parts.

Despite her almost impenetrable vagueness at times—which sometimes helped disguise a notable lack of hard knowledge—Neysa could be amazingly firm with friends and guests when she saw the need. George Abbott remembers the surprise of two young women whom Neysa turned away from her usually open door on the grounds that they were too drunk to be sociable and too far gone to judge their incapacity in that regard. Anyone who took Neysa's hospitality for granted was likely to discover that, as Ruth Gordon summarized her, "Neysa packed a lot of surprises."

Neysa's love of theater, opera, and music was not a simple liking, either. She loved them, first and foremost, as instances of art at its liveliest and most extroverted. About the opera she was, given her musical inclinations and taste for broad histrionics, particularly fond and knowledgeable. Yet she also loved the social side of the performing arts, the going there with friends, the being seen herself, the light chatter of the intervals. Particularly with her theatrical friends could she enjoy a sense of being on both sides of the footlights, knowing in close detail what went into mounting a performance, and, when the time came, experiencing a performance as a member of the audience. Not for her was the kind of dizzy logic that Bea Kaufman used on a male escort who was very late in getting her to a concert: "Hurry, or we'll miss the intermission."

Although Neysa was not without ego—some people, mostly outside her large, charmed circle, thought her haughty and even vain—she did appear, in contrast with the fair number of egomaniacs in her set, positively self-effacing. With the Algonquin wits often tripping over each

143
▼

other verbally, and getting their toes stepped on in the process, it was usually difficult to get a word in edgewise. Neysa, by contrast, hardly needed to uphold a continuously witty reputation—the occasional well-placed drollery was her chief verbal weapon—and so people could, with some discernible relief, talk to her easily and freely. Still, despite her offhand and accommodating ways, Neysa struck many persons, as, in the words of one of them, a "blazing personality." It is some major part of her mystery that she could seem at once so uncalculating and scattered as well as so vibrant and intense. That the decade which established her, the 1920s, had much the same odd combination of qualities helps explain why she was a genuine heroine of that decade, and one of its memorial figures thereafter.

Neysa prospered, for the most part, by her differences from her friends. In the unlovely, sometimes unloving, ways of the "Vicious Circle," Neysa's reputed lack of intelligence was a matter for periodic jests. Woollcott asserted, in so many words, that she "had no mind whatever," and sometimes treated her accordingly. FPA once described an evening in which the guests fell to conversing in a mixture of French, Italian, and Spanish, "much to Neysa's discomfiture, she understanding only a fraction of English, and the postage stamp flirtation and the language of flowers." Harpo Marx, obviously looking for spiritual allies, liked to relate the story of how in a spelling game of twenty-five words Neysa had eked out a victory over him, 1 to 0. Yet there was about Neysa, as about Harpo, an instinctive intelligence, a genius of sorts, that far exceeded their specific knowledge and was in a way greater than the more measurable intellectual talents of many in their group.

For example, Woollcott one summer decamped to the South of France with an accompanying entourage, his express purpose for the season being to make friends with George Bernard Shaw, who was summering in the area. And while Alec did manage to get Shaw to come over to dinner, it was Harpo, not Alec, to whom the Irish playwright took a great fancy. All summer, the clown, who had barely heard of Shaw before this, served as unofficial companion and chauffeur for the playwright and his wife as they gaily toured the winding roads of the Riviera in a rickety old car. We may justifiably suspect the basis of Shaw's choice:

that he discerned in Alec just a second-rate imitation of his own brilliant wit, but saw in Harpo's anarchic zaniness its true complement. Neysa, too, often made a stronger impression on the writers and artists visiting into the Algonquin set than did many of the group's writers and more professedly intellectual members. She had, as more than one who knew her has asserted, "a genius for people," and such is a genius beyond the power of intellect to cultivate. She allowed people to shine, and for this they were grateful.

Another factor that set Neysa apart, although not too far apart, from many in her set was her politics. If the Algonquin group was, as a whole, slightly to the left of liberalism, Neysa was slightly to its right. Those who remember her political stance at all recall it as does George Abbott: "on the liberal side, but very, very vague." Certainly she took no strong part in the general group approval of Roosevelt, and only involved herself in one political campaign, that in 1940 for Wendell Willkie, whose liberal Republicanism and "one world" philosophy appealed rather neatly to her vague and sentimental political instincts. For the most part she personalized politics, favoring tolerant attitudes, because they reflected her own approach to life, and cautious stances, because they reflected the politics of her origin.

Despite her sometimes political differences from her friends, Neysa never would have considered political views a serious enough matter over which to quarrel. Yet, in that querulous group, Neysa did not wholly avoid quarrels—or rather, breaks, for Neysa was not one for squabbling, preferring instead to break off a relationship rather than naggingly prolong it. Evidently one of those who asked Neysa to take more than she would tolerate was Dorothy Parker. One day Neysa returned home in an absolute, and atypical, fury, telling Jack that Dottie had said something so vile that she would never repeat it and that she would never speak to her again. Neysa kept the first resolve literally, at least as regards Jack, and the second in spirit. Relationships between the two women, once fairly intimate and fun-filled, became rather frosty, and remained so until Neysa's death. Despite Neysa's reticence, we can make a fair guess at the substance of Parker's insulting remark: it was probably some cutting reference to a vulgar kind of promiscuity which Parker attributed to Neysa, very possibly along with herself. In any case, the woman who once described her residential needs as just "room enough to lay a hat and a few friends," and who expressed her delight in a party by asserting, "Why, one more drink and I'd have been under the host," had a decided want of sexual delicacy. Neysa McMein might, like Dorothy Parker, be experiencing the new sexual freedom, but she was not suffering from it nearly so much—and would not have wanted Dottie's neuroses and guilts concerning it so freely projected onto her.

As opposed, on one hand, to the neurotic heterosexual dependencies of Parker—the consequence, as Marc Connelly put it, of her "always falling in love with some bum"—and, on the other, to the overt feminism of Ruth Hale and Jane Grant, Neysa calmly if firmly established a middle ground. She took the men she knew as the very imperfect creatures they were. Unlike someone such as Ruth Hale, who came more and more to feel stifled in her marriage—of course, Heywood Broun's fame *was* overwhelming—Neysa could take the freedom she necessarily had to afford Jack Baragwanath as the compensatory measure of her own. However, if she succeeded in maintaining her essential independence, that maintenance was not without some compromises of which, in her un-reflective way, Neysa was probably unaware. For one, she was professionally what she hardly was personally: a thorough creature of a narrow women's world. The illustrations (and advertisements) she drew were, at base, images of domestic felicity much more traditional and tame than obtained in her own life. She may have lived her life more among men than women, but it was ultimately by selling her wares in a world of women that she was able to do so. As the years went by, this once ardent suffragist seemed to think less and less frequently about the general position of women: having, in a sense, mastered, even beaten, the traditional system, Neysa was less inclined to be critical of it. Socially, sexually, and financially—if not wholly artistically—she was a success, and she came to take a serene pleasure in that success.

At the Dempsey-Willard fight in 1919, women were, at their insistence, rather grudgingly admitted, but they were confined to a small area in the rear of the grandstand. Within a few years, some women at prizefights were allowed to join the men down at ringside—and join them

Neysa enthusiastically and boisterously did. In a symbolic sense, she never afterwards gave up her seat: she continued to hold her privileged position, surrounded more by men than women, and she continued to view life from the perspective of a fan anxious to see what developments, surprising and amusing, were coming next. Withal, she never really challenged the notion that life, like boxing, was essentially a male sport.

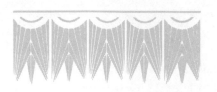

=9=

Sands Point and the House That Jack Built

Within a few years of their marriage, an important part of Neysa and Jack's life, nearly a full quarter of it, was taken up with a suburban summer existence. This was a yearly interval that differed markedly in tenor and pace from the busy rest of the life that they led, separately or together, in town.

For the summer of 1925, Jack's friend Bob Barbour lent them his place in Manhasset, on the North Shore of Long Island, half a dozen miles out from the city line. Here Neysa and Jack greatly enjoyed themselves: the Lardners' permanent home was just down the road, as was the Swopes' rather fabulous summer place; a literary-artistic life flourished in the area; Jack found it an easy commute to work during the week (and even easier to stay in town some nights); and Neysa was able to effect a transfer of her studio to the summer home. The leisurely, bright life of the North Shore struck both Neysa and Jack as a most viable alternative to the often blazing heat of mid-summer in the city, and so they determined to become permanent summer residents of the area.

The following year, they bought a lot and built a house at Sands Point, up the bay from Manhasset. The house, in a modified French provincial style, was a pleasant, airy structure of a fair size, but by the standards of the area a very modest house indeed, although its views, from a bluff overlooking Manhasset Bay, were fine. Jack, in the self-help ways of those dry times, made a bathtub of (highly praised) gin to celebrate the opening of their second domicile, and immediately, Neysa established their North Shore place as one of the necessary stops on the Algonquin-Broadway summer circuit. So immediately, in fact, that the house at once began to appear too small for the kind of offhand but busy enter-taining Neysa and Jack were likely to do as a matter of course weekend after weekend.

In time—actually just in time, for Neysa was about to relocate to a larger place—one of the American magazines devoted to hearth and home came knocking at Neysa's summer door to get a glimpse inside the house of this minor, but genuine, American celebrity. The February 1929 issue of *American Home* carried an article on "What My Home Means to Me," Neysa McMein as interviewed at home by one Wilma Van Santvoord. No doubt put to the test by Neysa's very hazy domesticity, the author of the piece told her readers that Neysa's place was, in a word, "unpretentious." Upon close inspection, the supposed photographs of Neysa's home have large areas which were airbrushed out, with some furnishings reinserted as line drawings meant to counterfeit a certain order and lack of clutter that the camera eye obviously could not find. The garden was described as full of sunflowers, those hearteningly gi-gantic and easy plants. And the routine of the place included mention of Neysa's current pets, her Irish wolfhound, Donegal, and her Persian,

Gooseberry, who, along with a small contingent of unnamed dogs and cats, were given free run of the place.

The summer community in which Jack and Neysa had landed themselves—and their establishment there was, more than almost anything else they did, a joint venture—was itself rather beyond the boundaries of their still considerable prosperity at the time. Sands Point, the area on the northern part of the peninsula between Manhasset Bay on the west and Hempstead Harbor on the east, just north of the cozy town of Port Washington, was in fact one of the wealthiest communities in the country, exceptionable even by the high standards of life on the North Shore of Long Island. Along this coastline, well into the next county and for miles inland, loomed the six hundred estates of the "barons" of the land, each set on hundreds, if not thousands, of acres—demesnes large and continuous enough to allow for the fox hunting that was regularly pursued across them. Here were Whitneys and Morgans and Guggenheims and Astors aplenty. On his estate, Otto Kahn built, for the fun of having it, a mountain. Amid these estates were the smaller, but still most attractive, parcels of land allowed to people like Neysa McMein and Jack Baragwanath, people who represented about as much of "the public" as these wealthy landowners were willing to tolerate. On the North Shore of Long Island, dotted with coves and bays all through Nassau County and far into Suffolk County, there were less than five miles of public beach.

In those days, Nassau was not what it has since become, a bedroom community, essentially a container for the overflow from the metropolis, an area packed with nearly a million and a half residents. In 1920, all of Nassau had barely enough of a population to rival that of a medium-sized city (126,120), yet it had, through its great concentration of the wealthy, an influence out of all proportion to its size. In the 1920s, for instance, the Republican Party had forty-nine delegations at its national conventions: one from each state, plus one from Nassau County. Such was the powerful world in which Neysa and Jack had chosen to make their summer way.

It was a choice both odd and explicable. If Neysa and Jack (and Joan) constituted the poorest family in their very wealthy community, it was

150
▼

not a community into which they had settled with the idea of competing with their near neighbors, which included, by way of daunting competition, three household-estates of Guggenheims. Rather, they sought only to establish themselves, in a pleasant style to be sure, in a comfortable, convenient, and very pretty summer locale. As it turned out, they also came to represent the most bohemian element in their small, elite community. Some of their neighbors took a very positive liking to the carefree, entertaining atmosphere they found at Neysa and Jack's, such that the couple could soon claim to have the most popular, if far from the most stylish, household in their very exclusive neighborhood. Theirs was a home dedicated, above all, to fun.

It was when, in 1929, Neysa and Jack built their second house that they established themselves firmly as a fixture of their summer community, freely conceded their special, entertaining social position. From their first establishment at Sands Point they realized the need for a place large enough to host the numbers of their friends that their free-and-easy summer life would inevitably draw to them. So they bought, very near the original house, a plot well forested with clusters of oaks and dogwoods—Neysa loved, and was very knowledgeable about, trees—and built a new, much larger house, one on the more usual scale of things at Sands Point, if hardly at the top of that scale.

The arrangement for this second house tells us something about the respective management of their independent incomes: the "bargain," and surely it was a bargain for Jack, was that he would design the house and Neysa would pay for its construction. What Jack designed was, according to surviving accounts, a most pleasing structure in the English style, its exterior in whitewashed brick and with vines sent climbing over it. The place had a score of rooms, and an extra large living room for entertaining. The facade of the front of the house, or the back of it—Neysa and Jack forever debated which was which—was dominated by a two-story window that let in the dappled sunlight in abundant quantities. And bohemian as they might have seemed, they were still sure to guarantee their privacy by maintaining a line of trees to block views from the passing roadway, a loop up from Port Washington Village which more than occasionally drew the curious along it in hopes of a glimpse of the rich and the near rich at play. A few years after the house was completed, Jack designed and built, with the help of several "village roustabouts" from Port Washington, a nice-sized swimming pool, which sat out beyond the terrace and completed their very comfortable appointments.

This second of their summer homes has been remembered with a fondness that almost equals the strong sentiment found in memories of Neysa's studio-salon. Unlike her salon, though, which gathered amusing and talented people into one large area to let them perform as they might in their various ways, Neysa's Sands Point house allowed for a much freer kind of association, with guests coming and going as they pleased and in whatever combinations they might choose. Some went down to the pool or for a stroll through the surrounding woods, while others went off for a swim in the bay or a visit to the houses of nearby friends. Freedom was the keynote, with guests left to their own, usually quite suitable, devices. To attend to the wants and needs of the guests there were four servants: three black women who were long-term employees, and a chauffeur-butler who was hired in for the summer, often with great hopes and less than fully satisfactory results. Most weekends the place was full, but unless there was a party on Saturday night, all the guests might never appear in concert. Sometimes, an impromptu act—George Gershwin sitting down to the piano or a parlor game that generated a lively, contagious excitement—would catch up those returning to the house and generate a sort of spontaneous group event. Their neighbors, as well as their visitors, realized the casual pleasure of the place: Neysa and Jack were probably the best-loved and certainly the most-visited couple on Sands Point.

This home was, in the manner of their other establishments, furnished in a charmingly haphazard and eccentrically mixed way. A few antiques mingled with examples of "Grand Rapids modern"; old-fashioned and overstuffed Victorian pieces were cheek by jowl with some fine Chinese lamps and these with nondescript bric-à-brac saved from Neysa's several studios. A shawl, getting dustier with each passing year, remained draped over the back of the grand piano. Not a few of the pieces were in need of repair, and guests had to be careful not to displace a table leg or chair arm that had been delicately propped in place. Animals, including for a time one mixed-breed proletarian type called by the generic "Mack the Dog," wandered about as freely, if not as numerously, as the weekend guests. A quaint sort of disarray was the general, and for the most part happy, result of all this, although Neysa's laissez-faire housekeeping, like her laissez-faire marriage, had its occasional critics. And while it was true that the lampshades tended to gather cobwebs, books and papers to pile up and tumble over, and a general dustiness to obtain, Neysa and Jack had never wanted a showplace anyway.

Between the rounds of weekend guests, a quieter, more leisurely schedule defined the daily routine. Neysa had breakfast in bed about eight, while Jack breakfasted downstairs in the dining room with whatever guests might be staying on from the weekend. At the table there was usually some small talk about the most recent gatherings and doings of the North Shore set. Then Jack was off to Port Washington and the train into Manhattan and work. Soon after, Neysa came down to the terrace to read the morning paper, have a chat with her guest(s) and, if the occasion warranted, play a game or two of backgammon. There was a late morning swim, then luncheon on the shady, cool terrace. After this Neysa might put herself to work for a few hours or might be off for a visit with some nearby friends or might settle down with a book, usually "the current thing," which often meant something written by someone who had been there the weekend before or would be coming the weekend after.

Unless he was staying over in town for a date, Jack would arrive home in the late afternoon, generally filled with some good-natured bluster about the nearly infernal heat of Manhattan or the exasperatingly slow and hot ride out on the Long Island Railroad. Neysa and whoever else was staying on at the moment would take his complaints as a sign, in those pre-air conditioning days when even the rich could only achieve comfort by a shift in locale, of the wisdom of their lazy, slow, and surpassingly comfortable day's regime. Neysa and Jack then took a quiet stroll through their full woods—Neysa fought back every attempt to have her beloved trees thinned—for what was their daily, if rather brief, time alone together. After this they dined, or went to dine, or were off to

153

▼

some other gathering, together or apart, as their inclinations or invitations dictated. It was—particularly for Neysa who lived it round the clock—a very relaxed and less intense life than the kind the two led in town from fall through spring. It was also a life very different in its tone from the one they had each lived in their childhood and adolescent years. Here was none of the seriousness and quiet sense of duty that marked Jack's ministerial home; and here was none of the looming disaster and manic depression that often made Neysa's a worrisome place.

With Jack barely excepted, the most important man in Neysa's Sands Point life was George Abbott. When George met, and was enchanted by, Neysa in 1929, he had just embarked on a second life that would, among other things, make him one of the most important personages in the history of the American theater. In 1910, shortly after graduating from the University of Rochester, he had married his high school sweetheart, Ednah, the sole twist in this traditional mating ritual being that his wife was not his classmate but his French teacher. Their life together was staid and regular, for the older Ednah had a "Puritan streak" which strongly conditioned their marriage and which brought out George's own Puritanism, the residue of a tense, narrow family life in a small town in upstate New York and, for a period, in the still largely uncivilized and demanding reaches of Wyoming, where the family had decamped in an attempt to reclaim his father from his alcoholic ways and give them a chance for a new beginning. From 1913 to 1924, George had struggled as a Broadway actor (he had a small part in the touring company of *Dulcy*), but he had only become a real success when he turned to other things in the theater: writing, producing, directing, and even "doctoring" ailing plays. *Broadway* (1926), which he co-authored and directed, was the first of several dozen big hits with which he was to be associated over the next six decades.

When Ednah died in the late 1920s, George, just past forty, found himself strangely but excitingly "on the loose" again. If he was not to be a bore, he had to learn to shed his lingering intolerance for those who drank and who, of necessity, must break the law to do so. He must also learn to enjoy the rewards of his long-postponed success. And he must get to know some new people. It was through a friendship with Charles Brackett that he was first brought into the Algonquin circle, but it was through meeting Neysa that he really came to know and like this world. His life, which had yet run only two fifths of its long course, was never to be the same, or as quiet, again.

For several years George was chiefly Neysa's friend, soon achieving a privileged position among the men she "dated." He especially liked taking Neysa to the movies and seeing her find delight in even the silliest offerings. At first, though, Jack, with his perfect ease and his suggestions where George might take his wife on their date, made him "uncomfortable." But when George realized the genuineness of Jack's casual attitude, and Neysa's perfect reciprocity, he could only conclude, with some admiration, that Jack "was a man of the world all right"—and one well worth emulating in his carefree ways.

Jack thought Neysa's new friend unduly reserved and in need of some loosening up, but he took a quiet liking to the tall, blond ex-actor nonetheless. When Neysa had George out to Sands Point for a few weekends, Jack was able to penetrate his surface reserve and discover what "a great asset" George could be socially, "good at all sorts of games" (though still enough of a Puritan to refuse to play card games), and a witty and attractive man for the ladies. Even the fact that George did not drink proved a benefit, for it meant there was always someone to drive the entourage home safely after late parties. Within a few years, George had become such a regular summer visitor that Neysa and Jack's friends were jokingly referring to their summer place as the "Abbottoir." However, what turned George from a good friend into a real intimate was a little business arrangement devised by Neysa and, in terms of its designated subject, crucially modified at Jack's suggestion.

Bernard Baruch's misgivings aside, Neysa could be surprisingly practical about money matters for so uncalculating a woman. In 1933, when she suggested to Jack that it would make good financial sense to take on a paying boarder at their large summer home, he half-agreed: he liked the idea, but hated her proposed candidate, Alec Woollcott (who, in any case, might not have been interested, since he tried to spend as much of the summer as he could up on Neshobe Island in Vermont). In Woollcott's stead, Jack nominated the more obvious and infinitely more acceptable George Abbott, and Neysa immediately agreed to the change. George, who could hardly believe his luck and who knew how to watch, and stretch, a penny, jumped at the opportunity. Over the next thirteen years, he, Neysa, and Jack shared a joyous summer existence; for George, that summer life was a yearly "carefree" interlude in a life otherwise much conditioned by the work ethic.

Looking back decades afterward in *"Mr. Abbott,"* George would see those summers as a turning point in his life. Although he would continue to work long and hard in the theater (and from time to time in the movies) right through the 1980s, he learned in those Sands Point summers to relax and enjoy himself in the necessary intervals: "I wish I could find words to convey the idyllic nature of the life we lived. My childhood had been one of strain and stress; as a married man my life had been filled with love and togetherness, but also with struggle and scrimping and saving and planning. Now I was in a house dedicated to gaiety and fun." Once he permanently settled in as a member of the summer household, George became as close to Jack as he was to Neysa, with the eventual result that in town he ended up a more constant companion for Jack than for Neysa. What made George a great friend to both was that his personality was a blend of the characteristics and likings of his two friends, people whom he saw as "very different" from one another, although in a highly complementary way. George moved easily, of course, through the world of Neysa's theatrical and literary friends, but he also liked playing the role of the handsome, very eligible man about town in Jack's world of young women. George was drawn to Neysa because she was an attractive woman, and to Jack because Jack was, like himself, drawn to attractive women—like Neysa.

Considering Neysa and Jack's well-known marital arrangement, George's presence at Sands Point raised some questions—and not a few eyebrows. When a dinner guest once innocently referred to George as a "house guest," Jack snorted good-naturedly, "House guest! The son-of-a-bitch has been here eight years. The first four years they thought he was Neysa's lover. Now they think he's mine." For Jack, another of the benefits of George Abbott's residence was that it tended to discourage visits from Alec Woollcott, who thought George something of a "hick" and had no desire to view Neysa's intimate relation with him at first hand.

One summer, George suffered an appendicitis, and Neysa made the melodramatic most of his minor crisis. Raoul Fleischmann, who was a Manhasset neighbor and amused onlooker, reported "Neysa's dramatic statements as to the astonishingly high temperatures George enjoyed," and lightly scored her great partiality for friends, whether in sickness or in health: "By God, no friend of hers can have anything that isn't just a bit out of the ordinary." In actual, more mundane fact, George was quite undelirious enough to pack his bag and otherwise calmly make ready before Neysa drove him to the hospital—although the appendicitis was perfectly genuine and the festering organ had to be quickly removed.

That hospital, in fact, did a fair trade in Neysa's house guests, what with the hectic sport there, to say nothing of the occasional mendings it had to do of the house's often ebullient and always injury-prone hostess. One afternoon, as she floated lazily around the pool on her back watching her guests take turns diving from the board into the water, Neysa began discoursing on the remarkable construction of the diving board. It was especially designed to have a lively give, she explained, but never, never to touch the water. She would demonstrate: one of them must dive while she, in perfect safety, floated under the board. The guests protested, but Neysa insisted. Finally one agreed and dove: the board shot up, then down, creasing the water, and with it Neysa's skull. When her head cleared—she had a mild concussion—Neysa loudly protested the unlikelihood, in theoretical terms, of her mishap: "It *shouldn't* have hit me. It's built *not* to."

One of the more sustained and tangible results of the intimate, if not always triangular, relationship between Neysa, Jack, and George was, for a time in 1938, to be seen on Broadway. At a luncheon the year before, Neysa had outlined for George the idea she had for a play, a piece of fluff about the misadventures of a Spanish "tart" who comes to New York in search of her fortune and gets herself farcically involved in the social battle between a handsome young man and a society "trout"

157
▼

who snubs his fiancée because she is an actress. When George offered his encouragement, but pointed out that the play still lacked a third act, Jack volunteered that he had "an idea" and that he would like to "take a crack" at writing the piece. Neysa freely handed over her as yet incomplete story, and George promised to do his theatrical best to get the result on the boards.

Jack's first step, or rather misstep, was to take on a co-author, Kenneth Simpson, whose chief recommendation was that he, like Jack, was a mining engineer and that "two mining engineers could write a better play than one." The dubious truth of that proposition was proven almost at once: Simpson dutifully arrived at Sands Point each Saturday morning, ready and eager for, but hardly capable of, the dramatic work. As the summer waned, so did Simpson. By the end of the season he had stopped coming entirely. Jack was left with a great deal of the writing still to do, which he managed with, as he gratefully put it, "a good deal of assistance from George." By early 1938, the piece, called *All That Glitters*, was complete enough to be cast and rehearsed. George was kind enough to put up half the money, with Sonny Whitney putting up the other half, but George was also cautious enough about his investment to make himself both producer and director.

The flimsy entertainment, at George's behest, was cast shrewdly, with Arlene Francis playing the key role of the Spanish "countess." What started off as something of a lark for Jack turned into something more than hard work. The novice playwright soon discovered, to his dismay, that his completed script was not nearly so "finished" as he thought. Every night there was tedious, endless rewriting. Jack's particular weakness was curtain lines: he could never seem to manage them to George's satisfaction and had to rewrite them by the carload.

By the time the play opened in Baltimore, Jack was, very uncharacteristically, "a nervous wreck." The response to the first act offered little cheer: the audience laughed politely and briefly, and Jack could see George, in his aisle seat across the theater, scribbling furiously on a notepad. The second act, however, brought long, loud belly laughs from the Baltimoreans—and Jack, out of sheer relief, went off to a bar and had a double Scotch. The reviews the next day proved Jack's new-found confidence in the main fate of the piece justified: they were glowing enough to stimulate a large advance buy on the part of the New York brokers. George, though, was dimly pleased at best. Assuming his rigorous posture as "Mr. Abbott," he would assemble the cast after each performance and, as he consulted his always long list of notes, tell them in his "pleasantly severe way" just what and how much still needed to be done. Jack, too, was given his tasks, and had to be up and rewriting by eight o'clock the next morning so the cast might have the revised script when it began its rehearsals at eleven. Jack was learning just why the hardworking George so much appreciated those idyllic summer months at Sands Point.

On the train back from the Baltimore tryouts, George confided to Jack that he thought they had a hit on their hands—but for once in his long theatrical life George was wrong. The New York audience gave the play scattered applause and scant laughs; these demanding, and hardened, theatergoers, as Jack immediately realized, were clearly "not impressed" by his effort. When, after ten weeks, the initial sales stimulus provided by the brokers' advance buy ran out, the play closed.

In retrospect, George Abbott decided that *All That Glitters* was "not sufficiently sophisticated" for New York, and that it might well have been a success if they had kept it on the road. Yet, in light of the fact that the story was basically one of Neysa's contriving, it could hardly be called an improbable New York tale, for the essential plot was really Neysa's own life cast in the conventions of farce: the story of a clever, attractive young woman from the provinces who comes to New York intent on being a success and making her way in society, and who, in her offhand way, achieves her aim.

What George Abbott came to discover as he settled in at Sands Point was what Neysa and Jack had discovered several years earlier themselves, namely, that the rich, as F. Scott Fitzgerald famously put it, "are different from you and me. They possess and enjoy early, and it does something to them, makes them soft where we are hard, and cynical where we are trustful, in a way that, unless you were born rich, it is very difficult to understand." At first, George tended to shy away from contacts with the wealthier members of Sands Point and the other nearby communities, preferring instead the comforting friendliness of Neysa and Jack's home and the lively, unpretentious guests—many of them known to George through his Broadway work—who filled the house so amusingly each weekend. When George finally became comfortable enough to move into the wealthier reaches of Sands Point society, he always seemed to protect himself by maintaining an air of almost scholarly detachment: "I studied with interest the morals and manners of these children and grandchildren of the strong, ruthless men who had made fortunes in the preceding century." What George discovered through this "study," besides the expected insularity and political conservatism of the set (FDR was "That Son-of-a-bitch in Washington . . . out to get them"), was that he was repeatedly "shocked at the amount of bad grammar and mispronunciation heard in this circle." At Neysa and Jack's, people, thankfully, spoke better and more brightly—and even Jack, who could purposely be coarse, would usually put in some stylistic twist to prove his linguistic mettle, like adding "retromingent" ("that urinates backwards") when he called one of his cronies a "son-of-a-bitch."

Although he was specifically referring to the large, sparkling Thanksgiving weekends at Harriman's Arden House, the mock title Heywood Broun offered to describe such a life, *The Upper Depths*, might just as well have served to describe North Shore summer life in the 1920s and 1930s. If, as George Abbott eventually came to feel, there was something empty about the lives of these people who "had too much," there was also a certain arrogant splendor (soon to be eclipsed) about their elaborate dinners and gorgeous parties and fanciful yacht expeditions up Long Island Sound to watch the Yale-Harvard boat race at New London, where they rooted, with adolescent glee, for the crew from one or the other of the schools from which the male members of the various important clans had almost invariably, if none too grammatically, graduated. Donald Ogden Stewart, who summered with the Whitneys at Manhasset for several years in the 1920s, had to admit in his autobiography, long after his sharp turn to the left, that North Shore life had its simple luxurious joys: "This was the world of youth, of fun unending. Not the cultured elite of which I had once dreamed, but yachts are very nice as a means of transportation, and so are private railroad cars."

North Shore social life, even for persons as accustomed to associating with the famous and rich as Neysa and Jack were, could be rather fantastic—probably never more so, on a regular basis, than at Herbert Swope's mansion. If Neysa was more famous than rich, and people like the Whitneys were more rich than famous, Herbert Bayard Swope was both in equal, and very full, measure. His enormous, lavish parties, with their variegated lists of guests, were a great magnification of the lively entertaining Neysa and Jack did at Sands Point: everyone eventually came to Swope's, and usually had a very good time there. At one of these gatherings, Neysa was standing in a group when one member, seeing their tall, red-haired host stride majestically through his "Swope-filled room," remarked in admiration, "He has the face of some old emperor." To which FPA could not resist adding, "And I have the face of an old Greek coin," an over-assessment which Neysa immediately, and quite accurately, amended to "You have the face of an old Greek waiter."

Neysa, for the most part, shared in the general sentiment that Swope, in some mysterious way, embodied a sort of ancient nobility, even as he played his part as master of the modern revels. But she also found one of Swope's habits—his chronic, cavalier tardiness—infuriating. With his unbounded energy and nearly unbounded egotism, the powerful and influential Swope simply held to his own expansive daily schedule and could be quite oblivious to the hours his more regular friends kept. He once called George Kaufman at ten o'clock in the evening to ask what the playwright was doing about dinner and received the reply he probably deserved, namely, "digesting it." When Swope and his wife showed up a full two hours late for a dinner at Sands Point and the meal was ruined, their hostess made the best of the following few hours, but quite firmly told the Swopes as they were leaving that she would never invite them to dinner again. Apparently, she never did, although she continued to see the Swopes as part of her North Shore rounds.

Of course, in a practical social sense, Neysa could not have completely cut off someone as powerful on the North Shore scene as the editor of the *World*. Besides, Herbert Bayard Swope was probably the leading figure of an inner circle of North Shore croquet devotees among whom Neysa counted herself. Swope's estate, in fact, boasted one of the finest, and probably the most often used, croquet grounds in the area. To the extent that this prime area of the North Shore was its own little nation in summer, croquet was the national game—and virtually everyone had either to be a player or a fan. Since Neysa greatly preferred to play in the sun rather than sit in the shade watching and drinking, it was necessary, in some measure, to stay on Swope's good side, for he dominated the arrangement and progress of the matches as surely, and by the same means, as he dominated many another thing: through the sheer force of his personality.

There were some North Shore visitors, like Donald Klopfer and Don Stewart, who could not, try as they might, stimulate in themselves a passionate interest in croquet. For the "ungamely" it was only the talk of the company that saved the life from being dull and boring—and when the company was at some croquet match for an exasperatingly long time, there was little salvation to be had. Some guests, like Helen Hayes, noted another drawback to the romantic life the rich were trying to lead: the Sound and the Bay were lovely to look at and contemplate, but they were sometimes too oily and garbage-filled to allow a swim. The privileged might be able to bar the invasion of tawdry, workaday reality by land, but they could not stem its invasion by sea.

Perhaps the most splendid view along the whole "Gold Coast" of the magnificent-looking, if sometimes dirty, Sound was to be had from Falaise, the estate on the eastern side of Sands Point which belonged to Harry Guggenheim and his wife, née Alicia Patterson. Perched on a very high bluff, the house and terrace looked out across Hempstead Harbor and commanded a view of the Sound in both directions. From the broad terrace, looking down from the balustrade, those on the estate's beach below seemed tiny moving figures, almost as miniature in scale as the scores of sailboats that dotted the waters on a weekend afternoon, the whole forming a brightly colored scene of serene leisure. The estate's large manor house had been designed to incorporate dozens of architectural bits and pieces taken off from the ruins of Europe, and the estate boasted several other large structures as well, including "Castle Gould," a piece of gimcrackery built in rough imitation of Killarney Castle at the turn of the century by Jay Gould, who originally owned the property. Over the course of fifteen years, Neysa had become not only a good friend of Alicia (the co-founder, with her husband, and long-term owner, after his death, of *Newsday*), but sufficiently intimate to enlist her as a traveling companion on a trip to visit Jack in Cuba, where he was superintending a nickel-mining operation. But by then the Guggenheim estate had become a naval training station and the sometimes dazzling North Shore world of the interwar years just a memory.

During its heyday, the high point of North Shore life, its most magical moment, was the annual July costume party given by Charlie and Joan Whitney Payson. Thousands of trees on their estate were strung with lights, and lanterns were set twinkling in the surrounding hills. Hundreds of guests strolled about in elaborate disguises. One orchestra played in the glittering ballroom and another on the terrace, at the end of a carpeted, blue-lit path leading down from the house. Masked couples danced and passed in and out of the mansion and walked arm in arm through the surrounding gardens and woods. As the night wore on, the more elderly guests gradually slipped away, and the couples on the dance floor became fewer and fewer, until at dawn, with the lights dimming in the trees, the last remaining guests, now weary and satiated, finally made their way to their cars and drove home. For days after, at Neysa's and in dozens of other North Shore homes, the great costume ball was the main topic of conversation, with speculation running high as to the identity of some of the more notorious, secretive, and intriguing guests.

Free of social-climbing instincts and far too "poor" to compete at the Sands Point version of "conspicuous consumption," Neysa and Jack (and George) set up, if very unofficially, an alternate version of social life for the community, one defined chiefly by the considerable talent, as opposed to the considerable fortune, of their guests. Visitors who dropped in at their summer home, as did Jack's teenage son, might find George

Gershwin holding forth at the piano: "I didn't know who the hell he was. Neysa gave me the sign to sit and be quiet. This fellow continued to play this light, tuneful stuff and I found out." Another time, a Fourth of July weekend to be exact, it would be the fledgling young cartoonist, Walt Disney, talking about his revolutionary animation techniques.

A fellow with a different sort of talent starting coming out to Sands Point in the early 1930s, a handsome young man whom Neysa introduced to Jack as someone able to install a radio in an automobile. He promptly gave proof of his ability by installing one in Neysa and Jack's runabout, much to the Jack's surprise. The surprise was diminished, however, when Jack learned just who the young man was: only a few years before, William Paley had organized a large group of independent radio stations into the Columbia Broadcasting System and had been presiding over the immensely successful company ever since. If anyone should have known all about radios, it was Bill Paley.

Most often, though, it was less a single guest who was the center of interest than the whole assemblage. Neysa McMein was, in the estimation of George Abbott and not a few others, "the greatest party giver who ever lived." While the historical veracity of the claim is debatable, or at least unprovable, its great sweep does indicate just how much her guests valued their beautiful hostess's ability to make fun and excitement for them without seeming to strain herself. People came to Sands Point for the same reason they went to any other place over which Neysa presided: to participate in the fun they were almost sure to find there.

One who did strain, and so much embarrass himself, at Neysa's was John O'Hara, then a young writer still pantingly eager to get a look at and make his way in "society." Like a number of other talented young artists on the New York scene, he eventually was tendered an invitation to Sands Point. Immediately, he took himself off to a swank clothier, to outfit himself for what he fantasized would be a very stylish North Shore weekend. He showed up at Neysa's door dressed to the sporting teeth, resplendent in a new boater, blue sailing blazer, and white duck trousers—an outfit to whose bright colors were immediately added the red of his face when he gazed on the casually, almost shabbily, dressed crew at Neysa's. After ten minutes, O'Hara, having had enough of the stares and amused laughter, fled, murmuring angrily, according to one eavesdropper, as he stormed down the path away from the scene of his social defeat.

Despite her largesse and her overtures toward social aspirants like O'Hara, Neysa did not welcome everyone to Sands Point. Among those for whom she had little time and less hospitality were the Quincyans who occasionally called at her summer door under the mistaken impression that she would enjoy reliving some hometown memories with them. One of these would-be reminiscers made his way to Neysa's indirectly— and most obviously and nostagically drunk. Having gotten as far as the house of that other North Shore Quincyan, Ruth Fleischmann, he was directed on to Neysa's by Ruth's teenage son, Gardner Botsford. But when the tipsy guest arrived, full of hometown cheer, he was none too gently received and even less gently sent on his way. Young Botsford was afterwards given a lecture about the sensible thing to do with visitors from the hometown, most especially drunken ones: they should be gotten rid of as expeditiously as possible. Like many of her wealthier neighbors, Neysa came to have a limited tolerance for the general public, Quincyan or not, even as her tolerance for her friends and acquaintances grew broader and more catholic by the year.

Certainly, tolerance was called for concerning perhaps the most unusual feature of her life at Sands Point: "Freedom Week." One week each summer—usually a week Neysa was up at the Neshobe Island retreat, but always a week when she readily agreed to absent herself— Jack, George, and Will Stewart, one de facto and two real bachelors, "entertained" a different group of women each evening. These groups were loosely organized and recruited by theme: there was "Models' Night" and "Actresses' Night" and "Salesladies' Night" and "Chorus Girls' Night" and even "Neurotic Women's Night," this last, quite predictably, not their greatest success. Among the more popular women on their large roster was one Mrs. McFeeters, a spirited and exotically pretty young woman who would later succeed as a Hollywood actress, in a series of hokum adventures, under the more mellifluous name of Maria Montez. The weekend would often be a reprise of the previous week nights, with the three favorite women brought back for an encore.

The Freedom Week routine was a fixed thing, with a long list of mostly silly rules, such as that the men must always be the first to sit to table. Each weekday afternoon, Will Stewart's chauffeur would pick up that evening's group in Manhattan and bring the women to Sands Point for a formal twilight dinner, followed by an evening around the pool. "Freedom" meant, among other things, freedom from the normal constraints of workaday adult life. There was much horsing around and adolescent humor, with Jack as the group's rowdy toastmaster. They would play charades or "Kangaroo," a Cuban elaboration of Chinese Checkers, or one of the intricate parlor games the men knew so well. At some point, Jack or George usually managed to set off a firecracker under Will's hammock. George, who might go so far as to have a glass of wine with dinner, was the group's taskmaster, ensuring that no one slipped half-drunkenly into the pool and that one and all were up early the next morning, so the women were ready to return to town after lunch, when the chauffeur would drive them in and pick up the next group.

If Jack and George, both of whom have left fairly full accounts of Freedom Week, are to be believed, the week was one of "innocent" fun and no sex. However, more than a few surviving bits of evidence belie the totally innocent character of the weeklong saturnalia. One of the groups had a high-priced call girl in it, reputedly in a failed attempt to convince George that such women were not as awful as he, in his lingering puritanical ways, thought them. Jack kept in his photo album, interspersed with dutiful pictures of family groupings, any number of photos of the women of Freedom Week, many posed quite artistically but also quite nudely, beside the pool. (As Loos's Lorelei, who would have been most welcome at Freedom Week, put it, "family life is only fit for those who can stand it"—and Jack had his own, peculiar ways of seeing through the trial.) George Abbott recounts the common playing of "Corks," a simplified version of strip poker, protesting the while about those who saw such typical Freedom Week activities as part of "a series of wild, pagan orgies" instead of just plain, high-spirited fun.

It is probably true, though, that the yearly event was more important in terms of social than sexual intercourse. It was, in fact, during one of the more respectable Freedom Week events, "Decent Women's Weekend," that Will Stewart met the woman he would eventually marry (although the marriage did not put an end to his participation in Freedom Week). These handsome, middle-aged gents were indulging themselves—with the ready, if now somewhat puzzling, assistance of many young women—in a prolonged, almost giddy rite of heterosexual passage. Despite the banter and hilarity that went on between the sexes, "it was," as Abbott has judged, "the men that made the party," and they made it night after night, all week. Neysa, for her part, allowed "the boys" their week, what Jack called "our fiesta," and insisted that it was a simple, non-sexual sort of hijinks; but she also knew that it was not quite as innocent as she and Jack and George made it seem.

Despite the institution of such rituals as Freedom Week, life at Sands Point did not remain exactly the same year in year out. For one thing, Raoul Fleischmann and Ruth Gardner divorced, thereby depriving Neysa and Jack's house of its most frequent visiting couple. In the late 1930s, Raoul arranged to be taken in at Sands Point à la George Abbott, as a paying summer boarder. On weekends, Raoul's teenage son, Peter, would come to visit, and at Sands Point he often found other bright, athletic young people, like King and the younger Joan. As these adolescents and young adults began to make an impact, if not a great one, on life at the Sands Point house, they must have reminded their parents and their parents' friends they were aging. Still, as long as Neysa, Jack, and George remained a devoted threesome, summers at Sands Point were defined by their union and remained a pleasant, carefree idyll. However, when a fourth party intruded, the idyll was shattered; the resulting estrangement was to constitute one of the lingering regrets of Neysa's last years.

10

Games and More Games

Both George Abbott and Howard Dietz, no mean games players themselves, freely accorded Neysa the title of "the queen of the party games." While her illustrations and portraits might betray a want of invention and imagination, these traits were never lacking in the games she invented or, more usually, crucially modified. As her daughter and stepson recall vividly, Neysa's instinctive response to the question of what should be done next was to invent a game, or to dredge up and reshape one from the hundreds she kept in mind. If many in the Algonquin crowd were drawn to games, indoor and outdoor, because of an almost unhealthy desire to prove themselves at competition, Neysa was the group's main representative of those who delighted in games chiefly for the fun and entertainment, rather than for the victories, they provided. Of course, she was good enough at games, and abnormally lucky in the balance, to make competition worthwhile and winning a regular thing.

That a goodly share of Neysa's mental energy went into gamemaking did not strike her friends, many of whom were almost as addicted to play as she was, as abnormal, although her devotion sometimes led to strange scenes with the uninitiated. Her stepson once came upon her clipping out sections of the *Encyclopaedia Britannica* for a game she had just invented and was getting ready for her guests that evening. Such gutting of the family reference work struck the Princeton student as "rather shocking," if also rather typical of his stepmother's playful priorities.

Although it was chiefly indoor party games for which Neysa was known, it was actually at croquet, until then a rather tepid and polite game, that she made her first mark as a games innovator and strategist. During a 1920 match on a New Jersey field, flanked by thick woods and swampy stretches, Neysa suggested that it might enliven the game if they agreed to play without any boundaries. The suggestion was taken up—with devastating results. When an opponent's ball could be sent flying several hundred feet, so that he or she was forced to play it back from the rough and rugged reaches beyond the field, the game took on a wholly new aspect: a fierce, vengeful, dangerous quality. Neysa had found the secret that turned the mild lawn sport into what Alec Woollcott, one of the great devotees of the newly enhanced and more vicious game, characterized as a "cunning, devastating battle of wits, strength and strategy."

This new kind of croquet quickly took on ritualistic aspects for its regular players, a group that eventually counted, in and around the Algonquin set, FPA, Dorothy Parker, Bea and George Kaufman, Harpo Marx, Alice Miller, Marc Connelly, Raoul Fleischmann, Howard Dietz, Mary and Robert Sherwood, Averell Harriman, Edna Ferber, Frank Sullivan, Harold Guinzburg, as well as Jack Baragwanath, George Abbott, and Will Stewart, together, of course, with Neysa, Alec, and the major-domo of the sport, Herbert Swope. In his "Conning Tower" column, FPA regularly announced his "trouncings" of various croquet opponents, and sometimes acknowledged his own defeats on the field.

Soon the players shifted to heavy, brass-bound mallets, which pulled one's arms downward and required two hands and considerable strength to swing precisely; cast-iron wickets with but a ⅜″ clearance (which they set at odd, difficult angles); and large composition balls capable of withstanding the frequent and gleeful poundings they were given. All this paraphernalia was imported at great expense—and at great profit to Abercrombie & Fitch—from England, but having devised their own highly explicit and unconventional version of the game, those in the Algonquin set would use no other. For years after, Averell Harriman, one of the most loyal and steadfast players, would tote his heavy, custom-built croquet mallet all over the world on his diplomatic travels, ever hopeful of a game in some far reach.

Once the game took hold in this set, a short summer season was hardly sufficient to satisfy the members' appetite. In 1923, Neysa petitioned the Parks Department for a permit to play in Central Park, and the group took avidly to the field at the first thaw. A few years later, Harpo spotted a large empty rooftop near his Upper West Side apartment building and proposed that it should be rented and made into a croquet field to carry the players through the winter months. The project was just about set when Swope self-importantly decided that he would use his political influence to get all the necessary permits so the sport might be played legally, as well as literally, above the crowd. The ensuing red tape and confusion—no one could figure out just what permits *were* needed— eventually killed that plan. The Algonquin set, it seemed, would have to settle for an eight-month croquet season, with the winter given over to glorying in and gloating over the season's triumphs, a fitting verbal reprise of an activity that was, as Jack Baragwanath described it, "a tough, acrimonious sport which was played bitterly."

Neysa could hold her own, like only a few other women players, with the more fanatical and expert players among the men. Her size and not inconsiderable strength were great assets, as was her general understanding of the strategy of games. Janet Flanner admiringly described her as an outstanding player with a fine sense of strategy and the requisite strength for long shots. According to Woollcott, Neysa took her croquet more seriously than glamorously, often wearing a pair of oversized sneakers to increase her leverage on long driving shots, a piece of sporting dress that gave rise to her purported nickname on the field, "Little Miss Webfoot." (Alec's description of Kaufman carefully bending over a shot, "a morning glory climbing a pole," is even more evocative of the comic seriousness with which the players pursued their croquet pleasures.) But Alec did admit that Neysa's equipage for the croquet ground, together with her skill, made her a formidable and surprising player, "unquestionably the shrewdest, most powerful and most malignant among the women players."

At Herbert Swope's North Shore place there was no such thing as a casual and friendly round of croquet. There croquet was always, as Edna Ferber judged it, "a bloody and bitter game," bearing no relation whatever to its polite Victorian ancestor. When Swope and Woollcott played, inevitably on opposite sides, they argued so loud and long over minute points and minuscule advantages that they were dubbed "the Katzenjammer Kids." And when Swope played with anyone but Alec, he dominated the proceedings with such a high rhetorical flourish that no one else could get a word in edgewise. Once, Swope gleefully smashed what he believed to be an opponent's ball far into the rough, much to the consternation of his partner, Bill Paley, whose warning that the ball about to be dispatched was their own went unheeded in Swope's running commentary on the game. (Several other of Swope's one-time partners also report similar misplays brought on by the editor's headlong verbal rush.)

The waning of daylight was never allowed to interfere with play: before Swope had permanent lights installed, he would have his guests pull their cars round the field and shine their headlights on it so play might continue; after the course had lights, matches were likely to start up almost any time of the night, one of them beginning at 2:00 a.m. and running through to dawn. A long downhill gutter, which could route a player's ball beyond shouting distance, adjoined the field and made every game tense and potentially vindictive, with disaster ever threatening.

Neysa was Alec's partner for probably the most legendary, and certainly the most quarrelsome, match ever held at Swope's, a five-game set at $1,000 a head against Swope and Charlie Schwartz, the dapper financier and sportsman who first introduced the group to the heavy English equipment it soon made regulation. Alec, unmindful of the axiom, "Don't Swopen until Swopen to," bickered with his host over every detail of the game, endlessly protesting the advantages Swope enjoyed on his home ground. After four games, the match was tied, and Swope finally acquiesced to the barrage of Alec's demands that the deciding game be moved to a neutral field, obviously aware that Alec would insist that any Swope-led victory on his own course would be impossibly compromised. The fifth game was held, with great fanfare and before a considerable audience, on the field at the Locust Valley estate of Paul and Lily Bonner. Alec and Neysa won this deciding game by a narrow margin. In victory, the rotund Alec literally and exuberantly jumped for joy—a sight as awesome as it was comedic. Neysa just smiled and pocketed her winnings.

Alec clearly respected Neysa's skill with the mallet, for it was his ability at croquet that gave him greater and more immediate pleasure than anything else. (Likewise, his near contemporary, Hemingway, would assert, just as outlandishly and with no trace of self-mockery, that his writing counted as nothing next to his boxing.) On his home grounds, the erratic and eccentric L-shaped course up on Neshobe Island, Alec was nearly unbeatable, since it took months to learn the rugged nuances of that ground, and only Alec ever spent the requisite time on the island to achieve full mastery. One visitor, at first scoffing at the unkempt grounds and seemingly exaggerated devotion of the players who would often rush back to their interrupted game the moment lunch was done, soon came to realize that "on that haphazard terrain a contest was taking place as deft as an operation on the human heart." With steeply sloping woods on three sides of the narrow field and the lake at its long end, it often took three strokes to get a well-smashed ball back onto the field, more if the ball was driven through the woods and into the water. As a result, games often lasted three hours. Neysa, one of the island's regular players, learned to play calmly and defensively when pitted against Alec, the croquet demon of that ground. And in triumph, she was more likely to laugh—and laugh till she cried if the victory were particularly lucky—than gloat.

Harpo Marx, who was more than once thrashed by Alec on the Neshobe course, has left a memorable portrait in *Harpo Speaks!* of the tyrant of Neshobe in his full croquet glory:

> Nothing . . . ever gave Woollcott a greater joy of pride and fulfillment than a good shot at croquet.
>
> When Aleck sent an opponent's ball crashing down through the maples . . . he would swing his mallet around his head like David's slingshot and whoop, "Buckety-buckety! Buckety-buckety! Buck-ket-ty-buck-ket-ty-in-to-the-*lake!*"
>
> When Aleck pulled off an exceptionally tricky shot—hovering over his mallet like a blimp at its mooring mast, while he aimed with profound concentration, then hitting his ball so it sidled through a wicket from a seemingly impossible angle or thumped an opponent after curving with the terrain in a great, sweeping arc—he was in his own special heaven.

Harpo had good reason to recall the fervor of Alec's game on Neshobe, for Harpo was more than once the victim of Alec's cruel and vengeful style of play. During one game, when Alec for the third time sent Harpo's ball deep into the thick woods that abutted the course, Bea Kaufman found the clown bent over the ball, weeping in sheer frustration. Harpo, though, sometimes got his own back: once, while his partner, Charlie Lederer, diverted the other players, Harpo slipped off, found an automobile tire which he sawed in half, then returned and quickly played his ball through it and right around a tree, sending Alec's ball caroming off into the woods—much to the apoplectic rage of the croquet bully of Neshobe, who threw down his mallet and stormed off the course.

173
▼

In time, as with so many of the Algonquin activities, this Neysa-inspired version of croquet became something of a norm, at least for those who could afford the equipment and had the large grounds necessary for its employment. Jack Baragwanath's roll call of the places to which this new, more open variation of the standard game spread—"all over Long Island, then to Connecticut, Bucks County, and Palm Beach. Beverly Hills followed"—is itself an indication of the socioeconomic level that had to be attained before the game might even be attempted. By the early 1930s there was much talk of a grand challenge match between an East Coast and a West Coast group (the latter enthusiastically led by Samuel Goldwyn), but nothing more came of the proposed match than a long correspondence full of dreadful puns, such as "with mallets toward none." By the onset of the Depression, croquet had become what George Kaufman early on had dubbed it: "pedestrian polo." He might have added: "for the nouveau, or near, rich."

Neysa's great reputation as a gameswoman, together with the fact that she gladly admitted, "I seem to have been inventing games and writing clues . . . for the past hundred years," has led to her being credited, at one time or another, with the invention of any number of parlor games. These include "Cops and Robbers," "Psychology," "Sentences," "Scavenger Hunt," "The Portfolio Game," "Corpus Delicti," "The Adverb Game," "Treasure Hunt," "Market Place," "Books," "Sex Appeal," "Cut-outs," and "Murder." In actual, strictly inventive, fact, she originated only the last five of these, and of them only "Murder" gained any real currency. More often, as in the case of croquet, Neysa suggested rule changes that made the games more wide-open, exciting, and engaging. Her genius for games was an adaptive rather than an inventive one.

Neysa's most successful invention, "Murder"—or "The Murder Game"—was inspired by the infamous Snyder-Gray trial of 1927, the case which served as the prototype for a score of subsequent fictional treatments, James M. Cain's *Double Indemnity* among them, of the story of a scheming, clever wife tricking her lecherous, dull-witted lover into killing her husband for the insurance money. It was Neysa's impression, which she first conveyed to Fannie Hurst, who was attending the trial along with her, that the defense witnesses, particularly Mrs. Synder, had an unnatural and uncanny command of the minutest details of the events, a command which made their whole reconstruction highly suspect. The jury apparently agreed that no one who could remember events down to such small particulars could be telling the truth and sentenced the two murderous lovers to death. Neysa had her idea for a game.

"Murder," as Neysa originally designed it, is simple in concept, but exasperatingly precise in execution. Two or three persons act out, the more ludicrously the better, a short scenario in which one of them ends up being murdered. Then the audience is asked a long series of questions about the scene (e.g., "What position was the body lying in?" and "What was the last thing Jeff said?"), the sum total of the answers supposedly pointing out just why, how, and by whom the victim was murdered. Normally, no one in the audience gets even half the answers correct— and many recall less than a fifth of the scene's details—with the result that even the "winner" of the game can feel stupidly unobservant and is, along with the other players, anxious to put his or her observational powers to the test again. Neysa knew that a successful party game needed to be pitched between satiation and desire, between triumph and an eagerness to play it again. With "Murder" she achieved just the right balance, and the game, like her version of croquet, spread through game-playing circles from coast to coast.

Elsa Maxwell might have invented "Scavenger Hunt," reputedly in Paris, but it was the diligent Neysa McMein—who would spend days constructing teasing lists of items for the hunters to scavenge (without ever once going on a hunt herself)—who Americanized the game and helped make it enormously popular in the 1930s, particularly with the North Shore set. In a 1932 letter to Lily Bonner, Raoul Fleischmann gives a telling description of the most famous of the many hunts Neysa orchestrated:

> There was quite an amusing party Saturday night at
> Millicent Hearst's. We were invited over with our week-

end guests to take part in a scavenger hunt. This game consists in teams of searchers who are given baskets and a two and one-half hour stretch of time in which to bring back as many as they can of thirty items. Among the items which come to mind are a peanut; a fire-cracker; a vase de nuit; a live animal (dogs and insects barred); three needles strung with green silk; a cabbage; a sausage; an autographed photograph of a living artist; a photograph of a nude; a black silk stocking; a strip of lavender toilet paper; a pair of lace drawers auto-graphed by the owner. . . . I started off with Katharine Cowdin but when we got to Port Washington Village in search for a live fish and were unsuccessful and heard that all the stores of the village were closed, we became disheartened and gave up. The winners were Jack Bar-agwanath and Gwladys Whitney with twenty-nine out of thirty items, and Herbert Swope and Marjorie Newton second with twenty-eight.

The finale of that evening, as Neysa herself recalled it in her games pamphlet, was a piece of high society foolery, with Sonny Whitney riding in on one of his polo ponies as his live animal:

> There were cats, goldfish, lobsters, crabs, climaxed by C. V. Whitney, who rode into the hall on a big white horse. There were tiny American flags, and one so big, brought by one of the Hearst boys, that it took three men to carry it. Some people who had put blonde hairs in matchboxes for safekeeping, lost them, and Sonny Whitney's horse ate up the hay that someone else had taken so much trouble to get.

As Neysa noted, one of the points of the exercise lay in its very arbi-trariness and freely chosen absurdity: "Almost as much fun as the hunt itself will be the stories told when the hunters return." As so often with the Algonquin crowd, the doing could quickly and permanently pass into the telling.

Most of the indoor games that Neysa favored were expressive of her social sense—that is, they involved and amused a fair number of her guests at once rather than, like the games many of her friends prized (bridge, hearts, backgammon), dividing them into small, discrete units. At Neysa's, games were always a group activity, and one that she put her willing guests to lightly and gaily. Neysa, for instance, explained her championing of "Scavenger Hunt" on simple, familial grounds that could be appreciated, if not exactly approximated, far beyond her Manhattan–North Shore world: "It's a wonderful game for the holiday season when family and friends are gathered together in the country and want something especially larky to do." For "Treasure Hunt," a somewhat similar game that she perfected—it consists in following from one to another a series of increasingly difficult (and pun-filled) clues until the "treasure" is found—Neysa had dozens, and once as many as 150, players questing, and muttering, about the grounds at Sands Point.

A number of Neysa's games demanded a certain verbal cleverness and dexterity that made them a close complement to the verbal fireworks at the Round Table. One of them, "Sentences," guaranteed a degree of verbal absurdity as well: each of two players has to work into a conversation an odd and generally quite obscure sentence (like "The women of Burma are very fond of betel") without his or her opponent spotting it. Needless to say, the other players, who form the audience while the two participants battle, are usually greatly amused by the contortions of the conversation as the two players work to maneuver the talk to a point where the designated sentence does not appear too outlandish, or at least no more ludicrous than those preceding or following it. It is a game that requires the players, much like the sitters at the Round Table and the frequenters of Neysa's studio, to create an atmosphere in which outrageous statements are taken as the norm and non sequiturs as the ordinary stuff of conversation.

Neysa's greatest game triumph, and the one with which she is identified above all others, is known simply as "The Game," a fittingly archetypal name for this ultimate in parlor games. Like so many of her other games, this too was a matter of Neysa's intervention rather than her invention. In June 1937, Jack, on his business travels, stopped a week at the Sherwoods' home in England. (The Algonquin crowd had by then dispersed itself as far afield as Britain and Hollywood.) During the visit, Jack was introduced to an old "historical" party game: a group is divided into two teams and a referee, with the latter picking a list of ten historical events ("Hannibal Crossing the Alps," "The Beheading of Charles I," etc.). The captain of each team gets the first event and then must, through a series of rapid sketches which provoke "yes-no" questions, induce a teammate to guess it. The correct guesser then rushes up to the referee, gets the next event, begins "drawing" it and so on, until one team gets all ten events.

What was amusing in England proved bland and dull in New York: as Jack remembered his initial American foray with the game, "no one died laughing." Then Neysa and Howard Dietz, the lyricist and publicist, hit upon a series of modifications. First, phrases need not refer only to historical events: they could be book and song titles, mottoes, slogans, proverbs, or just about anything else. Second, teams would be put in separate rooms—with an observer from the opposing team in attendance if bets had been placed—so players might carry on boisterously and frantically without disturbing their opponents or giving away their correct choices. Third, and most importantly, clues could be conveyed either by drawing or pantomime, with a combination of the two being preferable. The result of these modifications was an instant, contagious hilarity. Clifton Webb wriggled across the floor in his white piqué waistcoat doing "The Tortoise and the Hare"; players yelled and screamed their guesses as their prompter frantically alternated between outsized mime and rough sketches. The non-artists, according to Jane Grant, "quickly executed something crude but effective," while "Neysa and her artists friends . . . were too taken up with line" and so usually lagged behind.

When someone guessed correctly, he or she would dash from the room in search of the referee and the next phrase. Since this was no simple game—e.g., players were forbidden to use letters or numbers in their drawings—it often went on for fifty minutes or an hour or longer, always at a frenzied pace. Early on, some conservative souls tried to insist that phrases should either be drawn *or* mimed, but it was Neysa's free-for-all version—she did pause long enough to write down the rules of the variation she and Howard had devised—that quickly won out. That this version was soon prompted, almost glorified, in the pages of *The New Yorker*, where Jack declared George Abbott the best of its players, did not hurt in imparting a sense of madcap glamour and a distinct aura of being "in" to "The Game."

" 'The Game'," in Jack's words, "spread like a disease. The whole country was soon playing it"—a rank overestimation only if one insists on including in the tally those millions of citizens who did not inhabit one or another of the interlocking circles in which Jack and Neysa moved. In any case, Algonquin stalwarts immediately transplanted "The Game" to Hollywood, where many of them were then working. In Hollywood, like that earlier Algonquin export, croquet, it quickly became and remained the rage. Robert Montgomery, Fredric March (once a model for Neysa), and Charlie Chaplin, not surprisingly accounted the best "actor-outer," were among its first partisans and enthusiasts. Marc Connelly was such a devotee that he would rehearse his team all afternoon in his rooms at the Garden of Allah. Nor did "The Game" prove a passing Hollywood fancy: its hold on the movie community persisted over two decades, long enough to make enthusiastic players of the likes of Gene Kelly, Grace Kelly, and, rather unexpectedly, Marlon Brando.

Some indication of how thoroughly Neysa came to be identified with "The Game" is the assertion of her good friend Jane Grant that Neysa "invented from scratch The Game"—a claim Grant might not have made had she relied strictly on her memory and not just on her impressions. A decade after Neysa's death, Cleveland Amory proclaimed "The Game" to be "the most durable American contribution to the history of parlor games." As with her drawing, so too with her games: Neysa McMein had an acute sense of what would be popular, a sense derived from her willingness to expend her mental energies on things some thought inconsequential, but which her friends found relaxing, engaging, even compelling.

Because she took on games and related matters easily, and because she was more than half-superstitious herself, Neysa once agreed to do

179
▼

a numerology column for a newspaper syndicate—or rather, because she was particularly busy at that moment, she convinced Jack, who was always inclined toward such foolery, to handle the column and split the profits fifty-fifty with her. Jack actually boned up on the subject and launched himself wholeheartedly into the writing, but he was soon brought up short by the hundreds of letters—heartfelt, trusting, abject, miserable—that poured in from "gullible people, mostly women, who felt that 'Neysa' might provide some magic formula that would cure a crippled child, straighten out a worthless husband, or bring happiness and success to a home that would never be happy." When he showed a sample of these piteous letters to her, Neysa was appalled, and she agreed with him that they must give up the column straightaway, which they did. "Neysa" may have been something of an artificial creation, but she was no fake, particularly in the face of genuine misery and unhappiness about which there could be no "playing."

Games were, to put it simply, extraordinarily important in the Algonquin and its allied sets. Games were also the means by which sometimes members of the Algonquin crowd got to know one another: it was, for example, through backgammon at Woollcott's that the brash young Oscar Levant met the person who had preceded him as the group's "visiting boy genius," Noel Coward. Yet not all the members shared the games mania. Don Stewart, whose almost surreally comic "Haddock" books would seem to make him a likely enthusiast for the verbal play of parlor games, found instead that "guessing games of any kind produce in me a sort of malignant apathy." Benchley too disliked such games, although, typically, he admired others' prowess at them. Ross, so Thurber assures us, would have been made positively ill at the "merest suggestion of games" at *The New Yorker*, although he was an avid, if ungainly, croquet player and still carried with him, from his days as tramp newspaperman, a reputation as an outstanding cribbage player. But for the likes of Woollcott, FPA, Parker, Kaufman, Connelly, Sherwood, Broun, Swope, and of course Neysa (and Jack), games were a crucial part of day-to-day existence—and obviously an important means of self-definition. As

Helen Hayes recalled recently, still with some wonder, decades after the Algonquin crowd had broken up and most of its members had gone to their graves, "My God, they loved games. It was their life." It is not surprising then that when Alec impulsively chose to offer himself in marriage to Neysa back in 1923, he presented himself to her with a brand-new Parcheesi board in his lap. This was as close a vision of marital felicity—the two playing some game all their days—as he could muster.

For some in this crowd, a person should play a game excellently or not at all. When George Kaufman, who played bridge as well as most professional players, realized that his daughter was no more than competent at card games, he strongly discouraged her from them; instead he urged her to concentrate on croquet, at which she was quite skilled, and took great pride in her development at that game. (Fortunately, Joan Baragwanath grew up tall and athletic, and, as she came to them, managed her mother's various parlor games with passing skill.) And when in his later years Kaufman found his memory beginning to dim, he gave up playing cards entirely. Raoul Fleischmann, who was very good at croquet and who played games of chance with almost as much expertise as compulsion, was nonetheless irritated by his lack of skill at badminton, another North Shore enthusiasm. As he wrote to Lily Bonner, "It's really a swell game and I wish I weren't such a dub at it and also did not become practically apopletic after running around for a few minutes." Those in the Algonquin crowd played their games hard, they played them well, and they played them to win. What Woollcott wrote was the point of croquet—not merely to "excel your neighbor [but] . . . to damage him"—often became the point of many of their other games as well.

Herbert Swope may have been, Woollcott possibly aside, the most competitive of all of them. Once, and perhaps only once, Swope was bested at "Ask Me Another," the trivia game named after his incredible zest for and ability to answer questions ranging from the obscure to the absurd. (With his photographic memory and the several hours he spent each day reading newspapers from around the world, Swope had an incredible number of facts always in mind.) A young man who was visiting a North Shore friend was caught up in the usual whirligig of rounds out there and eventually found himself at Swope's, where he was dazzled by the houseful of celebrities he saw. Not wanting to be impolite, he answered the apparently meaningless questions—about American Indian burial rites, unfamous Teutonic poets, et al.—that were periodically put to him and which briefly interrupted his starry-eyed pursuit of Ethel Barrymore. When the results of the game were tallied, and the score of this unsuspecting player just edged out Swope's, the young man suddenly found a blustery, red-headed man looming over his small but now very conspicuous self.

Swope asked him point blank, "Who the hell are you? And why?" The young man politely, if nervously, explained that he was nothing more than a recent law school graduate looking for a job. Swope, still smarting from the defeat, but knowing a well-informed fellow when he met one, brusquely told him to report to the *World* the next afternoon, which the young man did and where he was immediately put on the city staff. Thereafter, William L. Laurence saw very little of the editor he had bested at his own game—but after Laurence, as a science writer for the *Times*, won a Pulitzer Prize in 1946, Swope began referring to him as "one of my boys." Herbert Bayard Swope, like so many of his Algonquin friends, often got in a final winning volley, even if he had to wait several decades to do it.

Although betting was not, all things considered, the chief point of their games, most in the Algonquin set, Neysa included, were willing to risk just enough money on their daily games to make them exciting. Small but not inconsiderable amounts of money did change hands with some regularity and rapidity. In his rounds of March 1921, FPA reported with satisfaction that he had gone "to Neysa's, and won $60 at craps from her and A. Woollcott and R. Ives in a few minutes." Several years later, FPA retailed a less triumphant day's gambling: he lost $17 in a card game at Neysa's, after which he and Alec adjourned to the Turkish baths, with FPA, on a losing coin toss, having to foot the fees ($7.25, duly noted) for both of them.

What often was at risk in these nearly constant games and wagers was whether one might get through the day free or end up having to pay double or triple the toll. As Alec evidenced in a letter to Lily Bonner, the principle of being clever enough and lucky enough to force one's competitors to pay your charges was a sort of constant goad to games: "On the way over [to Europe] I hope to make enough at backgammon from Noel Coward to pay for the expenses of the trip." Except for persons on the very fringes of the crowd—such as the writer-scenarist Herman Mankiewicz, a compulsive gambler with bad luck—the Algonquinites usually gambled at just the level their incomes, sizable but not grand, would allow. Neysa could afford to play croquet at $1,000 a match, a figure which should at least be sextupled in today's money, but she could not afford to lose regularly at such rates. Winning, of course, was even better—and helped provide for a few luxuries.

If "The Game" was the Algonquin group's most successful private contribution to the history of American games, *Information Please,* the popular and demanding radio quiz show of the 1930s and 1940s, was the most public expression of its game-playing spirit. Whether or not its lineage traces back directly to those trivia games in which Swope and many other Algonquinites gloried, the radio game was clearly expressive of the Algonquin spirit. From the outset, FPA established himself as a regular panelist, and others in and around the Algonquin crowd, like George Kaufman and Deems Taylor, appeared with some frequency, along with guests from a surprising variety of American milieus, including a young senator on the rise (William Fulbright) and a former presidential candidate on the decline (Wendell Willkie). In the 1940s, the rapidly aging enfant terrible of the Algonquin set's later years, Oscar Levant, well-informed high school dropout that he was, also became a regular panelist. After two years of pleading, Swope, the spiritual godfather of the game, agreed to come on for a "star turn" and did very well, missing only, and oddly, a newspaper question. (Which New York paper then liked to put a period after its name? The *Times.*) In all, the kind of instructional public play that was *Information Please* reminds us that the English word "school" traces its origin back to the Greek *skole*, which means "leisure." As one of Neysa's friends and admirers, Arthur Krock, said about her parlor games, they "test the imagination, intellect, quick recall, and informational scope of the players." *Infor-*

mation Please allowed the public to eavesdrop on this sort of fun—and to pick up tidbits of information, significant and trivial, in the process.

Neysa's approach to games, like her approach to the rest of life, was calmer, if no less fervent, than that of most of her friends. For Janet Flanner, the explanation for Neysa's devotion to parlor games was simple: she remained at heart a small-town girl who never forgot how much her guests, however sophisticated and worldly, enjoyed party games. Such an interpretation is supported by Neysa's own assertion that "there is no getting away from the fact that, at a party, people would rather be participants than audience." Yet to some extent Neysa must have shared—because she was a very good player as well as a devoted one—some of the motivations that impelled others in the Algonquin set to the games: the desire to exhibit cleverness, the need to excel, the compulsion to "play," and the desire to win. When, as part of their regular routine in town, Neysa and Jack would sit to some game before going their separate evening ways, the activity was more than just an hour's totally forgettable diversion, for they kept a running score that stretched over the months and years. The result of each evening's round was, in some way, a permanent part of their history together.

Wit, as Freud delineates it, has aspects which belie the notions of "sophistication" and "polish" that are commonly attached to it. For him, wit's closest comic type is the *naïve*, with which it shares a strong dependence on innocence and spontaneity. Very many instances of Algonquin wit—like the parody sentence, "I had two soft-burlesque for breakfast"—depend upon the same kind of quick but limited word association called for in Neysa's games. Emblematic of the close connection between Algonquin wit and Algonquin games was the fact that guests who sat to dinner at Swope's table often found a pad and pencil beside their place setting.

"All play means something," asserted the cultural historian Johan Huizinga, in what remains the classic study of "the play element in culture," *Homo Ludens (Man the Player)*. One need not assent to Huizinga's most sweeping claim that "civilization arises and unfolds as play" to perceive that Neysa and her friends were proclaiming, in their absorption with play of all sorts, the significance of "ludic time." Their games were not merely a diversion from, but rather a vital part of, the conditions of their existence. The very concentration with which they played was a kind of standing, and often public, affront to the "Puritanism" they believed, probably with more fervor than accuracy, still infected American society. Still, if their devotion to play was one of the key things that drew them together and defined both their lives and their work—as Huizinga notes, play "produces many of the fundamental forms of social life"—that devotion was also, ironically, one of the main underlying causes for their lack of lasting artistic success. One of the attractions of games, as Michael Novack observes in *The Joy of Sports*, is the possibility of "a momentary attainment of perfect form." The deftly placed witticism, the wickedly clever pun, the astoundingly ingenious croquet shot, the brilliantly instinctive correct guess in some word game— all these things have a certain enclosed perfection of form, but a perfection that is much more circumscribed than the one to be sought, if rarely attained, in the larger forms of poetry, drama, fiction, painting, and music. It may be that so many small, instantly acclaimed "perfections of form" had the effect of satiating the Algonquinites and so dissuading them from seeking perfection in the larger forms, or it may be that their talents condemned them to be miniaturists. In any case, miniaturists, often sparkling miniaturists, they remained.

Concerning the Algonquin preoccupation with games, there is another, but complementary, explanation that also serves. Many who came to be a part of the Round Table set experienced success fairly early and fairly easily. That they came to New York and so handily achieved their provincial vision of literary-artistic fame must have inclined many of them to see their life as something of a fun-filled and triumphantly played game, so much so that they often had difficulty distinguishing where the actual living broke off and the "playing" took up. Such, obviously, was the case with Marjorie Moran McMein, late of Quincy, Illinois, an artist of sorts, but for three decades the undisputed "queen of the party games" in and around New York.

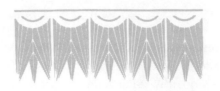

=11=

Neshobe, India, Egypt, and Other Expeditions

Neysa was an insatiable traveler, and ofttimes an oblivious one. According to FPA, she once sailed for Antwerp and "felt aggrieved to learn on arrival that it was not in Italy." Over the years, though, she did, by hap and mishap, manage to make her way across a fair part of Europe, and to several parts of Africa and Asia as well.

Travel was never an end in itself for Neysa, an attitude which made her hazy geographical sense less of a problem than it might otherwise have been. Rather, travel was most usually a variation, filled with new sites and places, on the determinedly social life she led in and around New York. The New York to which she had aspired and in which she had earned her success was the center of her world, and she never really went beyond its boundaries, far as she might travel beyond its borders.

For her domestic travels she had a routine so fixed—always some weeks up on Neshobe Island in summer and fall, usually some winter weeks at Palm Beach—that she was assured the same kind of New York company she kept at home. In the winter of 1933–34, for instance, she spent several weeks at Palm Beach with George Abbott and Charles Brackett, perhaps playing her old game of balancing potentially over-zealous "suitors" one against the other, and undoubtedly giving Brackett an earful of information for use in *Entirely Surrounded*, which he was then completing.

Palm Beach, in the period Neysa came to know it, was enjoying a second great flourishing, dating back to 1917. Seventy miles north of Miami, Palm Beach was the last developed and in some ways the most stupendous of the great nineteenth-century American resorts. Henry M. Flagler, using his Standard Oil money, financed the whole of its build-ing in the mid-1890s, including construction of what was then the largest hotel in the world, the Royal Poinciana. (It could accommo-date 1,750 guests and had, in the more ambulatory ways of nineteenth-century hotel life, over seven miles of hallways.) By Neysa's time, Palm Beach had become, in the much-esteemed judgment of Frank Crowninshield, reported in Cleveland Amory's *The Last Resorts*,"not exclusive, but merry, sumptuous and expensive." Like the North Shore of Long Island, it was, if more impermanently, a colony where the new and the old rich—and the near-rich friends of both—mingled and sported. It was also the American resort which had the strong-est attraction for wealthy foreign visitors, particularly titled ones, the social result sometimes being as one "old" Palm Beach poem had it:

> People whose parents came over in steerage,
> Here entertain only the peerage.

In Worth Avenue, Palm Beach had possibly the most exciting resort thoroughfare in the country—indisputedly, it had the most expensive. Excitement of a different, if still expensive sort, a trip into the "jungle" verging on the resort, was also daily available. Here one was propelled along the trails in the ill- but tellingly named "afromobile," a cross between a sedan chair and bicycle which was pedaled from the rear by a black driver. Then it might be back to the Poinciana's Coconut Grove for tea and coconut cakes, possibly a few tangos before dressing for dinner, and usually more dancing after it. Neysa and her companions were hardly stalwarts of the exacting daily rituals of the place, but neither were they recluses. Besides, anyone with George Abbott could hardly expect *not* to go dancing.

Needless to say, Palm Beach could be a thoroughly demoralizing resort if one lacked the funds to afford its overpriced pleasures, but it was an exhilarating place if one had them. As at Sands Point, Neysa's funds were just ample enough to pass muster—and in so doing she was permitted to hobnob with those who, in the resort's many exclusive gambling clubs or at its indigenous, and merciless, three-handed version of bridge, "Towie," could gamble away in a night or two what Neysa made in a year.

In all, Palm Beach was comically ostentatious and genuinely grand, beautiful with its Ocean Drive swerving out to the sea, and silly with its constant circulation of rumors of the latest reshufflings among its rather small set of leading, if always variable, couples. Scott Fitzgerald, describing the place in its 1920s heyday in "The Rich Boy," caught all the vagaries of its conspicuous, fun-filled consumption and its mildly loony atmosphere:

> Palm Beach sprawled plump and opulent between the sparkling sapphire of Lake Worth, flawed here and there by house-boats at anchor, and the great turquoise bar of the Atlantic Ocean. The huge bulks of the Breakers and the Royal Poinciana rose as twin paunches from the bright level of the sand, and around them clustered the Dancing Glade, Bradley's House of Chance, and a

dozen modistes and milliners with goods at triple prices
from New York. Upon the trellised veranda of the Break-
ers two hundred women stepped right, stepped left,
wheeled, and slid in that then celebrated calisthenic
known as the double-shuffle, while in half-time to the
music two thousand bracelets clicked up and down on
two hundred arms.

At Palm Beach, Neysa and her friends easily fell into much the same
role they played at Sands Point—that just slightly bohemian one of artists
cavorting among the wealthy.

Palm Beach, of course, was only an incidental, momentary place on
Neysa's journeying, but Neshobe Island was very nearly an inevitable
one. With its innate clubbishness and insularity, the Algonquin set
needed a rustic corollary to the Round Table and its other privileged
metropolitan haunts—and, in 1924, it found one. Enos Booth, a young
lawyer friend of Neysa's studio neighbor in the 57th Street building,
Sally Farnham, suggested that Woollcott, Neysa, and their friends might
consider renting as a summer place the seven-acre island, with its
clapboard "shack," that he had recently purchased up in Vermont. Alec,
Neysa, and several others took the five-and-a-half-hour drive up there
and, under the powerful sway of Alec's instantly nostalgic vision, agreed
that the island, in the middle of Lake Bomoseen, would be just the place
for them: isolated, beautiful, and self-contained, a ground they could
command entirely to themselves, a place where they could rest from
being, but never forget that they were, metropolitan celebrities.

Woollcott, in what proved to be a prophetic gesture of self-declared
leadership, drew up a charter for a summer "club" there: it would have
but ten permanent members, each paying an initiation fee of $1,000;
members could bring guests, but everyone coming must make reservations well in advance; and there would be a $7.50 charge per person
for each day spent on the island. Besides Alec and Neysa, original
shareholders included Alice Duer Miller, Ruth Gordon, insurance man

Ray Ives, Bea Kaufman, publisher Harold Guinzburg, Raoul Fleischmann, and two others, variously named as Howard Dietz, Janet Flanner,
Marc Connelly, and newspaper publisher George Backer. In 1926, taken
with the success of this summer encampment, and grateful that the
taciturn Vermonters left them pretty much in peace, the "corporation"
purchased the island from Booth—or so its members thought until events
a decade later made them question, and eventually establish, their total
claim to this summering place.

The rusticity Alec and Neysa found, and joyed in, on Neshobe was
not so much a primal quality as a reestablished one. The island's present
designation—it was named after an Indian chief—dates back only to
about 1880, hardly the legendary romantic past. Moreover, in the late
nineteenth century the Lake Bomoseen region became part of the busy
East Adirondacks–Vermont resort belt, and there were three fairly large
hotels on the shore, just opposite the island. For a brief time there was
even a small hotel on the island itself, although it burned down not too
many years after being built. Before and after its hotel days, the island
served variously as a site for Indian ceremonies, as a pig farm, and as
an ice-fishing center, until it slipped slowly back into the rather pleasantly overgrown condition in which Neysa and Alec discovered it.

A surprising variety of trees and shrubs—among them oak, maple,
pine, hemlock, basswood, hardhack, birch, cedar, cherry, shagbark
hickory—covered most of the seven acres. On all sides the island sloped
up steeply from the waterline toward the high point on its northern end.
Thus, from every vantage point, except right along the shore, one looked
both out and down on the sparkling lake, usually with sunlight streaming
down through the trees and mottling the forest floor. Besides the chatter,
often pleasant, sometimes strident, of one's familiars, the air offered
only the subdued sound of the wind in the trees and an occasional
muffled shout from some boat out on the lake. It was a perfect place to
be alone—with friends.

Harold Ross once asserted that Woollcott had "the soul of an inn-
keeper," and nowhere was that soul more in evidence than on Neshobe.
Although all shares in the island club were theoretically equal, Alec
made it apparent from the first that his was more than equal. According

to Marc Connelly, whose enthusiasm for Neshobe gradually waned, Alec simply "took everything over" up there. Even two of Alec's great partisans, Bea Kaufman and Joseph Hennessey (Alec's man of all help who ran the island for the visitors), described Neshobe as Alec's seven-acre kingdom, where guests had only the recourse of being his willing or unwilling subjects: "He ran the island like a benevolent monarchy, and he summoned both club members and other friends to appear at all seasons of the year; he turned the island into a crowded vacation ground where reservations must be made weeks in advance; the routine of life was completely remade to suit his wishes."

Among the things Alec demanded of all but his most recalcitrant guests was an early morning swim in the still chilly lake (his fat kept him warm), followed by a two-hour breakfast at which he would hold grandly forth; a willing devotion to the proposed activities of the day, almost always croquet in the late morning, perhaps badminton or boating in the afternoon, with "Cops and Robbers," "Murder," cribbage, or some word game in the evenings; and a willingness to bear the more than occasional insults arising from the chiding, mocking tone he set. Except by monarchial dispensation, guests were not to do any of their own work on the island. (Alice Miller reportedly found a way round this proscription by retreating to a corner with a jigsaw puzzle, piecing together in her head the plots of her romances as her fingers pieced together the puzzle.) Those guests who needed relief from the capriciousness of Alec's rule normally had only one recourse, to walk out on the broad trail that looped the island, since Alec pretty much dictated when guests could go over to the mainland, and he often went along with them when they did go.

More covertly—some would say more insidiously—Alec demanded allegiance to his vision of Neshobe as an idyllic, very nearly perfect vacation spot, a view some visitors felt obligated to challenge. For instance, Howard Dietz insisted, in an autobiography written three decades after the Neshobe Club ceased to exist, that Alec's tyrannically blissful view of the place conditioned visitors' perceptions so thoroughly that many ignored the island's rather mediocre reality: "The Island, as it was intimately called, was not really beautiful. The water around it was not too invigorating and the foliage was a dusty green, as in a city park.

Despite its lack of features, it was romanticized by the cast of characters who lived there in the summer."

Children were, for the most part, prohibited on the island, and made rudely unwelcome by Alec, remembered by one visiting child as "mean and vicious," when they were brought. Once, though, Alec, in his arbitrary way, completely reversed his policy. When Paul Bonner, Jr., then twelve, was brought to the island while recovering from rheumatic fever, Alec, in the typically sentimental way of bullies, insisted that the suffering boy be treated with loving attention by everyone and even trundled him all over the island in a wheelbarrow, although not without complaining about the weight.

If Alec was the king of Neshobe, Neysa was about as close to a queen as the island club had—although her role was really more that of a consort, enjoying the freedoms and privileges accorded royalty but none of its power. To be sure, Alec had a few mildly insulting "bits" on Neysa, like his repeated references to the island's "Neysa McMein Memorial Cesspool." And apparently he did sometimes play Neysa against another of "his" women, Ruth Gordon, who was also a frequent visitor to the island. But for the most part, Alec excused Neysa from the full tyranny of his rule: if she wanted to do a little sketching, that was fine; if she wanted to beg off croquet or badminton to take a nap, Alec would not insist that she play; or if he had offended her, he might go so far as to try to make amends. Once, after several times landing his three hundred pounds on her during a wild badminton game, Alec took the bruised and battered Neysa out for a con- ciliatory row on the lake, an apologetic gesture made rather ineffective by his capsizing of the boat. Neysa's nickname on the island, "Miss Beauty Queen," was emblematic of the special status that the other guests, fol- lowing Alec's lead, granted her. Next to Alec, Neysa probably spent more time on Neshobe than anyone else in the Algonquin crowd during the two decades it served as the group's northern outpost.

There is every evidence that Neysa, who had a sentimental streak nearly as strong as Alec's, thought of the island with the same nostalgic fervor as Woollcott. In 1937, she avowed, in a letter to him, that she dreamt of the island "as Mohammed dreamt of paradise—or was it Moses?" And throughout her sometime residence there, Neysa was usu-

ally a supporter of Alec in those many battles, meaningful or insignificant, that inevitably arose wherever Alec was. The most important of
these, for it settled the issue of exactly how different life on Neshobe
should be from "Algonquin life" elsewhere, was the battle between the
"Masses" and the "Classes." The former wanted to keep the island as
primitive as possible, preferring to maintain an environment created by
kerosene lamps, outdoor plumbing, and a wood stove, while the latter
pushed for at least the minimal comforts of electricity, modern plumbing,
and some basic appliances. When Alec shifted his allegiance from the
Masses to the Classes, the battle, for all intents and purposes, was over:
Neshobe became a "modern" summer club, and several members resigned their shares, which were quickly taken up by Woollcott partisans
like Harpo Marx and Harold Ross. As she indicated in a letter of 1931,
Neysa grew not merely to tolerate Alec's high-handed rule of Neshobe,
but actually to like and depend on it for her vacation amusement: "We
had one wild, hectic and beautiful week at the Island, which was the
top as far as vacations go . . . Aleck running us all as usual, and well."
For Neysa, Neshobe was indeed a benevolent monarchy.

Despite the added comforts, the island was still a place of rough
accommodations and one where, as a visitor put it, a "bravura disorder" always obtained. Around the largish living room of the "clubhouse," dominated by a fieldstone fireplace, were mounds of sporting
gear and equipment, game paraphernalia, and clothing, together with
assorted, very miscellaneous pieces of rustic furniture, scattered in con-
fusing, seemingly random fashion. Piles of books were everywhere, and
Alec's voluminous correspondence, brought over by boat each morning,
took up virtually all of the table and shelf space. Disheveled beds and
cots filled the small, sparse rooms off the main one. Sometimes, a
gimcrack, creaky bed—nicknamed "the informative double" by one of
the bridge-playing wags in residence—had to be set up in the main room
to handle the overflow of guests. Since trees grew close onto the house,
its interior remained shady even in the blaze of noon. Meals were cooked
by dour, grumbling locals, and were of the simple variety, usually some
variation on steak and potatoes, which Alec favored and so everyone
had. Most who came to Neshobe were by then accustomed to those of

life's small comforts which were in short supply on the island, and so could say, with Ruth Gordon, that time on the island "was very different from any other part of my life. Different from any other parts of anyone's life, I suppose." Neshobe was, in terms of its living accommodations, a frank indulgence in "country living" for a quintessentially "big-city" group.

Despite Alec's tyrannical ways, one kind of freedom that did exist on Neshobe was sexual freedom. Bea Kaufman might come up with her "feller"—whatever young man she then had in George's long-vacated sexual place—in tow. Dorothy Parker once showed up with a gorgeous new garden hat, and proceeded to wear it and absolutely nothing else for the whole weekend. Neshobe was no trysting place for Neysa, but she did attract to her, without half trying, many of the occasional male, particularly the young male, visitors to the island. One of these was Richard Carver Wood, a young Hamilton graduate whose burgeoning career as an architect had been interrupted by the Depression and whom Woollcott, in a gesture of old school loyalty, had arranged to serve as a sort of paid photographer to the group. Wood, who found this sudden immersion in "semi-Broadway life" to be "fascinating," was especially taken with the attractive, older Neysa, so much so that he "would have done anything for her." What particularly captivated him was her charm and "softness" in a grouping where hard, brittle wit was the going thing. With him, Neysa kidded easily, almost lovingly. And if the young man who is the main character in *Entirely Surrounded* is based on any sort of reality, then on Neshobe Neysa must have created a virtual epidemic of puppy love.

Because Alec did not much like the male attention given Neysa, he made a special point of tormenting island visitors who looked on her admiringly or desirously. Not the least of these was George Abbott, who, probably unwisely, accepted an invitation to Neshobe even though he was already aware of Woollcott's animosity. Alec had decided early on that George was an irredeemable hick, and so always, in feigned forgetfulness of his name, called him "Elmer." In fact, Alec had already gone so far as to attack him in print, implying that George's name hardly deserved to appear before the title of *Coquette* since, as co-author and director, George's contribution to the success of the piece was only a minor one. It was, however, on this ill-advised Neshobe visit that George managed some measure of revenge and gained the grudging respect of the powerful petty tyrant. During a croquet match in which Alec was taunting him mercilessly, George slowly began constructing an insulting limerick in his head. When the match was concluded so was the limerick:

> A waggish old madcap named Alec
> Was only a weeny bit phallic.
> 'Tis true girls would groan
> When he got them alone
> But 'twasn't for matters italic.

Instead of attacking directly with this ditty by making it public, George passed it on to Alec through Ruth Fleischmann, then waited for a burst of anger and a typically nasty reply from the "viper-tongued Führer" of the island. He got neither, but found instead that for the rest of the visit (and thereafter) Alec treated him, if not exactly kindly, at least less caustically and condescendingly. For all his bullying ways, Alec could appreciate the slashing, cruel retorts to which he sometimes drove his opponents—and usually accorded them more respect afterwards.

If Charlie MacArthur or Ruth Gordon or a dozen others are to be believed, "no one," including many of the Algonquinites who were not intimately involved in the vacation project, turned down an invitation to Neshobe. Benchley, tame suburban creature that he was, came simply because he was invited, knowing he would be bored silly by the over-abundance of nature. Kaufman, generally not one given to inconveniencing himself, came a few times and was remembered for being precisely, slyly witty. Dorothy Parker came often, and more than once was "expelled" for being drunk. Neurosis was freely tolerated on Neshobe—how could it not be?—but drunkenness, because Alec despised it, was rudely and summarily treated.

Harpo Marx and Charlie Lederer, two island stalwarts, made the shortest of all possible visits to Neshobe, especially considering their great efforts to arrive at the place. Sitting around the pool at William

Randolph Hearst's San Simeon estate one summer afternoon, the two men decided it would be a good thing to give "the old fraud" (Alec) a thorough scare. First, they commandeered a limousine to get them to the San Francisco airport, then took a long cross-country flight to New York City, after which they made their way to the island via seaplane, hired car, and motor launch.

Landing on the far side of the island, Harpo and Charlie disrobed and steathily crept up on an intent croquet foursome of Alec, Neysa, Alice Miller, and Bea Kaufman. Suddenly, screaming and screeching, the two naked men burst out upon the players, but hardly caused the great disruption they had envisioned. Alec, for his part, merely gave them a quick, cool glance, filled with a steely non-recognition, and the other players followed his lead. "Alice, it's your shot, my dear," Alec insisted, and the game continued. Deflated, the two men skulked back to the woods, dressed, left the island, and retraced their route back to the coast, without a word ever being passed between the four croquet players and their two would-be disturbers.

Neshobe was also something of an outpost for the Anglo-American theatrical/film community of which Alec, as so influential a critic, was a prime member, and in which Neysa had many friends. In the late 1930s, Charlie MacArthur brought Ben Hecht up to the island, so the two might finish, in as playful an atmosphere as possible, their screenplay for *Wuthering Heights*, in which another island visitor of the period, Laurence Olivier, was to star. At Alec's gentle but persistent urging, and much to Neysa's delight, Noel Coward became one of the most regular visitors among the non-shareholders, and several times brought his frequent stage partner, Gertrude Lawrence, with him. The Lunts visited often, and Vivien Leigh came with Olivier. Ruth Gordon, of course, was almost as constant a visitor as Neysa. And Cornelia Otis Skinner, whose father lived in Woodstock, Vermont, was a regular drop-in, for she delighted in walking to the far end of the island to practice declaiming her lines into the wind. The island community even boasted its own playwright manqué: Gus Eckstine, an eccentric professor from the University of Cincinnati with whom Alec was strongly taken, not the least because of his wild and amusing theatrical schemes. Relaxing with all these actors and actresses and other theatrical luminaries, Neysa found, much to her amusement as a ingloriously failed thespian, that they were usually among the most awkward and unconvincing "players" of those elaborately dramatized parlor games that flourished in her set, particularly on Neshobe.

Thornton Wilder, chiefly because he was so close to Ruth Gordon, was for years a shareholder in the club, despite the fact that the Algonquin crowd in general, and Woollcott in particular, sometimes induced in him a frustrating sense of literary inferiority that he knew was unfounded. One evening, when he chose to stay in Rutland for dinner rather than return to the island, Wilder ended up getting a thoroughgoing interrogation from Woollcott, who wanted to know precisely where and what he ate and why he would choose a solitary repast over a lively communal meal at Neshobe. The very tenor of Alec's lordly questioning might itself, had Alec been sufficiently self-aware, have been taken as answer. When he was on the island, Wilder would talk endlessly with any fellow visitor he could interest (or corner) about his great literary obsession, Joyce's *Finnegans Wake*, which was coming out in installments during the 1930s. Despite the general disinterest in such "highbrow" literature and the decidedly light literary tastes of the Algonquin crowd—while Thornton was championing Joyce, Alec was making a bestseller of *Goodbye, Mr. Chips*—Wilder's critical compulsiveness was easily forgiven him. When his *The Skin of Our Teeth*, the play so strongly influenced by *Finnegans Wake*, premiered, Alec was quick to trumpet his approval, declaring, "It is not so easy to think of any other American play with so good a chance of being acted a hundred years from now." Thornton, after all, was a friend, if a sometimes errant and over-intellectual one.

The roster of Neshobe guests was, more than anything, the measure of Woollcott's influence, which grew to legendary, if now perplexing, proportions in the 1930s. Dorothy Thompson, whose acquaintance with the Algonquin crowd was of the most passing sort, would come to the island as a break from her journalistic wanderings. Rebecca West visited a number of times, and then sent her bright young cousin, David Ogilvy, for a taste of witty rustification. Ted Roosevelt would fly up from Oyster

Bay in his seaplane. In a way, all these visitors came to pay homage to
Alec, as did Bill Fields and Francis Robinson, who sometimes visited
the island to work over Alec's upcoming lecture tours, during which the
general public would get to pay him much the same sort of homage. If
Neysa overestimated Alec's importance, it is little wonder: on Neshobe
she regularly saw his power in its purest form.

Those who were not summoned to Neshobe, on the other hand, were
made distinctly unwelcome when they appeared. Most intrusive were
the summer tourists, who often approached the island under the vague
notion that it was full of celebrities and that it housed a group given to
wild orgies and like behavior. Confusions were rife. One group peering
through binoculars mistook the corpulent Alec descending to the water
for a swim for Marie Dressler. Another group made so bold as actually
to land and begin a picnic. This latter group received such a greeting
that its report must have scared away many potential trespassers: a naked
character smeared with mud, swinging a hatchet, a maniacal look on
his face and a red fright wig on his head, came charging out of the woods
at them, whooping and hollering. It was Harpo, making his "gookie"
face and doing what seemed to come naturally to this most uninhibited
of the Marx Brothers. The interlopers beat an ultra-hasty retreat to their
boat, and Harpo swept up the picnic supplies they had abandoned and
carried them up to the clubhouse. These celebrities, as trespassers soon
discovered, were persons who defended their privacy with fervor—and
with comical imagination.

It was, however, an insider who invaded the privacy of the island
club most completely and who pilloried the group's weaknesses most
thoroughly. Although the several headnotes to Brackett's *Entirely Surrounded* protest that "the characters and situations in this work are wholly
fictional and imaginative," amounting to no more than "some caricatures," any reader who knew even a little something about the Algonquin
crowd—which is to say, a good many readers in 1934—would have had
no difficulty in matching the fictional characters with their real-life
counterparts, for they were all, as Woollcott judged, "painfully recognizable." "Mr. Hulbert," described as "one gigantic drop of human
flesh," is Alec Woollcott at his testiest, most mincing, and nastiest. He

even "groans," not entirely good-naturedly, when Leith O'Fallon (Neysa) calls him to see the sunset.

Most of the characters are shown as opportunists of one sort or another. Clyde Fitch, modeled on Brackett's sometime boss at *The New Yorker*, Harold Ross, is forever flattering and conniving to get contributions to his magazine, *Man About Town*. "Cooch the Clown" (Harpo), it is implied, is a creature pumped to unmerited importance by the influential effusions of Hulbert, who has made him into an idiotic clown-in-residence for the group. Agnes Sterner (Alice Miller), although kindly and pleasant, insists on drawing an absolute class line between her patrician self and the literary-artistic bohemians among whom she is slumming. And Daisy Lester (Dorothy Parker) is depicted as such an uncontrollable neurotic that she disappears and lets the rest of them assume for several days that she has drowned herself. The book's naive young hero, Henry Cook, who had worshipped the "first wits" from afar through the columns that contained them and the works that expressed them, and who came expecting to find a "magic island," finds instead a self-centered group of egotists who treat him in a fashion that ranges from sarcastically tolerant at best to abominable at worst. As Henry gazes on Hulbert, he notices that "his mouth was like a shark's, a small, savage crescent"— a momentary vision that portends the cruel treatment the young man is to receive from the group. Close up, as Brackett pictures them, most of these celebrated personages are not kind, or even decent, people.

Neysa, though, generally escapes Brackett's scathing, if often overdone, satire. There are, to be sure, a few swipes at her: Leith is not given the minimal dignity of being a cover artist, but is instead a designer of cheap statuettes, reproductions of which "flooded the gift shops of the country"; and she is described, in marked understatement, as being "somewhat deficient in book-learning." But she is the only one of the characters who is not meanly etched. Among these poseurs, endlessly set squabbling with each other by the "acid, Sunday-school superintendent . . . voice" of Hulbert, Leith calmly but firmly insists, "I never make scenes," and remains unperturbed among the much perturbed. Instead, she rests "secure in her agelessness," with a definite, intriguing "style" that is all, and simply, her own. Even her self-absorption is cast

199

▼

in benign images, suggestive of the "feline" sensuality that so easily and attractively clung to her: "Leith O'Fallon would always be where the sunlight was warm." Among these "caricatures," only Leith/Neysa emerges as a "character," drawn with real sympathy and a genuine understanding of her rise from provincial obscurity to metropolitan eminence, if not with any great depth. When Alec opined that Neysa "comes off best" in the novel he was, for once, underestimating the matter, for she is the only one who survives it.

In the mid-1930s, members of the Neshobe Club were startled to find the foundation for a house being laid on the high ridge overlooking their clubhouse. It seemed that Enos Booth, who drew up the papers when he sold them the island, or what proved to be most of the island, had inserted an inconspicuous clause giving him rights to build on this parcel of land. Alec roared loudly, but not for long: conceding the legality, if not the honesty, of Booth's claim, he bought out the lawyer's portion; then, for his radio celebrity had made him wealthier than ever, picked up the mortgage on the place. When all these dealings were completed, Woollcott ended up owning half the island, and the club the other half.

With Booth's foundation already in, Alec decided to go ahead with a plan he had been cherishing for some time: building a larger, more comfortable, year-round house on the island. He set Joe Hennessey to the task of arranging its construction and ended up with a commodious fieldstone-and-wood dwelling in an elegantly rustic style: a large L-shaped living room, with an oversized fireplace, facing onto an ample terrace that looked down on most of the island, comfortable bedrooms off a long hallway, a kitchen capable of supporting haute cuisine, two maids' rooms and, perhaps most importantly, ample space for Alec to display the memorabilia—drawings of celebrated friends by other celebrated friends, Sir Henry Irving's gold-knobbed cane, a pocket knife belonging to Dickens, Duse's gold beads, a score of famous theatrical posters—he had collected or been given over the years. When the house was completed, Alec started spending as much of the year up on Neshobe as he did in New York.

Alec's love, and his need, of the island seemed to grow stronger with each passing year. In fact, in his later years Neshobe became very much

the measure of his whole existence. After spending several weeks at the
Roosevelt White House—his championship of FDR did not go unnoticed,
or unrewarded—Alec told everyone it was "just like Neshobe," a puzzling
remark until someone figured out that he meant simply that there was
always a fresh, warm pot of coffee available. As Alec's life grew more
and more to center on Neshobe, Neysa's changed accordingly, for her
ties to Alec remained as strong as ever. Now she would be up at the
island late enough in the fall to see the foliage turn golden and early
enough in the spring to see the trees renewing themselves. Apparently,
her more frequent goings to the island necessitated faster, and rather
more thrilling, means of getting there. In a note to her adolescent daughter, Neysa wrote, with a sense of small triumph, "we had quite a trip
up in the plane as it kept getting darker and mistier, but it only took
an hour and twenty minutes to fly from Long Island to Vermont!"

During the last decade of Woollcott's life, more and more of Neysa's
time with him was time they spent together on Neshobe. Some measure
of their not-quite-sexual intimacy was a sketch of Neysa he kept on his
study wall: a cheery cartoon of an "intimate moment in the life of a
lady" in floppy robe and "new red bath slippers." Alec's life became
more settled and regular as he spread himself out in the new house, and
it was mainly on the island that the last part of Alec and Neysa's "life
together" was lived. It was also here, four months before his death, that
Neysa had her last bitter battle with the "nabob of Neshobe"—a man
she loved after her fashion, but also a man she could not, and would
not, abide when he was at his most horrid.

In the 1930s, Neysa took several trips much further afield than Vermont.
Ralph and Peggy Pulitzer convinced her to join them on a three-month
tiger shoot in India, the great inducement being that they would be
transported everywhere by elephants, those beasts for which Neysa had
an exceeding fondness. In December 1934, the three were given a
spirited sailing party by Art Samuels, with FPA urging Neysa, for sentiment's sake, to take along a bottle of Hudson River water to mingle
with the Ganges, since it was India the explorer was seeking when,

rather off-course, he discovered that river named after him. Although the trio was joined by the Duke and Duchess of Sutherland, lunched at the vice-regal palace with the Viceroy, and was entertained at every turn by maharajahs and other potentates (one of whom, in a gesture of monarchial modernity, kept a frigidaire in each corner of the state dining room), it was almost entirely of pachyderms that Neysa spoke when she returned: of the strong, loyal elephant she rode daily, "one of her warmest friends," of the "tiffin elephant" which carried the supplies for the elaborate tea the group had each afternoon, and of other assorted, friendly elephants with their traveling party.

Of all her longer jaunts, in many ways the most typical was one to Egypt in the early 1930s. The impulse behind the trip was Neysa's desire to be reunited with Paul and Lily Bonner, then in the first years of their removal to Europe. Egypt recommended itself as a meeting point because it was cheap: "if you can get together $1.50—this is the time to go," Neysa wrote the Bonners. They replied that they could handle the going toll and would have the five weeks or so necessary for the journey. Early on in their avid planning, there was some talk that Nelson Doubleday would join them, and Neysa, knowing from her honeymoon and other journeys how likely Alec was to insert himself into and completely reshape others' travel plans, warned the Bonners that she "wouldn't be a bit surprised if he joined us at the last minute." As it turned out, Alec did not add his considerable traveling presence to the entourage, but Alice Miller and George Abbott—the latter surprised and delighted by the invitation of his still new friend, Neysa, to join the party—did come along. George's extended account of the trip, in his autobiography, is the most complete picture we have of Neysa the traveler. According to George, she was "enthusiastic, romantic, imaginative, sensitive and urbanely witty and charming," everything an ideal traveler should be, save perhaps for "curious."

George, Alice, and Neysa landed at Nice, where they had lunch with some of Neysa's "friends" and where George was able to try his tango on Enrico Caruso's widow, then made their way by train to Naples to join the Bonners (who immediately began to get on George's nerves with their insistent enthusiasms). From Italy, it was a boat trip across the

202
▼

Mediterranean, with Neysa quickly establishing herself as "the captain of our crew" and lightly setting out a proposed travel and sightseeing agenda. In Cairo, Neysa organized them for a night ride out into the desert to see the Pyramids, "green and blue and mysterious" under a full, eerie moon.

In the middle of their Egyptian sojourn, the group took the long boat ride up the Nile, with George, who was already feeling something of an "oddball," daily becoming more sulky. When he announced to Neysa that he intended to leave and go back to the Cairo hotel to write, she would have none of his malcontent traveling and made clear his obligations to the others: "instead of dismissing me as a difficult fool, she talked to me calmly and said . . . that if I wished to stay on the boat and write, I could do so, but I must not do anything so drastic as to leave the group." Gracefully coaxed by Neysa, George not only abandoned his grudging moodiness, but actually caught much of her enthusiasm for the sights and smells and sounds of the great muddy river, for the plaintive chants of the boatmen who propelled them along, for the vast tombs far up the Nile. In all, the whole river journey then took on from George's view the "dreamlike quality of an idyl" produced by the slow, steady going of the boat up the ancient, busy river.

The party arrived back in Cairo just a month to the day after it had first landed in that city, and Neysa, recalling that the moon would again be full, proposed another night ride out to the Pyramids. George begged off, wanting to go nightclubbing after his several weeks away from metropolitan civilization, but the others agreed to accompany her. However, they pulled out on Neysa at the last moment, preferring instead to play bridge, and George, recognizing Neysa's genuine distress, gave over his dancing plans and went, much to his pleasure, to the desert with her: "Again it was beautiful, and as seen through Neysa's eyes, it acquired a double magic: not only beautiful, but weird, mysterious, like a scene under water."

A few days later, the group sailed to Athens, and then Neysa, George, and Alice, feeling homesick, abandoned plans for a Paris visit and sailed on to New York. Almost immediately, variable, conflicting, fabulous, and amusing accounts of the trip began to circulate and become part of

Algonquin lore. Within a month, Alec was writing to Lily Bonner: "I feel sure Neysa's account of the flight from Egypt or whatever Moses used to call it, needs correction here and there. I have many things to ask you and some to tell you." By then, Neysa had already written of her latest travel intentions to this same correspondent: "I miss you and Paul something awful, and am going to start to plan another trip right away."

About her tentative plan we can be sure of at least one thing: that there was, as usual, no place for a husband in it.

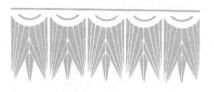

12

Neysa and the Withering of the Wits

Economically, the Depression proved a flush time for most in and around the Algonquin crowd. With the coming of sound to films, there was a great demand for those who could write sharp, crisp dialogue, and Kaufman, Parker, and Connelly all made large sums of money for movie writing that amounted to little real work. Benchley both wrote and starred in a series of short comic films. Woollcott became, at William Paley's urging, radio's "Town Crier": "This is Woollcott speaking," he began his broadcasts, and millions listened and were swayed mightily by his likings and dislikings.

Even Alice Duer Miller, who certainly did not need the money, had a great bestseller at the decade's end with *The White Cliffs*, her sentimental narrative poem urging American intervention in the war. ("But in a world where England is finished and dead, / I do not wish to live.") Neysa, too, did very well financially through most of the decade. The McMein girl, aging ever so slowly and now decked out in the slightly more somber clothes of the Depression years, continued to earn her keep handsomely.

Personally, though, many of the Algonquinites found the Depression years to be a marked contrast with the previous, so much more fun-filled decade. Despite their ongoing financial success and sustained popularity, they had reason to become somewhat dispirited, for they were no longer so bright and lighthearted, and certainly they were no longer so young. Moreover, their art and their brand of wit was gradually being displaced, in critical if not public esteem, by that of a group of younger writers and artists who had not shared the crucial experience of World War I. To one of these writers just coming to feel his power, E. B. White, Woollcott sitting at the Algonquin circa 1930 already "was just an old poop then."

Properly packaged, Algonquin art and personality might be as salable a commodity as in earlier years, but the need to sell at high prices was greater than ever, for many in the set, including Neysa, had adopted lifestyles that depended on means far beyond what most artists could rationally expect to earn at their trade. As Benchley's son observed, by the mid-1930s his father could no longer afford *not* to work in movies. And when Kaufman and Hart wrote of Sheridan Whiteside, their point-by-point parody of Woollcott in *The Man Who Came to Dinner*, that "he looks like every caricature ever drawn of him," they were hinting at that large element of self-parody that in the 1930s became Alec's most distinguishing characteristic—and perhaps his greatest selling point.

Woollcott, in one of those moments of introspection that redeems his character, mockingly dubbed himself "the greatest writer in America with nothing to say," a title for which Benchley or Parker, had the latter not abandoned writing almost completely, might have challenged. Connelly, with *The Green Pastures* amounting to a virtual life's sinecure, also wrote very little after 1930, so little that upon the publication of a recently discovered Dickens manuscript, Connelly's old collaborator, Kaufman, quipped, "Charles Dickens, dead, writes more than Marc Connelly, alive." Connelly could have responded that the fearful and insecure Kaufman, who could never rest content with his many theatrical successes and who only ventured one play without a collaborator, was the greatest half-dramatist in American theatrical history, and that it was only "his Hart" that was now sustaining him. Neysa as an artist, though, went on much as she had done from the first: incessantly and rapidly imitating herself. Only a technological revolution could stop her.

As they became richer and more famous, the Algonquinites no longer needed each other's help to keep their names before the public, and many of them drifted into new social groupings of one sort or another. Sherwood moved to England (although he still spent enough time in the United States to serve as a speechwriter for FDR), and Benchley became virtually a permanent resident of Hollywood, where he served as a kind of unofficial greeter and host at the Garden of Allah, the rather bizarre bungalow hotel which was about as close an equivalent to the Algonquin as Southern California could manage. Parker, as she moved leftward politically, cut off her non-leftist friends, like writer/publisher George Oppenheimer, and even her once inseparable companion "Mr. Benchley," in favor of new, more "politically correct" friends, like Lillian Hellman (whose influence over her Benchley, in turn, deplored). When Dottie wrote her scathing, if exaggerated, denunciation of the Round Table crowd from Madrid in 1937, Neysa, for one, was not surprised: she had already experienced how treacherous Parker could be, even when the motive was no more than personal.

In the mid-1930s, Heywood Broun and Ruth Hale, a union FPA had dubbed "the clinging oak and the sturdy vine," decided they must divorce after a decade and a half of marriage, insisting their need for freedom was greater than their obvious dependence on each other. Some years earlier, Harold Ross and Jane Grant had divorced, Ross's obsession with *The New Yorker* making him, as two subsequent wives would also discover, an oftentimes impossible mate. The gangly and seemingly unromantic George Kaufman, through the great embarrassment of the

Mary Astor trial, was exposed as rather a satyr and held up, mock-heroically, as "Public Lover No. 1"—Beatrice, though, stuck by him, but the couple did purchase Barley Sheaf Farm in Bucks County shortly after the incident, partly so they could have a retreat from the glare of New York (and Hollywood) publicity. Another kind of split took place between Woollcott and Swope, whose habitual quarreling eventually lost all friendly sense when Swope charged Alec with small-mindedness and anti-Semitism in blocking the application of Swope's sometime business associate, John Hertz (the car-rental man), for an apartment in Alec's swanky East Side cooperative. Alec retaliated by accusing Swope of political cowardice in not supporting LaGuardia for mayor and by hiring away Joe Hennessey, who had been functioning as a general superintendent at Swope's North Shore estate, to run the Neshobe Club.

Neysa and Jack's casual, calm marriage arrangement, on the other hand, was looking better all the time. "Neysa had a date and I was on the loose," Jack began one of his anecdotes of New York life in the 1940s, indicating just how easily—and guiltlessly—the two went their busy, separate social and sexual ways well into middle age. Not surprisingly, Neysa weathered the gradual dissolution of the Algonquin crowd better than most. Unlike many of them, she had never needed the enforced sociability of the Round Table, even in its heyday. As the Algonquin crowd began to split apart, she quite easily and quite naturally formed new relationships and developed older ones—while still managing to stay friendly with many from the old group, even when they were really no longer friends with one another.

Some of her great friends, like Noel Coward, had come to her through "Algonquin channels," but they eventually grew much closer to her than to other members of the slowly disintegrating group. Through Noel, Neysa cemented a strong friendship with one member of the Anglo-American theatrical community, Bea Lillie, and became a good friend of another, Gertrude Lawrence. Other newer friends, like Alicia Guggenheim, Millicent Hearst, and the young Jock Whitney, were part of the North Shore set in which Neysa and Jack had so firmly established themselves. Increasingly, Neysa's new friends were drawn from "society" and were rich.

Still other new friends were persons who casually floated into Neysa's orbit and remained there when they discovered how warm and generous a friend—and how indulgent a hostess—she could be. Of these last, the most important was Nicky de Gunzburg, a young Russian émigré baron, who seemed ever present at Sands Point in the late 1930s and early 1940s, and who was often Neysa's companion in town. Though he was later to make a reputation as a fashion editor at *Vogue*, when Neysa took him up, Baron de Gunzburg—his banking family had been ennobled by the czar not too many decades earlier—was little more than a handsome young man with exquisitely civilized manners and a romantic reputation for having helped squander the last of his family's fortune during its Parisian exile. As Neysa's stepson recalled him in 1984, de Gunzburg might well have been playing on Neysa's legendary tolerance for her friends, especially those with glossy manners and mysterious, foreign airs about them:

> He was one of the ballet impresarios who knew every-
> body. He was an international person. He knew all the
> Russians, White Russian nobility and Italian and French.
> Probably very much of a lounge lizard too. He lived off
> his name and reputation and his good looks and his
> manners. I don't think he had any real visible means
> of support. . . . He was very much around.

Surrounded by friends—old and new, famous and talented and ro-mantic—Neysa, for the most part, lived through the Depression years in the reassuring afterglow of the 1920s. For her, there was still the gaiety, and sometimes the splendor, of North Shore summer life, which flourished, unabated, right up to World War II, then vanished on the instant. There were the weeks on Neshobe, where the Algonquinites and their visiting friends could feel as if the small, mocking, bright world they had created in the previous decade had hardly diminished in these less hospitable times. There was still her noteworthy career as a cover artist, memorialized by the January 1934 *McCall's*, which celebrated Neysa's ten years with the magazine. And there were now even the occasional family moments, such as "Uncle Alec," on his best, most charming behavior, bearing Joan off to her first play.

Throughout the thirties and into the early forties, then, Neysa McMein continued to live out, with good grace and with a lightness of heart, the fantasy of metropolitan life she had conceived in her growing years and had come surprisingly close to achieving in New York by 1920. That many of her somewhat younger friends—like Helen Hayes and Charlie MacArthur, Richard Rodgers, Walt Disney—had far surpassed her own celebrity was for Neysa more cause for delight than envy. She could still feel that she knew the most important people, even if she might not quite qualify as one of them herself anymore.

In the summer of 1940, Neysa and Jack, despite a recent decline in Neysa's income, still had sufficient funds to make a move back to the more fashionable East Side from the West. Their new duplex apartment, at 131 East 66th Street, was large enough to contain studio space for Neysa (although she would use it less and less) and had a two-story living room, a piece of real metropolitan luxury. The apartment was to be her in-town home for the rest of her life, and Jack's for a decade beyond that.

Starting in that same year, Jack began spending a good deal of time in Cuba, helping to set up, and eventually serving as general manager for, a nickel-mining operation encouraged by a United States government anxious to find replacement sources for the valuable metal. (The enterprise would help to make Cuba for a time the world's second largest nickel producer.) When in Cuba, Jack would alternate between Nicaro, the site of the mine, for two weeks, and Havana for a week. Once the United States entered the war, he was caught up in the furtive air of amateur intrigue that hung over the foreigners in residence in Cuba. Hemingway, whom Jack had encountered fairly regularly and gotten to like on earlier visits, was now rarely to be seen: by report, "Papa" was out on his boat doing some "important hush-hush work for our government." Jack, for his part, reported on developments at Nicaro to the

American ambassador once a month. Back in New York, Jack, by then in his fifties, gave evidence that he had, not wholly unwillingly, lapsed back into the rougher ways—always boisterous and often bawdy—of day-to-day mining life. Neysa bore with the change.

Shortly after their transfer to the 66th Street duplex, Jack's son, recently graduated from Princeton and waiting to be drafted, moved in temporarily, at Neysa's invitation, for what proved a seven-month stay. With the exception of "Woody" Broun, who had a startlingly precocious existence in his father's and FPA's columns, children had rarely been an evident or important part of Algonquin life, although most members of the group eventually became parents. (It might, indeed, be surmised that the Algonquinites and their friends, with their endless play and jokes and "fun," never really vacated spots that their children could occupy.) Neysa, nonetheless, was occasionally given to such impulsive, if vague, "parental" gestures as inviting her stepson to become part of her household.

The ostensible purpose for having King move in was so that he might get to know his half sister better, although Neysa's plan apparently consisted of no more than putting the two—the recent college graduate and the sixteen-year-old high school student—together with some regularity. King and Joan normally had supper by themselves; sometimes they went off to play badminton or see a movie. More often, Joan had homework to do, and King was left to go about town on his own, as he very eagerly did. In the end, however, it was not so much Joan as his stepmother whom King came to know better. Neysa had, after a fashion, beguiled yet another young man.

Since Jack was often away in Cuba, Neysa and King soon established a daily tête-à-tête, "Breakfast with Neysa." Here they would analyze, with humor and candor, the day's news, the opera or ballet Neysa had likely been to the previous evening, who of talent and wit was in town and just what they were about. King's love life, such as it was, was thoroughly dissected—and one important young woman in it classified "an empty-headed drip" by Neysa. The young man, with his rather staid, old-fashioned upbringing, found this daily exposure to Neysa's "very wide attitudes" enlightening and exciting. Yet Neysa always dexterously avoided satisfying his greatest curiosity: precisely what the relationship was between herself and his father.

As Joan could have told her half brother, her parents were "very independent people," meaning essentially that their busy social routine often took precedence over their children. The confidences of the break-fast table were no pledge of Neysa's interest and attention later in the day. As King discovered, "If she had guests in, she'd very openly tell Joan and me to go to Horn & Hardart's and give us some nickels to go." And if, as he often did, King came home during a party or dinner, he was expected to make his way unobtrusively to his room. Only once, using the general mayhem of the situation as a cover, did he manage to stay on: "I did come back one night, and they were having a party for the cast of *Pal Joey* [which George Abbott had produced and directed]. I walked in and it was amazing, so many people, so much singing and yelling and going on that I stayed and nobody seemed to kick me out."

After King moved out—he was drafted in time to find himself at Pearl Harbor on December 7—and Joan went off to Wellesley, Neysa was essentially on her own for the first time in two decades, since operations at Nicaro now kept Jack in Cuba almost all the time. At Christmas in 1943, there was a brief family reunion when Neysa and Joan joined Jack in Cuba, where Neysa finally got to see what Jack's working life was really like. She declared herself "astounded" at the size and intricacy of the mining operation—and enthralled by the beauty of its mountain location. For twenty years Jack's stories had made his work seem more of a rollicking adventure than the hard, busy labor Neysa now understood it to be.

She and Joan contrived to have a "proper," if tropical, family Christ-mas that year, making do with a palm tree and some begged, borrowed, and improvised ornaments. Then Neysa and Jack got down to the sort of thing they were always having to do, namely, as Jack put it, "bringing each other up to date and bridging the gap in our lives."

The Round Table as an institution had died in 1930, when the last of
its members finally ceased their, by then, very occasional sitting to lunch
together. The finale of the Algonquinites as a group is marked by two
events in 1939, both, hardly by chance, concerned with Alec Woollcott,
who more than anyone else centered the group and who by then meant
much more to Neysa than all the rest of them combined. Kaufman and
Hart's fine, funny play, *The Man Who Came to Dinner*, was the cul-
mination of that strong Algonquin tendency to make its success, and its
living, through a retailing of each other's habits, wit, foibles, and consciously outsized personalities. Sheridan Whiteside is Woollcott at his
most hilariously impossible, fully deserving of the tirade to which he
drives his exasperated assistant, Maggie:

> I think you are a selfish, petty egomaniac who would
> see his mother burned at the stake if that was the only
> way he could light his cigarette. I think you'd sacrifice
> your best friend without a moment's hesitation if he
> disturbed the sacred routine of your self-centered, paltry
> little life. I think you are incapable of any human emo-
> tion that goes higher up than your stomach, and I was
> the fool of the world for ever thinking I could trust you.

Yet Whiteside is also, in an odd way, almost endearing in his imper-
viousness to any but his own concerns. Whiteside's childishness is so
monumental, so perfect, so complete that it is forgivable, though by no
means always bearable. He is a virtuoso of selfishness. As Edmund
Wilson, hardly a great partisan of Alec's, put the argument for Woollcott
in a memorial essay, "He did not hesitate to assert himself as a single
unique human being; he was not afraid to be Alexander Woollcott; and
even when Alexander Woollcott was horrid, this somehow commanded
respect." Neysa, and apparently a fair portion of the theatergoing public,
could not have agreed more.

The other public scourging of Woollcott in 1939, the three-part profile
"Big Nemo" in *The New Yorker*, made even *The Man Who Came to
Dinner* seem a fond indictment of Alec's petty, tyrannical, small-minded

213
▼

ways. The origin of the damning piece was very much an indication of just how much the old Algonquin ties had weakened. Not only had the author of the profile, Wolcott Gibbs, come to *The New Yorker* through the recommendation of his aunt, Alec's great friend Alice Duer Miller, but the moving spirit behind the debunking piece was Harold Ross, who freely admitted, after Alec's death, how calculated an insult the profile, for which Ross himself supplied a goodly number of the most damaging stories, was meant to be: "All the time Aleck wrote for us he was a trial . . . he was getting drunk with power and the magazine couldn't hold him." "Big Nemo" was, in essence, Alec's dismissal notice.

Woollcott never wrote for *The New Yorker* again. Nor did Woollcott and Ross ever speak directly to one another during the remaining four years of Alec's life. (Once, feeling very ill, Alec sent a request to Ross for a conciliatory meeting, but withdrew it the moment he felt better.) More than any other single event, then, "Big Nemo" signaled the end of the Algonquin group. What had been founded at, and partially in celebration of, the end of World War I, was put to rest on the eve of World War II.

The critic Robert Warshow, in "E. B. White and the *New Yorker*," voiced what is perhaps the most damning criticism of *The New Yorker*, not because it denies the enterprise its grace, charm, and wit, but rather because it ultimately makes of them negative virtues:

> The *New Yorker* has always dealt with experience not by trying to understand it but by prescribing the attitude to be adopted toward it. This makes it possible to feel intelligent without thinking, and it is a way of making everything tolerable, for the assumption of a suitable attitude toward experience can give one the illusion of having dealt with it adequately.

To the very considerable extent that this stance derived from the Round Table and the whole way of life of the Algonquin group, Warshow's critique also serves to point to the group's greatest limitation, a limitation that became more and more apparent as the Depression progressed and World War II came on: its inability to put its experience into any genuine perspective, whether historical, social, cultural, or literary. Group members were typically too busy tolerating, making light of, or adopting an attitude toward most things to be bothered trying to assess them critically. As Jack's son observed about his father and Neysa, "They just *didn't* discuss things. They were very busy making *badinage*, jokes, and witty comments, and kidding and razing."

Like so many of their friends, they had never gotten over the marvelous new sense of freedom and gaiety which they had helped establish as a sophisticated norm in the 1920s. As a result, many of the Algonquinites, not excluding Neysa, often found themselves, without quite realizing it, held for the rest of their lives in what the child of two of them, Heywood Hale Broun, ironically termed "the iron grip of freedom."

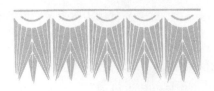

13

Passings

One Saturday night in Hollywood during the mid-1930s, S. N. Behrman was given a lively going-away party by his friends, many of them, like himself, temporary exiles from the New York theater world that bordered on, and in places overlapped with, what remained of the Algonquin world. However, just before he was to depart for New York the next morning, David Selznick called to tell him that Greta Garbo had pronounced herself unhappy with sections of Behrman's script for *Anna Karenina* and that the writer would have to stay on to alter them.

Walking to the studio commissary for coffee early on Monday morning, Behrman ran into George Kaufman, who had been at the party. Showing no surprise, Kaufman merely remarked, "Oh, forgotten—but not gone." With a few exceptions, such as Kaufman's own television celebrity through the quiz show *This Is Show Business* in the late 1940s, the line might have been applied to some, perhaps most, members of the Algonquin crowd from the onset of World War II until their deaths. "Forgotten but not gone" was generally the case, at least so far as the public was concerned, for Neysa McMein during the last decade of her life. Her celebrity was definitely passing.

In the 1930s, there were a number of casualties among Neysa's friends. In 1931, Ralph Barton, the great *New Yorker* caricaturist—he did a marvelous, stylish Christmas card of Neysa in all her 1920s glory—committed suicide. In 1937, George Gershwin, not yet forty, died of a brain tumor. In 1939, Heywood Broun died at fifty-one, still near the height of his fame as a columnist. But it would be the 1940s that would see the relatively early deaths of so many in the Algonquin crowd, that grouping which had epitomized the spirit of metropolitan brashness and youth just two decades earlier.

In 1938, Neysa experienced another kind of "death": the end of her career as a cover artist. Throughout the decade, four-color process printing for photographs was being steadily improved—and *Life* had already, with its outstanding black-and-white photographs, crucially influenced magazines in favor of the more dramatic and "lifelike" photograph. By the late thirties the process was nearly perfected, and magazines could substitute much lower priced color photographs for expensive cover sketches. *McCall's* made plans to switch over to photographic covers and canceled Neysa's contract as of April 1938.

George Abbott, who was with Neysa when she received the news, was amazed that she moped but for a day or two, then returned to her usual high-spirited self. But, for once, her determinedly carefree attitude could not fully overcome an unpleasant reality. Losing the *McCall's* contract really meant the end of Neysa's chief career. No longer having a well-paid monthly commission also meant, as Neysa's daughter vividly recalled, a decided, although not immediate, change in family fortunes. Starting in 1938, Neysa and Jack had to calculate the cost of things more closely.

Neysa did a few covers for the *Saturday Evening Post* after leaving *McCall's*, but soon the *Post* could no longer use her, either. Within a few years almost every popular magazine—save *The New Yorker*, whose cover style was very much outside Neysa's purview, and the *Post*, where Norman Rockwell reigned supreme—had switched to photographic covers. By 1939, her career as a magazine artist was over, and Neysa, who once had had more work than she could handle even at her rapid pace, had to worry about making a living for the first time in over two decades. As she confessed to William Paley some years after, losing the *McCall's* contract was a shock from which she never fully recovered, try as she might to shrug it off.

Fortunately for Neysa, her rich and well-to-do friends were available, and willing, to have their portraits painted, and she was able to expand her career as an oil portraitist accordingly. Yet, if she had more than occasional work as a portraitist, she no longer had a full-time artistic career. Moreover, her work in oils, while quite professional, for the most part lacked the style, verve, and good color sense of her work in pastels. Slowly, her income began to decline—and with that decline a certain kind of life gradually became unaffordable. Neysa, not for want of spirit or want of ease, thus shared somewhat in the withering of brightness and gaiety that afflicted so many in the Algonquin crowd as they moved into middle age and found it not so agreeable and cheering as their much-prolonged youth.

During the last three years of his life, 1940–43, Alec Woollcott was far sicker than he let on: his heart, from bearing the strain of his obesity, was starting to fail him. In February 1942, Neysa, always injury-prone, fell down the stairs while sleepwalking and broke her back. It was the conjunction of these two illnesses that defined, most unfortunately, the last phase of Alec and Neysa's relationship.

A piece of Neysa's hip had to be grafted to her spine, and she was forced to spend several very painful weeks in a cast at St. Luke's Hospital. When she returned home, her recovery continued to be slow, painful, and tedious, although made cheerier by a regular stream of visitors. Woollcott, who was feeling none too well himself (he was in the process of contracting pneumonia), was very much upset about Neysa's accident and wrote to Lily Bonner in terms that clearly show him as the devoted friend he could be when he let his sympathies rather than his self-concern dominate a relationship: "I don't know why it is that I should hear calmly of vast multitudes in agony in Russia and the Far East and then feel this highly localized disaster of Neysa's as if it were a blow on my head. Or rather, I have felt ever since as if someone were kneeling on my heart." In the same letter, Alec reported another, even more dire physical disaster concerning one of their intimates: "Alice Miller, who appeared to be in the pink . . . discovered something amiss inside her. It proved to be a malignant growth which involved deep and drastic surgery."

After getting out of the upstate hospital where he was being treated for pneumonia, Alec came down to New York to set up a "joint convalescence" with Neysa in "that damned duplex of hers." For a few days this partnership of the ailing worked well, but then Neysa and Alec's irredeemably social bent got the better of them, and they overdid their bedside entertaining. Alice Miller reported how the two "saw 18 people in one day. Then the doctor said no visitors, [Alec] had a slight gallstone attack, and was removed to the Island." Feeling low herself, Alice went on to identify herself with Neysa's evident, if less threatening, suffering. Rather suddenly, these three friends had to face the fact that they were quite ill and quite exhausted—and that they now lacked the easy healing grace of youth.

Alec, contrary as ever, insisted that his recuperation on Neshobe demanded the presence of friends, and he summoned many of them to join him. By early summer, as he wrote to Noel Coward, Neshobe resembled a "convalescent camp," with many of its aging guests nursing various minor illnesses and ailments. Neysa continued on in New York.

In the middle of an August night, word was brought across the lake to Neshobe that Alice Miller had died of cancer (with her so oddly matched friend, Harpo Marx, at her bedside). The coming of this grim news reminded Alec of a night seventeen years before, when Neysa had been awakened by a late night messenger bringing word of the death of Gregory Kelly, Ruth Gordon's young husband. At the earlier time, though, the guests had had the energy to sit up the rest of the night, talking about and remembering their friend. Now they just forlornly returned to their beds.

By the early autumn, Neysa felt well enough to make the trip up to Neshobe. Here she found Alec cranky and restless in his ill-health. Things did not bode well, especially since Neysa had to stretch out flat for a number of hours each day to relieve the pressure on her spine. Soon after her arrival, Alec proposed a drive through the Vermont countryside to view the fall foliage. Neysa agreed to go, but reminded him that she could sit up for no more than three hours at a stretch. The ride started merrily enough, but when Neysa and the other riders, Richard Carver Wood and Grace Eustis, began to worry Alec about the time, he grew petulant, insisted the best scenery was yet to come, and commanded the driver to go on, along bumpy roads that were beginning to cause Neysa agonizing pains. Neysa protested, first tearfully, then angrily, that her back ached, but Alec refused her pleas and took affront when she called him callous. Finally, they turned round and made their way back to the landing for the boat trip across to Neshobe, with Alec proclaiming to the other two, "It's lucky I *know* who my friends are. I'll never go to her place again." Back on the island, he continued to sulk self-righteously. Neysa, for once absolutely furious with him, left Neshobe, in great pain and aghast that Alec could be so impervious to her suffering.

When she got back to New York, Neysa wrote to him that although she was still fond of him, it would probably "be better" if they did not see each other for a while. Alec, vaguely admitting to his guilt in the incident, reluctantly agreed. However, this time their "trial separation" turned out to be a permanent one, for Alec would die within three months, after suffering a heart attack during a radio broadcast.

Neysa found the memorial service for Alec a melancholy affair. Nor was the gathering at the hotel of the remaining Algonquinites afterwards for a drink to Alec's memory any more cheering. A few days later, Alec's ashes were shipped up to Hamilton College, to be buried on the campus, out in the "provinces," far from the scene of his metropolitan triumphs.

One of Alec's nemeses, George Abbott, for over a decade an inseparable companion to both Neysa and Jack, figured in an important domestic change in their life the following year. By 1944, it had become apparent not only that Neysa and Jack would never again have the money to live as stylishly as they had in the 1920s and 1930s, but also that they needed to take some immediate steps to shore up their financial position. Rather than sell the Sands Point house on the open market, Neysa and George, he by then incredibly successful on Broadway, worked out a neat reversal: he would buy the house, and Neysa and Jack would become his summer "boarders."

The proposition worked quite well for several summers, but then George, nearing sixty, decided to marry Mary Sinclair, an actress half his age. Neysa, according to George, had sensed that the young woman, from her very first visit to Sands Point, was "a menace to our little domestic paradise," and when he broke the news of his impending marriage to Neysa and Jack, assuring them that they would be as welcome as ever at Sands Point, George was met with a "stony silence." At this point, Bill Paley offered her and Jack the summer loan of the ivy-covered cottage which served as the gatehouse on his nearby Manhasset estate. They informed George that they had accepted Paley's gracious offer and would not be returning to the Sands Point house the following summer.

During the ensuing few summers, Neysa and Jack grew close with Paley and his new wife, Babe. Many evenings, the two couples would dine together on the estate, Jack regaling the appreciative Paleys with tales of his mining, business, and other adventures. In Neysa, who had started taking on a certain middle-aged quietude, Paley found an "appealing softness" that much contrasted with Jack's still vibrant, bluff style.

Meanwhile, a definite summer coolness set in between the Baragwanaths and Abbotts. At a Sands Point luncheon to which Neysa and Jack had been invited as a conciliatory gesture, Mary carelessly began to speak of knocking down a wall to make a wider entrance to the terrace. It became clear to Neysa and Jack that the house they had lovingly designed and built had fallen into the hands of someone who did not at all care for its beauty and proportions. "They finished lunch in silence and then swept grimly and grandly out and into their car and away," George later wrote, adding that he felt "very distressed." Over the remaining years of Neysa's life, she and George would never rekindle their friendship. George's real "reunion" with Neysa came only fifteen years after her death, in the loving portrait he drew of her in his autobiography, *"Mr. Abbott."*

In April 1946, Neysa threw a great party in the New York apartment to celebrate the marriage of her daughter to Fred Leech, a young naval officer Joan had met on a train journey back from Miami in June 1944, after a visit to her father in Cuba. Directly after the wedding, the newlyweds moved to Neenah, Wisconsin, Fred's hometown. Neysa's only child had, very conclusively, traced her mother's steps back to the Middle West. Neysa's New York life was not to last into a second generation.

After the war ended, Neysa was again much with Noel Coward, whom she realized was greatly depressed by his war experiences and the decline of his reputation. In the spring of 1946 she spent a month with him in England, where he, now a thorough establishment figure, was able to present her to the king and queen after the performance of one of his plays, and where the two drove out to Windsor late one afternoon, for, as Coward floridly recorded in his diary, "a peerlessly beautiful evening with the castle looking peach-coloured in the late sunlight." Neysa spoke jauntily of getting Noel a press agent just to "start a campaign" in his favor and lightly kidded him out of the gloom and sense of harassment that seemed to settle all too easily on him in these years.

In the winter of 1946–47, Neysa gave her last large, and according to Jack her very best, party. A young cousin of hers was a member of the crew which had dropped the bomb on Hiroshima—and she invited his crew, as well as the crew that bombed Nagasaki, to New York. The young men, minor celebrities in an America still celebrating the end of six years of a world war, got to meet a host of major celebrities and, in Jack's telling, many "good-looking girls." By Neysa's estimate, these were all "people she thought they would like to meet," and all people she could still, in spite of her eclipsed fame, assemble under her roof. Cole Porter played the piano while Bing Crosby sang; then everyone, this being Neysa's place, played party games and became a bit giddy and hilarious. Edna Ferber primly recorded in her diary that the party was "very gay and pleasant." For the young airmen, there was probably little disputing George Abbott's claim that Neysa was "the greatest party giver who ever lived."

Because of the passing of her fame and the decline of her career, Neysa may have felt the need for some new, representative accomplishment, for in the late 1940s she began work on two largish projects. That these were writing projects shows how little she then hoped for any revival of her artistic career. The more sustained of the projects was a play, eventually entitled *Studio Story*, she co-wrote with her old friend, Jane Grant. Whatever Neysa's exact contribution—surviving manuscript versions give no indication who wrote what sections or whether both authors worked on each together—there is no doubt that Neysa's earlier life was the inspiration for the whole play. The studio of the title is Neysa's studio in its legendary days as a salon and a scene of great, often madcap excitement. The plot is a piece of pure nonsense, involving comic gangsters, a "hard boiled," wisecracking model (in one scene costumed as a drum), several journalists (ranging from the gossipy to the yellow), an "arrogant" society woman, a mild takeoff on Noel Coward ("a famous British author . . . genial with extravagant English mannerisms"), and a handsome young writer (very loosely modeled on Jack Baragwanath) who is in love with the heroine.

Most significantly, the play contains in "Barbie Brown" a portrait of Neysa as she (and Grant) saw her in her 1920s heyday. It is, however, a portrait that emphasizes Neysa's disingenuous and simple side—and lops ten years off her age in the balance:

> An artist in her twenties. She is good-looking, enthu-
> siastic about life, enjoys everything and everybody in-
> discriminately with a gay contagion which makes her
> extremely popular. A good many men fall in love with
> her. She is vague in her manner; is unable to stay angry
> very long, and can easily be diverted from her work.
> Combined with a naivete is a deep belief in the occult.

The portrait, to be sure, is something of an idealization of Neysa in the
years in which, to quote one of the play's characters, "she fails not at
all in making meek men strong." The qualities that Neysa had recently
lost in life she determined to recoup in art.

Despite its lightness, the play is not without a few, rather obvious,
expressions of the 1920s femininism that Grant espoused and with which
Neysa much sympathized. Barbie, for example, insists early on that "the
modern woman can have marriage—and all that goes with it—but for
fulfillment, she must also have her career . . . and independence." And
at the play's end, Barbie insists on giving the young writer half her
money, simply because he needs it, and then she asks him to marry
her.

Neysa was able to construct a stageworthy play just as she was able
to create "Neysa," that is, with a sense of the necessary artifice and
forced emphases involved. Withal, *Studio Story* has about it a curiously
embalmed quality, as if the two authors were relying unduly on its
audience to have the same abiding interest in the place and period it
chronicles as they did. The plot never develops even to the point of
farce, and the characters seem to appear on stage almost entirely to
assert their personalities—odd, extreme, comical, and blasé.

Neysa's other late project also attempted to draw on her reputation,
specifically on her identification with numerology and other superstitious
practices. She proposed a short book entitled *Keep Your Fingers Crossed!*,
which would be a compendium of common superstitions arranged by
topic (Animals, Birth, Names, the Theater) and discussed in a breezy,
half-skeptical tone. As her sample introductory chapter shows, the book
was to be a lightly mocking critique of the many "up-to-date . . . modern

. . . streamlined . . . scientifically-minded" people who, nonetheless, stubbornly and only half-consciously perform their little collection of superstitious rituals. "You have been guilty of the most unscientific, fact-spurning behavior" she mockingly warns such transgressors, and then goes on to make a vaguely historical, and celebrity-filled, case for superstition. Her argument reflected her own equivocal attitude toward superstitious practices: namely, that though there was probably nothing to them, they were harmless enough and very possibly efficacious on some occasions. She also put in, doubtless in thanks for "Neysa," a particularly kind word for numerology.

The proposal for *Keep Your Fingers Crossed!* breaks off suddenly with the promise of "MORE TO COME." And in her last decade, Neysa was, at some level, always hoping for "more" of what she had known in the prewar years: the bright, witty, energetic life in which successes came easily, friends were lighthearted and always amusing, admiration and celebrity were readily hers. In the postwar years Neysa could only think to recapture the mood by going back on her own tracks.

After her accident in 1942, Neysa had begun to show her age. She no longer had the jaunty carriage that was an important part of her attractiveness. One young man, who a few years before had thought Neysa a markedly attractive older woman, now noticed that her once honey-colored hair was dyed a rather brassy blond and that lines had begun to show in her face. Neysa, too, took note of the loss of her beauty and was, in Bill Paley's estimation, more than a little "disheartened" by its passing. To John Minary, one of Paley's assistants at CBS, who only came to know Neysa and Jack during the last five years of her life, the balance of liveliness and spirit between the two was obviously in his favor. Jack remained vibrant, hearty, and full of fun, whereas Neysa increasingly appeared listless, weary, and "faded," as if she were much older than her husband. Neysa also struck Minary as perhaps being ill, although she evidenced no explicit ailments or symptoms. Likewise, Peter Fleischmann, when he was out with Neysa and his mother, now Ruth Vischer, in 1948, thought Neysa "quite apparently ill," and very possibly dying. Neysa, who for decades so easily drew people's admiration, was now drawing their sympathy instead.

Seeing Neysa in New York in January 1949, Noel Coward found she "looked gallant and weary," a sure indication of her failing health and energy, since Neysa always made a special effort to be lively and bright for him. In March, she went to California, to fulfill a commission for a portrait of Walt Disney's daughter. After it was completed, she began feeling distinctly unwell and returned to New York and saw her doctor. The initial prognosis was not at all good, but she was not told the worst and, possibly, did not suspect it.

In mid-April, Jack, in Toronto on business, got a call from Neysa telling him that she was going into St. Luke's Hospital the next day for a minor operation and that he was not to worry. Despite her assurances, he was alarmed and contacted her doctor, who told him the truth: that she had an advanced cancer which would require two extensive operations, one in a week and another several weeks after that. When Jack saw her at the hospital, Neysa was fretting about not being allowed home while awaiting this first, supposedly minor operation, but otherwise she was quite cheerful. Her friends had filled the room with flowers. Bill Paley had telephoned, saying that he was sending a movie projector and some films she might like to see. She prattled with Jack, inquiring after the details of his Canadian trip, while he, dismayed, tried to remember "some of the cleaner Canadian jokes I had heard." Then, sadly, she told Jack that she had learned that Ruth (Gardner) Vischer, her old friend from Quincy, was also in the hospital. "Poor, dear Ruth," she confided, was suffering from throat cancer and was deluding herself that "everything will be all right." (Ruth would outlive Neysa, but only by a year.)

Neysa finally convinced the doctors to allow her home for a few days before the first operation, but when she got there she was listless and depressed, most of the time just "mooning" about in a bathrobe. Her cancer had done what sixty-one years of living could not: it had destroyed her insatiable appetite for life. Then it was back to the hospital for her first operation, which the doctors declared a success, but which left Neysa barely conscious most of the time. Often she did not recognize

Jack or the others who came to visit her. Her gaiety was gone. After the second operation, on May 12, 1949, Jack waited nervously for word. First he was told that the operation had been a success, then that Neysa was experiencing some respiratory problems, but that these were not unexpected. A few hours later two doctors came to tell him that she was dead.

Neysa's funeral was held two days later at Holy Trinity Protestant Episcopal Church, she long ago having outgrown her Baptist-Methodist origins. Several of her friends arranged to have truckloads of branches of white dogwood, her favorite flower, brought in to fill the church. A choir sang "The Battle Hymn of the Republic," a particularly apt piece, at least in historical terms, for someone who came to make her New York success from a Midwestern town that had played a crucial part in the Civil War. Then the ceremony was over. Neysa McMein had, for the last time, brought together dozens of her witty, interesting, charming friends.

Just one month after the onset of her final illness, Neysa's body was cremated.

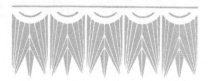

Epilogue

Neysa's obituaries made her sound like a decidedly more tame and prim creature than she was. Several stressed that she was a "gifted cook," one that she was a "gifted storyteller." Only one mentioned her clandestine marriage and her sailing for Europe without Jack the following day, but then, obviously relying on old, inaccurate newspaper accounts, made the incident seem less libertine and more respectable than it was by adding, "Her husband joined her there later, after she had attended to her business affairs." In another obituary Neysa was described as "sixtyish." Clearly, the era in which a willing public knew of and delighted in a gay, glamorous, free-spirited, and seemingly forever "young" Neysa McMein had passed.

Back in Quincy, the obituary writer for the *Herald-Whig* put on a brave face about the town's late, but hardly loyal, celebrity: "While few were in close touch with her, many who had known her in her girlhood followed her career and read with interest news about her and her work in newspapers and magazines." In the ensuing years, Quincy would forget Neysa McMein almost entirely. When an 800-page, double-column compendium of local history, the *People's History of Quincy and Adams County, Illinois*, was published a quarter century after her death, there was not a single mention of Neysa in it (although the editors saw fit to include some words on, and a picture of, Robert Earl Hughes, the "world's largest man," at 1,041 pounds, merely because he lived in Pike County across the river and "was widely known here"). Perhaps Quincy, which had been designated *Look's* "All-American City" for 1962, had become more concerned about the lives of those who remained—and achieved their success—close to home, or perhaps there was simply no one left to recall Neysa, or no one who thought her story at all important in the larger scheme of things Quincyan.

Neysa did continue to be remembered fondly, though, in recollections of the Algonquin group. Indeed, she came to assume something of a place of honor in the tales of that witty, competitive, often quarrelsome, and proudly neurotic group of minor talents. As Alice-Leone Moats, who attached herself to Neysa's set in the 1930s, wrote to Margaret Case Harriman, Neysa, seen in perspective, had qualities the others in the Algonquin crowd lacked, most especially kindness, calmness, and a boundless appreciation for her friends' talents.

Those friends remained extraordinarily loyal to Neysa's memory. In 1955, sixty-eight surviving friends contributed to the establishment of the Neysa McMein Memorial Fund at the Whitney Museum of Art. They included George Abbott, Bernard Baruch, Irving Berlin, Charles Brackett, Howard Deitz, Walt Disney, Mrs. Nelson Doubleday, Janet Flanner, Raoul Fleischmann, Ruth Gordon, Jane Grant, Alicia and Harry Guggenheim, Averell Harriman, Moss Hart, Jascha Heifetz, Ray Ives, George Kaufman, Arthur Krock, Fredric March, Bill and Babe Paley, Joan and

Charles Payson, Cole Porter, Richard and Dorothy Rodgers, Robert Sherwood, Cornelia Otis Skinner, Clifton Webb, Sonny Whitney, Jock Whitney, and a large number of the society friends Neysa had made over her last two decades.

Jane Grant, in working on the draft of a capsule biography of Neysa for her *Ross, The New Yorker and Me*, struck out the only really critical phrase in an otherwise adulatory portrait: "a skill for cultivating those who could further her" became "a skill for cultivating interesting people." Asked about her, Marc Connelly said simply that "Neysa was superb." And Noel Coward, according to his intimate and biographer, Cole Lesley, "did miss her always. Over the years he would from time to time say, 'I could have done without Neysa dying, you know.' "

Sources

BOOKS AND ARTICLES

Abbott, George. *"Mister Abbott."* New York: Random House, 1963.

Adams, Franklin P. *Diary of Our Own Samuel Pepys.* 2 vols. New York: Simon & Schuster, 1935.

Adams, Samuel Hopkins. *A. Woollcott: His Life and His World.* New York: Reynal & Hitchcock, 1945.

Amory, Cleveland. "The Gaming Crowd." *Harper's Bazaar,* November 1957.

————. *The Last Resorts.* New York: Harper & Brothers, 1952.

Atherton, Gertrude. *Black Oxen.* New York: Boni and Liveright, 1923.

Baragwanath, John. *A Good Time Was Had.* New York: Appleton-Century-Crofts, 1962.

————. *Pay Streak.* Garden City, N.Y.: Doubleday, Doran & Co., 1936.

Behrman, S. N. *People in a Diary: A Memoir.* Boston: Little, Brown & Co., 1972.

Benchley, Nathaniel. *Robert Benchley: A Biography*. New York: McGraw-Hill, 1955.

Benchley, Robert. *The Benchley Roundup*. Edited by Nathaniel Benchley. New York: Harper & Brothers, 1954.

Bernstein, Burton. *Thurber: A Biography*. New York: Dodd, Mead, 1975.

Brackett, Charles. *Entirely Surrounded*. New York: Alfred A. Knopf, 1934.

Broun, Heywood Hale. *Whose Little Boy Are You? A Memoir of the Broun Family*. New York: St. Martin's/Marek, 1983.

Brown, John Mason. *The Worlds of Robert E. Sherwood: Mirror to His Times*. 2 vols. New York: Harper & Row, 1965.

Caro, Robert. *The Power Broker: Robert Moses and the Fall of New York*. New York: Vintage Books, 1975.

Chaplin, Charles. *My Autobiography*. London: The Bodley Head, 1964.

Connelly, Marc. *Voices Offstage: A Book of Memoirs*. Chicago: Holt, Rinehart & Winston, 1968.

Coward, Noel. *Future Indefinite*. Garden City, N.Y.: Doubleday & Co., 1954.

⸻. *The Noel Coward Diaries*. Edited by Graham Payn and Sheridan Morley. Boston: Little, Brown & Co., 1982.

⸻. *Present Indicative*. Garden City, N.Y.: Doubleday, Doran & Co., 1937.

Daiches, David. *The Present Age in British Literature*. Bloomington: Indiana University Press, 1969.

Dietz, Howard. *Dancing in the Dark*. New York: Quadrangle, 1974.

Ferber, Edna. *A Peculiar Treasure*. Garden City, N.Y.: Doubleday, Doran & Co., 1939.

⸻. *So Big*. Garden City, N.Y.: Doubleday, Page & Co., 1924.

Fitzgerald, F. Scott. "Echoes of the Jazz Age" in *The Crack-Up*. Edited by Edmund Wilson. New York: New Directions, 1956.

⸻. "The Rich Boy" in *The Stories of F. Scott Fitzgerald*. Edited by Malcolm Cowley. New York: Charles Scribner's Sons, 1960.

Flanner, Janet. *The Cubical City*. Carbondale and Evansville, Ill.: Southern Illinois University Press, 1974.

Ford, Corey. *The Time of Laughter*. Boston: Little, Brown & Co., 1967.

Freud, Sigmund. *Wit and Its Relation to the Unconscious* in *Basic Writings of Sigmund Freud*. Edited and translated by A. A. Brill. New York: Modern Library, 1938.

Gaines, James R. *Wit's End: Days and Nights of the Algonquin Round Table*. New York: Harcourt Brace Jovanovich, 1977.

Geronsky, Rev. Landay, O.F.M. *People's History of Quincy and Adams County, Illinois*. Quincy: Jost & Kiefer, 1973.

Gilbert, Julie Goldsmith. *Ferber: A Biography of Edna Ferber*. Garden City, N.Y.: Doubleday & Co., 1978.

Gill, Brendan. *Here at The New Yorker*. New York: Random House, 1975.

Goldstein, Malcolm. *George S. Kaufman: His Life, His Theater*. New York: Oxford University Press, 1979.

Gordon, Ruth. *My Side: The Autobiography of Ruth Gordon*. New York: Harper & Row, 1976.

———. *Myself Among Others*. New York: Atheneum, 1971.

Grant, Jane. *Ross, The New Yorker and Me*. New York: Reynal & Co., 1968.

Harriman, Margaret Case. *The Vicious Circle: The Story of the Algonquin Round Table*. New York: Rinehart & Co., 1951.

Hart, Moss. *Act One: An Autobiography*. New York: Random House, 1959.

Hayes, Helen (with Sandford Dody). *On Reflection: An Autobiography*. New York: M. Evans & Co., 1968.

Hinkle, Beatrice M. "New Morals for Old: Women and the New Morality." *The Nation*, 19 November 1924.

Hoyt, Edwin P. *Alexander Woollcott: The Man Who Came to Dinner*. Revised edition. Radnor, Penn.: Chilton Book Co., 1973.

Huizinga, Johan. *Homo Ludens: A Study of the Play Element in Culture*. Boston: Beacon Press, 1955.

Irwin, Inez Haynes. "The Making of a Militant" in *These Modern Women: Autobiographical Essays from the Twenties*. Edited by Elaine Showalter. Old Westbury, N.Y.: The Feminist Press, 1978.

Kahn, E. J., Jr. "Plenipotentiary—II." *The New Yorker*, 18 May 1952.

———. *The World of Swope*. New York: Simon & Schuster, 1965.

Kaufman, Beatrice, and Joseph Hennessey. Introduction to *The Letters of Alexander Woollcott*. (See Woollcott entry below for particulars.)

Kaufman, George S., and Moss Hart. *The Man Who Came to Dinner* in *Six Plays by Kaufman and Hart*. New York: Modern Library, 1942.

Kazin, Alfred. "The Background of Modern Literature" in *Contemporaries*. Boston: Little, Brown & Co., 1962.

————. *On Native Grounds: An Interpretation of Modern American Prose Literature*. Revised edition. Garden City, N.Y.: Doubleday/Anchor, 1956.

Keats, John. *You Might As Well Live: The Life and Times of Dorothy Parker*. New York: Simon & Schuster, 1970.

Kramer, Dale. *Heywood Broun: A Biographical Portrait*. New York: Current Books, 1949.

————. *Ross and "The New Yorker."* Garden City, N.Y.: Doubleday & Co., 1951.

Krock, Arthur. *Memoirs: Sixty Years on the Firing Line*. New York: Funk and Wagnalls, 1968.

Lesley, Cole. *The Life of Noel Coward*. London: Jonathan Cape, 1976.

Levant, Oscar. *The Memoirs of an Amnesiac*. New York: Bantam, 1966.

Loos, Anita. *Gentlemen Prefer Blondes* and . . . *But Gentlemen Marry Brunettes*. New York: Vintage Books, 1983.

————. *A Girl Like I*. New York: Viking, 1966.

McMein, Neysa. "Games I Like to Play" (pamphlet). *McCall's*, n.d.

————. Monthly film reviews. *McCall's*, June 1932–June 1933.

————. "We Do the President." *The Ladies Home Journal*, August 1921.

————. "What My Home Means to Me." Interview by Wilma Van Santvoord. *American Home*, February 1929.

————. "The Woman Who Is a Design." *Arts & Decoration*, October 1923.

———— and Jane Grant. *Studio Story*. Unpublished play, copyright 1950. Jane Grant Papers, University of Oregon Special Collections, 31/4.

Marx, Harpo (with Rowland Barber). *Harpo Speaks!* New York: Freeway Press, 1974.

Meryman, Richard. *Mank: The Wit, World, and Life of Herman Mankiewicz*. New York: William Morrow, 1978.

Miller, Alice Duer. *The White Cliffs*. New York: Coward-McCann, 1940.

Miller, Henry Wise. *All Our Lives: Alice Duer Miller*. New York: Coward-McCann, 1945.

Nin, Anaïs. *The Early Diary of Anais Nin. 1920–23, Vol. II*. Edited by Rupert Pole. New York: Harcourt Brace Jovanovich, 1982.

Novack, Michael. *The Joy of Sports: End Zones, Bases, Baskets, Balls, and the Consecration of the American Spirit*. New York: Basic Books, 1976.

O'Connor, Richard. *Heywood Broun: A Biography*. New York: G. P. Putnam's Sons, 1975.

Oppenheimer, George. *The View From the Sixties: Memoirs of a Spent Life*. New York: David Mackay, 1966.

Paley, William. *As It Happened: A Memoir*. Garden City, N.Y.: Doubleday & Co., 1979.

Parker, Dorothy. *The Collected Poetry of Dorothy Parker*. New York: Modern Library, 1936.

———. *Laments for the Living*. New York: Viking Press, 1930.

———. "The Seige of Madrid" in *The Portable Dorothy Parker*. Edited by Brendan Gill. New York: Penguin, 1973.

Reed, Walt, ed. *The Illustrator in America: 1700–1960*. New York: Reinhold Publishing Co., 1966.

Rosmond, Babette. *Robert Benchley: His Life and Good Times*. Garden City, N.Y.: Doubleday & Co., 1970.

Showalter, Elaine, ed. Introduction to *These Modern Women: Autobiographical Essays from the Twenties*. Old Westbury, N.Y.: The Feminist Press, 1978.

Stewart, Donald Ogden. *By a Stroke of Luck! An Autobiography*. New York: Paddington Press, 1975.

———. *Mr. and Mrs. Haddock Abroad*. New York: George H. Doran, 1924.

Teichmann, Howard. *George S. Kaufman: An Intimate Portrait*. New York: Atheneum, 1972.

————. *Smart Aleck: The Wit, World and Life of Alexander Woollcott*. New York: William Morrow, 1976.

Thurber, James. *The Years with Ross*. Boston: Atlantic Monthly Press, 1959.

Time Capsule/1923. New York: Time Inc., 1967.

Warshow, Robert. "E. B. White and the *New Yorker*" in *The Immediate Experience: Movies, Comics, Theater and Other Aspects of Popular Culture*. New York: Atheneum, 1971.

Wilson, Edmund. "Alexander Woollcott of the Phalanx" in *Classics and Commercials: A Literary Chronicle of the Forties*. New York: Farrar, Straus and Giroux, 1967.

————. *The Twenties: From Notebooks and Diaries of the Period*. Edited by Leon Edel. New York: Farrar, Straus and Giroux, 1975.

————. *Upstate: Records and Recollections of Northern New York*. New York: Farrar, Straus and Giroux, 1971.

Woollcott, Alexander. "Croquet." *The New Yorker*, 20 September 1930.

————. *The Letters of Alexander Woollcott*. Edited by Beatrice Kaufman and Joseph Hennessey. Garden City, N.Y.: Garden City Publishing Co., 1946.

————. "Mr. Wilder Urges Us On" in *Long, Long Ago*. New York: Viking Press, 1943.

————. "Neysa McMein" and "The Death of Thanatopsis" in *Enchanted Aisles*. 2nd ed. New York: G. P. Putnam's Sons, 1924.

———— et al. "Neysa McMein." *McCall's*, January 1934.

Yardley, Jonathan. *Ring: A Biography of Ring Lardner*. New York: Random House, 1977.

NEWSPAPERS AND PERIODICALS

McCall's, New York Post, New York Herald Tribune, The New York Times, New York World, The New Yorker, Newsday, Quincy Daily Herald, Quincy Whig, Quincy Herald-Whig, The Saturday Evening Post.

— SOURCES —

LIBRARY AND ARCHIVAL RESOURCES

American Society of Illustrators, Boston University Library, Brooklyn Public Library, Dartmouth College Library, New York Public Library, Princeton University Library, University of Oregon Library, and the public records of Quincy and Adams County, Illinois.

PERSONAL CONTRIBUTIONS

The following generously shared recollections of Neysa McMein and knowledge about her life and times:

George Abbott
Albert Kingsmill ("Barry") Baragwanath
Eileen Baragwanath
Paul H. Bonner, Jr.
Heywood Hale Broun
Gardner Botsford
Merritt Chandler
Peter Fleischmann
Malcolm Goldstein
Elise Goodman
Sidney Harl
Helen Hayes
Jeannie Kay
Donald Klopfer
Joan Baragwanath Leech
John Minary
William S. Paley
Anne Kaufman Schneider
Irving Schneider
Howard Teichmann
Brenda Wineapple

239
▼

Robert T. Williams

Richard Carver Wood

A number of the remarks by Marc Connelly are drawn from an interview conducted by Aviva Slesin for *The Ten-Year Lunch*, a documentary film on the writers of the Algonquin Round Table.

PERMISSIONS ACKNOWLEDGMENTS

ABOUT THE AUTHOR

Brian Gallagher holds a doctorate in American literature from the University of Pennsylvania. He has been a National Endowment for the Humanities Fellow in Residence at Brown University and an Andrew W. Mellon Fellow in American Civilization at the Graduate Center of the City University of New York. He is presently Professor of English at the City University of New York (LaGuardia).

He lives with his wife and daughter in an 1870s brownstone in the Park Slope section of Brooklyn.